Kosher Feijoada and Other Paradoxes of Jewish Life in São Paulo

New World Diasporas

UNIVERSITY PRESS OF FLORIDA

Florida A&M University, Tallahassee
Florida Atlantic University, Boca Raton
Florida Gulf Coast University, Ft. Myers
Florida International University, Miami
Florida State University, Tallahassee
New College of Florida, Sarasota
University of Central Florida, Orlando
University of Florida, Gainesville
University of North Florida, Jacksonville
University of South Florida, Tampa
University of West Florida, Pensacola

Kosher Feijoada and Other Paradoxes of Jewish Life in São Paulo

MISHA KLEIN

University Press of Florida

Gainesville · Tallahassee · Tampa · Boca Raton

Pensacola · Orlando · Miami · Jacksonville · Ft. Myers · Sarasota

The publication of this book was made possible in part by a grant from the University of Oklahoma.
All royalties from the sale of this book are donated to the Memorial Foundation for Jewish Culture in support of future research.

This book may be available in an electronic edition.

21 20 19 18 17 16   6 5 4 3 2 1

First cloth printing, 2012
First paperback printing, 2016

Library of Congress Cataloging-in-Publication Data
Klein, Misha.
Kosher feijoada and other paradoxes of Jewish life in São Paulo / Misha Klein.
p. cm. — (New world diasporas)
Includes bibliographical references and index.
ISBN 978-0-8130-3987-9 (cloth: alk. paper)
ISBN 978-0-8130-6211-2 (pbk.)
1. Jews—Brazil—São Paulo—History—20th century. 2. Jews—Brazil—Sπo Paulo—History—21st century. 3. Sπo Paulo (Brazil)—Ethnic relations. I. Title.
F2651.S29J539 2012
305.892'408161—dc23
2012001104

University Press of Florida
15 Northwest 15th Street
Gainesville, FL 32611-2079
http://www.upf.com

To the memory of my grandparents:
Nadejda (Remenchik) Malbin
Morris Malbin
Philip Klein
Anne (Adickman) Klein
and
Professor Alan Dundes
with *saudades* . . .

Contents

Acknowledgments ix

❖

1. Departures 1

2. Braided Lives 35

3. Kosher Feijoada 69

4. The High Cost of Jewish Living 99

5. Inscribing Jews into the Nation 132

6. Doubly Insecure 163

7. Cosmopolitans at Home 191

❖

Notes 209

Bibliography 233

Index 247

Acknowledgments

This book represents my thoughts on identity for a heterogeneous group in a particular place and what that says about other transnational ethnic groups with other histories in other locales. In the process of thinking about these themes, I have also reflected on my own transnational networks. For those who have lived for extended periods far from home, the sensation of being out of place never fully disappears. While it may be possible to go "home" to a geographic place, to the physical location where we began a journey, our experiences change our core being such that while we may recognize our surroundings, we no longer recognize ourselves in them. While we can maintain relationships from a distance we also sustain a loss of intimacy; the technologies that make ongoing contact possible are poor substitutes for physical proximity. Instead, we leave pieces of ourselves scattered along our path.

It is a daunting task to try to reconstruct that path and make an account of the many people who have helped along the winding course of this project. It has been my very great privilege to have been guided and inspired by professors whom I admire as intellectuals and individuals and to have enjoyed the support and encouragement of scholars in the United States and in Brazil. Friends and family have provided all manner of emotional and material sustenance. Most extraordinarily, a community of people welcomed me into their midst and shared their experiences with me. I wish I could detail the myriad ways in which I am indebted, so it is my hope that the many people whom my path has crossed in the course of this project will recognize their influence on these pages. The errors and shortcomings are mine alone.

Over the course of this project I have received financial support from several institutions. Early research for this book was made possible by a Jacob K. Javits Fellowship from the U.S. Department of Education. My research in Brazil was funded by a grant from the Memorial Foundation for Jewish Culture and by grants from the University of California (U.C.), Berkeley's Center for Latin American Studies and the Department of Anthropology's Robert H. Lowie and Ronald L. Olson Fund. Additional field research and the preparation of this book were supported by Junior Faculty Research Grants from the College of Arts and Sciences and the Office of the Vice President for Research at the University of Oklahoma. Publication of this book was aided by a joint subvention grant from the Department of Anthropology, the College of Arts and Sciences, the Provost, and the Vice President for Research at the University of Oklahoma.

I am deeply grateful to several people at the University Press of Florida: John Byram sustained interest in this project, Amy Gorelick shepherded it, Jesse Arost guided the publication process, and the manuscript was honed by Kathy Bork's acute attention to detail. I also thank two anonymous reviewers and Robin Sheriff and Maxine Margolis for their astute guidance in the revision of the manuscript.

At the University of Oklahoma department chairs Pat Gilman and Susan Vehik gave unfailing support. It has been my very good fortune to have Lesley Rankin-Hill and Noam Stillman as my colleagues, mentors, and confidants. I enjoy the intellectual stimulation and wonderful friendship of colleagues in the Anthropology Department and across campus, in particular: Clemencia Rodríguez, Tassie Hirschfeld, Diane Warren, Rita Keresztesi, Nancy LaGreca, Laurel Smith, Hester Baer, and Ryan Long. My affection and gratitude go to the members of my writing group, present and past: Kristin Dowell, Marc David, Circe Sturm, Peter Cahn, and especially Mandy Minks.

I wish to thank the following members of the faculty at UC Berkeley: Gerry Berreman, Aihwa Ong, Bill Hanks, Donald Moore, Lawrence Cohen, Gillian Hart, and Candace Slater. I am especially grateful for support from Carol Stack and Percy Hintzen, and from Alan Dundes, whose loss I feel every day. Laura Nader continues to inspire. My most heartfelt appreciation goes to Nancy Scheper-Hughes for decades of guidance and for her commitment to an engaged anthropology and her fierce sense of social justice.

I have enjoyed the friendship and benefited from the knowledge of many colleagues over the years. From my years in Berkeley special thanks go to Linda-Anne Rebhun, Rebecca Dobkins, Jonathan Xavier Inda, Roland Moore, Catherine Macklin, Nancy Chen, Peter Redfield, David Eaton, Patricia Márquez, Tanika Beamon, Adrian McIntyre, Mabel Agozzino, Stephanie Sadre-Orafai, Jelani Mahiri, Liz Roberts, Moira Pérez, Kenji Tierney, Tim Plowman, Donna Lanclos, Bev Davenport, Theresa Álfaro-Velcamp, and Rob McLaughlin. A few relationships have bridged Berkeley and São Paulo; my warmest thanks to Karen Bond, Bibia Gregori and Tom, Silvia Fabiani and Heráclito Carvalho and family, Vanessa Rosa, and especially Fabrizio Rigout.

A few extraordinary colleagues deserve special recognition for their invaluable friendship: Maria Massolo, Naomi Leite, Cecília de Mello e Souza, without whom I simply would not be here. For over thirty years Joy Eden Harrison has been the deepest of friends, inspiring ongoing discussions about creative and life processes.

I have enjoyed tremendous emotional and material support from my far-flung family, especially my parents, Irina and Erik Gronborg, who insisted that I learn to write; I hope I have fulfilled my mother's wish that this book be readable and not too academic. Other family members who have had a hand in supporting this project are Tor Gronborg, Michelle Look, Naomi Klein, Avi Lewis, Sacha Klein, Henry Klein, and Cecelia Ford Klein. Fictive kin and new kin have also played a critical role, and I thank Dan and Peggy Hilberman, Jim Riis and Nancy Borge, and my mother-in-law, Judy Riis.

In Brazil, Jota and his family introduced me to Brazil, showed me a side foreigners rarely see, and forever changed the course of my life. I thank my colleagues at the Universidade Federal de São Carlos: Marina Cardoso, Gloria Bonelli, Oswaldo Truzzi, Roberto Grün, Terrie Groth, and Valquíria Padilha. Other colleagues in Brazil with whom I have engaged in sometimes lively discussion include Monica Grin, Renée Avigdor, Marta Topel, Ethel Kosminsky, Nancy Rozenchan, Rachel Mizrahi, Roney Cytrynowicz, Beatriz Kushnir, Bila Sorj, Ilana Strozenberg, Ruben Oliven, and Guita Grin Debert. Jeff Lesser provided important insights and advice while I was in Brazil. I benefited greatly from René Decol's course on Jewish Brazilian demography at the Universidade de São Paulo (USP). The library at the Centro de Estudos Judaicos at USP generously extended access to their collection on Jews in Brazil. Jairo Friedlin of the Livraria Sêfer has sustained an interest in this project and has continued to provide me with materials and answer my questions from afar.

None of this work would have been possible without the permission and generous cooperation of the directors of the Associação Brasileira "A Hebraica" de São Paulo, especially Gaby Milevsky and presidents Samsão Woiler and Hélio Bobrow, who allowed me unfettered access. As the club's "Director of Jewish Culture," José Luiz Goldfarb not only threw open the doors, but has also maintained ongoing discussions. I benefited from the assistance of the club's staff, including the editor of and writers for the club's magazine, Júlio Nobre and Magali Boguchwal; Tania Tarandach understood this project from the beginning and has continued to support it.

I am full of admiration for the inventive ways that Jews in São Paulo creatively navigate the contradictions of their lives. I am honored by their trust, and I hope I have been faithful to the spirit of their experiences. My promise of anonymity keeps me from naming the many individuals who participated directly in the research. I wish I could sing my gratitude to Maestro León Halegua and the members of the Jerusalém and Shir Ha Shirim choruses. Warm thanks to the following people for their support of this project: Eliezer and Esther Kashtan and family; Noemi Treiger and family; Bela Tamezgui and family; Einat Hausman and family; Daniel Grabarz and family; Ana and Moyses Fraiman; Sueli Farber; Leah Goldstein; Betty Boguchwal; Carla Sitton Berg; Chaim Ashkenazi; Danielle Fridman; Joyce Zimmerman; Keren Almeida; Fatima Serebrenic; Régis Karlik; Benjamin Steiner; Marcel Berditchevsky; Rosa Botkowska; Luiz Roberto Zitron; Alexandre Leone; Cláudio Goldman; *Moré* Carlos Dimant; Alberto Milkevitz of FISESP; Renato Guertzenstein of the Clube Israelita Brasileiro in Rio; Rabbi David Azulay; Rabbi Ádrian Gottfried; Rabbi Henry Sobel; Rabbis Chaim Biniamini and Adi Biniamini and *Morá* Rivka Biniamini of the Yeshivá Colegial Machané Israel in Petrópolis; Marcel Hollender and Brenda Turteltaub of Shalom Brasil; João Batista and Adelia Aoki of UNIBES; and Abrão Bernardo Zweiman of the Chevra Kadisha. Additionally, I have enjoyed the friendship of Ana Goldfarb, Márcia Ferraz, and Lícia Beccari. I am grateful to Tania Furman and her family and sad that Tania was not able to see this project to its end. My deepest thanks go to Lilian Starobinas and her family; Lilian is the *fada madrinha* of this project, and I am grateful for her friendship.

Finally, after so much prose I am left without adequate words to thank my son, Theo, who has brought unbounded joy into my life. My husband, partner, colleague, Sean O'Neill, inspires me with his passion for mindful anthropology and has sustained me with encouragement, challenges, and love. I am eager to see what comes next.

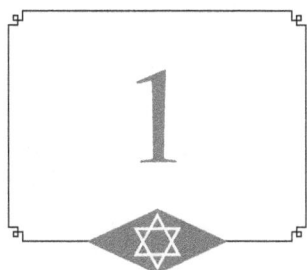

1

Departures

I have often been met with surprise or even utter astonishment upon telling people that I conduct research on Jews in Brazil. Though hardly a small population when compared with the tiny Jewish communities that are scattered about the globe, it seems as if the idea of Jews in Brazil—a country known for deeply held and celebratory Catholicism, for indigenous cultural and environmental resistance, for Afro-Brazilian religion and art, for entrenched poverty—contradicts these more familiar ways of knowing this continent-sized nation. While there are certainly contradictions inherent in being Jewish and Brazilian, I have found that Jewish Brazilians provide an intriguing window onto Brazil, a way of understanding the center from the margins, a way of examining the complex intersection between nation, race, ethnicity, and class. Considering the experiences of Jews in Brazil is also, of course, a fascinating way of thinking about the cultural construction of Jewishness, of the practices and meaning associated with being Jewish as it is lived and understood in a particular historical and cultural context, in this case, the metropolis of São Paulo at the turn of the twenty-first century.

In this book, I explore this set of issues from several perspectives: the intersecting histories of nation, city, and multiple places of origin; the multicultural constitution of the Jewish community; the way in which socioeconomic class is central to ethnic practices and identity; the economic constraints on religious and ethnic expression; the ways in which Brazilian ideology has created a particularly welcoming space for Jews and the ways in which Jews have created a community that reflects that ideology; the overlapping concerns with security that permit the Jewish community to build on existing practices in São Paulo to protect themselves against external sources of violence; the way these external threats place limits on Jewish belonging in Brazil; and the ways in which Jewish diasporic imaginings and transnational practices seek to overcome the contradictions inherent in multiple forms of belonging. Underlying this research is my own relationship to this project, the theoretical questions that frame it, the methodological approach taken, and the setting within which the research was conducted.

Classic ethnographies began with an arrival scene, drawing the reader into another world through the arduous travails of intrepid scholar-adventurers. Fieldwork in one of the world's largest cities offered challenges to be sure, but so much of what earlier generations faced is inverted in such a hypermodern setting, especially when the research is conducted among a community of people quite familiar with social science and even more likely to discuss the research process and outcomes. So it seems fitting to invert the order, to begin with the end, a departure scene.

Jewish Christmas Baskets

I left São Paulo at the end of 1999, just before Christmas. After a prolonged spring, summer had finally arrived: schools had let out, vacations had begun, and the hated *rodízio* (rotation)—a traffic-reduction measure that kept one fifth of the cars off the road each weekday—was suspended for the summer months. With the new season's popular music in the air, a collective joy spread in anticipation of *carnaval*.[1]

Having conducted field research at the Hebraica, the large social and athletic club that is a focal point for the Jewish community, I returned there for a final visit to make the rounds and say good-bye as I was preparing to leave. When I stopped by the office of the club's Department of

Jewish Culture, Sílvia and Kátia were busy as usual with preparations for the diverse events coordinated through this office.[2] Sílvia was one of the many non-Jewish employees at the club, while Kátia was a member of the Jewish community and an active participant, as well as an employee.

When I arrived, they had just received their *cestas de Natal*, the Christmas "baskets" distributed by the Personnel Department to all club employees, non-Jews and Jews alike. The Christmas basket is an extension of the *cesta básica*, the "basic basket," a package of household goods that many employers distribute monthly to their employees. The retail cost of the standardized contents (including foodstuffs such as rice, beans, and cooking oil, as well as personal hygiene and cleaning products) is used as one of the measures of the cost of living against which the national minimum wage is compared. For holidays, the packages usually contain additional items appropriate to the season. These holiday packages are such a mainstay of Brazilian celebrations that not only did the employees at this secular Jewish club receive Christmas baskets, but so did the employees at one of the major synagogues in the city.

I had been talking about this apparently incongruous practice with Miriam, a close friend who worked at this large synagogue. She thought it was "absurd" that Jewish employees should receive Christmas baskets, all the more so since they also received gifts on Jewish holidays while the non-Jewish employees did not. Given these ongoing conversations, and an appetite for contradictions whetted by fieldwork in this community, I was eager to see what was contained in these baskets distributed by the Hebraica club. Kátia was also curious, albeit for more prosaic reasons, and stopped her work to go through her basket with me.

Kátia's basket was actually a large cardboard box containing items typically consumed during the celebrations of Christmas and the New Year in Brazil:

- a bottle of champagne
- a bottle of red wine
- a bottle of olives
- a package of lentils
- a package of prunes
- a box of pineapple-flavored gelatin
- one *panettone* (sweet Italian Christmas bread)

- two *torrones* (Italian honey and almond nougat)
- hard candies
- Brazil nuts (*castanhas-do-pará*)
- ham pâté

The contents of the box were largely expected and somewhat amusing to us both. The champagne and red wine, and even the olives, candies, and nuts, fit easily into a holiday party menu. The same could be said for the pineapple gelatin and prunes, though these restorative items might also be associated with recovery from overindulgence rather than with the festivities themselves.

A few of the items in the package were ethnically marked. The *panettone* and *torrones* were evidence of the tremendous influence on local culture of the previous century's Italian immigration. So completely have Italians integrated into local culture that the custom of eating lentils on New Year's (in Brazil and elsewhere) to bring prosperity in the coming year has long since lost its association with its Italian origins. The box did not contain anything else that was clearly associated with a particular ethnic group, not even the large populations descended from twentieth-century Japanese and Middle Eastern immigrants to São Paulo; though many of their descendants are Christian, Japanese and Middle Eastern holiday foods have not been incorporated into the typical Brazilian Christmas menu.

Significantly, nothing in the box was particularly "Jewish" or acknowledged the Jewish context, nor was there anything associated with the celebration of Hanukkah, the minor Jewish holiday that coincides with the Christian holiday season. There was no "Hanukkah gelt," the golden foil-covered chocolates made to look like exotic coins, and no box of candles to offset the forty-four needed over the course of the eight nights of lighting the menorah (the eight-branched candelabrum used during the holiday).

In fact, the strong association of many of the items specifically with Christmas and New Year's celebrations heightened the incongruity of the employees of a Jewish club receiving gifts for Christian holidays. Kátia and I laughed out loud as we pulled the can of ham pâté out of the box; this definitively nonkosher item was proof that the boxes were not specially ordered for the club's staff, but were instead prepackaged *cestas de Natal* just like those received by employees throughout the region. Whatever ethnic markers contained within were presumably representative of the shared majority culture, effectively unmarked, except in this particular non-Christian context where the ethnic symbolism could not have been clearer.

Kátia and I discussed this practice of distributing Christmas baskets to employees at the Hebraica. Confirming that what Miriam had told me about the synagogue's policy was also true at the Hebraica, Kátia explained that Jewish employees additionally received chocolates for Rosh Hashanah, the Jewish New Year, while for Passover they received a box of *matzah*, the latter distributed by the Department of Jewish Culture. However, non-Jewish employees did not receive these "Jewish" gifts on Jewish holidays. Concerns over parity, it seemed, were one-sided.

In large part, this notion of parity was legislated at the national level. In accordance with federal law, all employees who work on national holidays must be paid overtime. Though there is legal separation of church and state, culturally, Brazil remains a Catholic country, and most major national holidays have Christian roots, even if they are not always particularly Christian in their mode of observance. Such holidays include Christmas, New Year's, and *carnaval*, as well as the day of Nossa Senhora Aparecida (Our Lady of the Apparition), the patron saint of Brazil, whose colonial-era black Marian apparition is associated with the national formation of Brazil. These are national holidays, regardless of the religion of the employee or employer. In the context of a Jewish institution, this logic was partially extended to Jewish holidays; Jewish employees of the club were also paid overtime if they worked on Jewish holidays, but non-Jewish employees were not. Federal labor legislation does not include Jewish holidays.

As I said my good-byes to Kátia and Sílvia, I was struck yet again by the deliberation and humor with which Jews in Brazil navigate the many contradictions in their lives. No one thought it particularly curious that a Jewish institution provided its employees with Christmas baskets and paid Catholic holidays, since these were standard Brazilian practices. That some people were critical of the apparently preferential treatment of Jewish employees on Jewish holidays was evidence that the relationship between Jewishness and Brazilianness remains in flux, and that the route to being both Brazilian and Jewish has not yet been fully charted.

Points of Departure

I never expected to do research on Jews. Although I always had a strong secular Jewish identity, I was not raised Jewish nor did I have a formal background in Jewish studies. My childhood Jewish education consisted of memorizing the transliterated blessings for the candles, wine, and bread for Shabbat (the Sabbath) when I was at my father's house in Canada, and spending my seventeenth summer as a lifeguard and swim instructor at a B'nai B'rith summer camp outside of Montréal,[3] where I learned the melody and faked the words to "Hatikva," the Israeli national anthem. As I later came to realize, the transnational implications of being a U.S. citizen in Canada (with landed-immigrant status) singing the anthem of yet another nation, where I had relatives but where I had never set foot, was symbolic of the modern Jewish condition.

In most respects, that summer camp looked like any other children's camp, albeit with a Jewish flavor. In addition to the usual dormitories and activities, there was a small equivalent section for elderly members of the community, a sort of "Golden Age" summer camp. One thing that caught my attention that summer was the sign at the entrance to the elders' portion of the camp; on it were written the words for "welcome" in well over a dozen languages from many points in the Diaspora. That sign did not represent any sort of abstract ideological internationalism, but was a pragmatic and respectful recognition of the many cultures represented by these immigrants and survivors who had come for a summer of organized recreation by the side of a bucolic lake. Over those summer months, every time I passed one particular elderly Russian man, he would look back and forth from my sweatshirt with my name ("Misha," a definitively masculine nickname in Russian) to my feminine face and shake his head and sigh, repeating in a heavy accent, "How can this be?" In spite of the gender reversal that has been so confusing for Russian speakers throughout my life, I have always found that in Jewish contexts my name has signified my Jewishness, at least among Ashkenazim.[4] At that point in my life, I had not had much contact with Jews from other backgrounds, but that summer spent in a wooded camp outside a city of immigrants gave me my first inkling of the tremendous diversity of Jewish cultures.

I grew up mostly in Southern California, where I acquired an interest in Latin America, which I sustained throughout my studies. During my early graduate training I developed a specialization in race and ethnicity, prepared to conduct fieldwork in Guatemala, and pursued research on what I have come to call "nonrepresentative minorities," people who are atypical in meaningful ways from the populations of the nations of which they are citizens. In retrospect I find it significant that while I was doing preliminary research on the national and transnational identities of Garifunas (an Afro-Caribbean group from the Central American coast), no one ever asked if I was of Garifuna descent. The Garifunas easily fit within preconceptions of appropriate anthropological subjects, and there was no need to verify whether my ethnic heritage justified my personal investment in the research project. The contrast with my later experience while researching Jews in Brazil was stark, as I found that my heritage and identity were both presumed and made explicit as part of the process and the justification for the research.

Although my first experiences in Brazil had nothing to do with Jews, those early encounters had everything to do with how I came to study Jews in Brazil. When I first went to Brazil at the end of 1992, for romantic rather than purely scholarly reasons, I was intrigued by the political transformations that were under way with the impeachment of the first democratically elected president following the military dictatorship. Although I was familiar with the particular racial constructs that have made Brazil such a compelling context for anthropological research, there was virtually no English-language literature on the variety of immigrants that have enriched Brazil's thick cultural blend. I landed in the interior of the state of São Paulo, in the southeast of the country, in São Carlos do Pinhal, a small city of roughly 100,000 about three hours inland from the metropolis of São Paulo, the state capital. Surrounded by cane fields and orange groves that had mostly replaced the coffee plantations that had brought wealth to the region, the town was dominated by the practicing-Catholic descendants of Italian immigrants (who came in large numbers at the end of the nineteenth century to pick coffee), making it an especially *Catholic* place, even within the world's largest Catholic country. I would not have been so acutely aware of the Catholic presuppositions of everyday life (in speech, in the weekly rhythms, in social presumptions) had I lived in the culturally diverse, cosmopolitan cities of Rio de Janeiro or São Paulo, for instance, where practicing Catholics have increasingly given way to nominal Catholics and practitioners of a surprising array of other spiritual and religious sects.[5]

Over the course of the more than five years that I lived in São Carlos, while I taught English, did translations, and taught anthropology at the Federal University, I was intensely aware of the predominance of Catholicism (and Christianity more broadly). I was not used to such religious assumptions and began to wonder about the experiences of non-Catholics, and especially non-Christians, and the meaning they found in being Brazilian.[6] Through forays into the state's capital, I gradually came to learn about the Jewish community there, a community that I found to be exuberant in explaining its comfortable place within Brazilian society, and the ways it was proudly "Brazilian" in distinction from the rest of the Jewish Diaspora. I found myself returning to the question of nonrepresentative minorities and national identity; I wondered what it meant to be Jewish in this Catholic country, and what it meant to be Brazilian when ethnic identity and practice placed the entire group outside of the norm of national identity. I found a community eager to explain, to celebrate its acceptance, to laugh at the contradictions, and to embrace its own transformations.

What I did not encounter was an anthropology that was entirely welcoming of this sort of research. Although a new generation of anthropologists was conducting research on Jewish communities around the world and examining the history of the discipline and the place of Jewish scholars and scholarship within it, when I returned to UC Berkeley in 1998 to prepare for formal field research I encountered warnings from faculty about barriers to funding and employment. It turned out that these informal impediments had their roots in the twentieth-century history of the discipline and a problematic relationship between Jews and anthropology (see Feldman 2004, Bunzl 2003).

Jews and Anthropology

In a biting review essay in 1993, Virginia Domínguez asked whether anthropology had a "Jewish problem." She interrogated the very minimal ethnographic research or writing on Jews, including that by anthropologists of Jewish descent, and the difficulties encountered by the few anthropologists who did write on Jews. By the early 1990s, the discipline had largely shaken off its colonial mantle and come to accept research done within the "core" countries of the world system as legitimately anthropological and no longer sought out only the apparently exotic as the proper subject of anthropological inquiry. Further, the discipline had become more comfortable with anthropologists conducting research on their "own" communities, including those who shared the same ethnic identity as their research participants. The fallacy of the "insider/outsider" dichotomy had been exposed as a complex continuum of subject position during the research process, and so-called insider research was no longer dismissed as reflexive self-indulgence, but welcomed for the important contributions scholars can make to the field through challenging our presumptions regarding subjectivity and authority.

Yet there persisted a caution against research on Jews, this in spite of some landmark research conducted by major scholars in the field. For instance, Barbara Myerhoff's *Number Our Days* (1978), about a community center for elderly Jews in Venice Beach, California, was a breakthrough in the development of reflexive anthropology (Frank 1995) and stands out as an exception to the general trends of North American anthropology.[7] In fact, some have argued that the very roots of anthropology as it developed in the United States found nourishment in the Jewish background of the founding scholars, most importantly Franz Boas and several of his most influential students, including Edward Sapir and Melville Herskovits (Frank 1997, Lewis 2001, Yelvington 2000). Nevertheless, on the few occasions when these scholars did address Jewish topics it was in minor publications and usually in the context of addressing the larger questions with which they were engaged.[8] Generally speaking, until very recently, whenever Jewish anthropologists addressed Jewish topics it was only once they were well established in the field, with secure jobs and publications that already made it clear that they were serious scholars with research agendas that engaged the core issues and traditions in anthropology.

The first generation of anthropologists in the United States was actively engaged in questions of "race" and culture; what is less well known is that they found fertile ground in the Jewish question because of the way race and culture intersect in the enduring conundrum over how to define Jews. Employing multiple methodologies, several of the discipline's best-known scholars, including Boas (1923), Kroeber (1917), and Herskovits (1927, 1960), questioned the existence of a Jewish race or attempted to define who was a Jew at a time when this was a major sociopolitical concern.

In his article "Are the Jews a Race?" (1917), Kroeber concluded that *Jews* were not a race, but then reified a biological basis for social difference by reaffirming racialized stereotypes for *other* groups. Kroeber can be forgiven for this argument because it was still early in Boas' process of dismembering the sociobiological concept of race.

Boas' (1912) studies of several immigrant groups (including Jews) added considerable weight to the nurture side of the nature versus nurture debate, since he found that the children of immigrants showed anthropometric differences from their parents. Although Boas' findings have been challenged by scholars who take issue with the particulars of his statistical analysis, the far-reaching impact of his research on the discipline in dismantling the notion of biologically distinct "races" is undeniable. Nevertheless, these findings still do not seem to have penetrated popular consciousness.

While recognizing the complex interplay between biology and environment (culture) on the body, Boas dismissed any biological determination of the "habits of life and cultural activities" for all people, Jews included, and he emphasized that cultural qualities "depend upon outer conditions that sway the fate of the people, upon its history, upon powerful individuals that arise from time to time, upon foreign influences" (1939:13). He understood the conditioning effects of historical circumstances and power relations on culture. Even in the context of a Jewish publication (the inaugural issue of the journal *Jewish Social Studies*), Boas' treatment of the Jewish question moved beyond the existence of a Jewish race by addressing the broader theoretical question of "heredity and environment," leading him to the precautionary conclusion that "the existence of a cultural personality embracing a whole 'race' is at best a poetic and dangerous fiction" (1939:14). His prescient use of quotation marks around "race" signaled an early deconstruction of the concept, an example of how thinking about Jews provoked an entire line of thinking about the human condition more broadly.

In keeping with the developing Boasian consensus, in his study of Jews in Cochin, India, David Mandelbaum concluded that "Judaism is a social and not a physical heritage . . . a matter of cultural conditioning and not of congenital acquisition" (1939:459).[9] None of these scholars considered the social meanings of "race," including the ways in which Jews themselves employ folk biological concepts in defining the Jewish people and Jewish identity; their major concern was to counter the prevailing notions of race that underlay the popular eugenics that would eventually fuel the atrocities of the Second World War.

Herskovits also employed physical anthropology to question the existence of a Jewish race (1960[1949]), but his most thorough exploration is found in his earlier article, "When Is a Jew a Jew?" (1927), in which he considered and discarded each of the various approaches to defining Jews as a unified group. Part of what makes this such an enduring question for Jews and scholars of world Jewry, and of particular interest to anthropologists, is that these attempts at definition include "race, people, nation, religion, cultural entity, historic group, [and] linguistic unit" (Herskovits 1960:1491), some of the most slippery and problematic of the concepts that together make up ethnicity.

That a consideration of Jews and Jewishness draws on all of these disparate elements makes Jews, in Lévi-Strauss' terms, "good to think with" (see Frank 1997:731). Thinking about Jews forces us to challenge conceptual categories, thereby contributing to general anthropological theory, especially where culture and identity are concerned. Nevertheless, in spite of developments in the social and biological sciences, it does not appear that any more satisfactory definition of a Jew has been put forward than that offered by Herskovits: "*A Jew is a person who calls himself a Jew, or is called Jewish by others*" (1927:117, original emphasis). This definition is completely social, and completely flexible, and implicitly allows for the kind of contextual variation that has filled the pages of scholarly research and troubled the minds of rabbis and philosophers.

Defining who is a Jew is a central and irresoluble question, posing a variety of historical, practical, methodological, religious, genetic, and even philosophical difficulties. While these definitional challenges are the focus of some research on Jews, they are not central to this research, where the focus is on the relationship between different sources of identity. Therefore, this question must be dealt with in the most pragmatic manner possible. Consistent with the approach taken by demographers of world Jewry (DellaPergola 1993), and following Herskovits' definition, for the purposes of this research a Jew is a person who identifies or is identified as Jewish (including by other Jews).[10]

For Jews, like other groups who are always in the minority (except in Israel), the question of self-definition has become incorporated into cultural (including religious) practices. Jews are constantly in interaction with other ethnic groups, and in the contemporary period, when most Jews in the world make their homes in cities, this usually means contact with many groups at once. Jews have become adept at finding a balance between fitting in and remaining distinct, and at understanding the nature of ethnicity in a flexible and comprehensive way.

Scholars have employed a variety of metaphors in an attempt to explain ethnicity. Although ideologically powerful, the "melting pot" view of cultural mixing as inevitably leading to cultural unity has given way to pluralist or multicultural approaches. Metaphors of blending or melting together are inadequate to describe experiences in which present-day reminders of the past keep Jews from entirely disappearing into the many places they have called home. In conceptualizing the historical experiences of Jews in Brazil, the metaphor of "braiding" allows a consideration of the way multiple strands are interwoven to create a whole, one in which the disparate elements are still evident. The metaphor of braiding describes the intersection of the lives of people who have come from so many places and created community, bringing together multiple histories, influences from disparate cultures, to create unity in difference.

Braiding (the process and not just the final product) can incorporate an almost infinite number of strands, and although the manner by which they have become intertwined is not always immediately evident, there is a logic to the relationship among the strands. Religious scholar Robert Orsi has also found braiding to be a useful idiom: "Braiding alerts us to look for improbable intersections, incommensurable ways of living, discrepant imaginings, unexpected movements of influence, and inspiration existing side by side" (2005:9). Braiding is particularly apt in this context, since it appears repeatedly in Jewish material culture as an element in Jewish ritual life, including at the beginning and end of Shabbat, the Jewish Sabbath. Shabbat begins at sundown with the lighting of candles and the blessing of wine and challah, the Sabbath and holiday bread, which is braided in the Ashkenazi tradition. (It is often sprinkled with seeds representing the manna miraculously sent from heaven that sustained the Israelites as they wandered in the desert). The braided form is said to resemble wheat on the stalk, wheat being one of many symbols of fertility. Wheat also represents stability, since it requires sedentary farming rather than nomadism as a way of life (Frankel and Teutsch 1992). As such, challah could be said to represent the aspirations of a people with a long history of wandering: the braiding of the strands of diaspora holds the hope of belonging, creating unity without losing the memories of the past. Additionally, the candle used in the Havdalah ceremony that brings Shabbat to a close is braided in the Ashkenazi tradition. The candle serves as a reminder of the unity (a single flame) that can form out of many lights (wicks).

Interwoven Identities

This notion of strands and braiding can be particularly useful for thinking about the related concepts of diaspora and transnationalism. For however much the usage of these terms overlaps, they refer to distinct, albeit related, phenomena and deserve some clarification, as this distinction bears directly on the question of belonging for people who are dispersed and for whom dispersal is part of their identity.

In the original Greek, "diaspora" meant dispersal. The trajectories of diasporic peoples are marked by multiple border crossings, layers of movement thickened through time, such that group identity incorporates and reflects this sense of displacement. Theirs is not an immigrant identity; diasporic peoples are wanderers who make their home in the world and have a "double consciousness."[11] Clifford explains this double "diasporic consciousness" in terms of a paradox (1997:248): "The empowering paradox of diaspora is that dwelling *here* assumes a solidarity and connection *there*. But *there* is not necessarily a single place or an exclusivist nation" (1997:269, original emphasis). Diasporic people have a dual identity where one part of them is grounded in the here and now and the other is held in the imaginary of what can never be recovered.

For the African Diaspora—the descendants of those who were sold into slavery in the Americas—"Africa" is mythic, not the continent divided up among nations that it is today. These descendants share an experience of displacement with no possibility of return to their original homeland, with profound implications for ethnic identity and "cultural nationalism" (Gilroy 1993). This is not unlike the process of imagining that Anderson (1991) has described for the creation of national identity, where people feel a strong connection and share a set of practices with people they have never met; in contrast to Anderson's "imagined communities," for diasporic communities their identity is not tied to a nationalized territory.

Similarly, the experience of Native North Americans is illustrative of how there can be *internal* diasporas as well; dispersed within a territory that is a single geopolitical unit in contemporary times, their place within that territory in no way corresponds to their original homeland. Another powerful example can be found in the Roma people (Gypsies), whose existence is defined by wandering and whose culture is detached from any particular geographic locale.

This common condition of *homelessness* is an experience shared by other diaspora groups. Rather than a temporary status, what unites the members of these groups is their identity as a *permanently* displaced people.

Jews are the prototypical diaspora,[12] a fact that is frequently overlooked in the more recent literature on diasporas (Gilroy 1993:205). The existence of a contemporary nation called "Israel" (occupying territory roughly corresponding to that ancient land occupied by Israelites long ago) does not erase the historical experience of the dispersal or the condition of diaspora as a fundamental part of their identity.[13] In his analysis of the history of the use of the term "diaspora," Jon Stratton contrasts Eretz Israel (the biblical Land of Israel) with the nation-state of Israel (1997:305). For most Jews in the world, while an important referent, modern Israel is not their country of origin. Significantly, as a multicultural, immigrant nation, modern Israel is a *product* of the Diaspora, not its *erasure*.

In spite of its long history, the term "diaspora" came into vogue in academic discourse only in the late twentieth century. Unfortunately, "diaspora" has come to replace other perfectly useful terms, such as "immigration," thereby collapsing phenomena and losing conceptual specificity. In its current usage, "diaspora" may refer to any group of people who have been displaced or relocated, whether by force or by choice, recently or in the more distant past, and whether or not there is a homeland to return to. Stratton argues for the importance of theorizing diaspora in a more rigorous way, distinguishing historical uses of the term from modern ones, which he sees as "fundamentally political . . . bound up with the nation-state" (1997:312). I am suggesting that this difference be marked with the use of the newer term "transnational" to designate these more recent nationalized and politicized meanings.

Glick Schiller, Basch, and Blanc-Szanton introduced the concept of "transnationalism" to refer to groups of people who operate across national borders, people who are "forging and sustaining *multi-stranded social relations* that [link] their societies of origin and settlement" (1992a:ix, emphasis added). They define as transnationals those whose lives are connected through "systems of social relations that are wider than national borders" (1992b:10). Further refining the concept, Ong emphasizes the political economic context of transnationalism, where this "condition of cultural interconnectedness and mobility across space . . . has been intensified by late capitalism" (1999:4).

Certain transnational practices are becoming increasingly common among all immigrants and include sending remittances, the exchange of cultural products such as music, publications, and foodstuffs, as well as the maintenance of ongoing business and familial relationships across national borders. These practices constitute what Guarnizo calls a "transnational *habitus*" (1997:311; following Bourdieu 1990:52–65), emphasizing the cross-border activities that define this phenomenon and how they inform identity. In contrast to the notion of the wandering diasporic subject, when Ong (1999) refers to the "nomadic subject," she is referring to the frequent and opportunistic movement of transnationals, as in the "flexible citizenship" of overseas Chinese who carry multiple passports as they move among nations. While this is a successful strategy for living in the contemporary global economy, their status as foreigners or citizens of multiple nations makes transnationals subject to scrutiny and mistrust by nationals, who are more firmly grounded.

It is the question of homeland or, more precisely, *nation* of origin that I consider most important in the distinction between "diaspora" and the more descriptive term "transnationalism." Recent use has seen a slippage between the two terms such that one is used to define the other. James Clifford offers important points for differentiating the diaspora experience: "Diasporas usually presuppose longer distances and a separation more like exile: a constitutive taboo on return, or its postponement to a remote future. Diasporas also connect multiple communities of a dispersed population" (1997:246). "Diaspora" is a concept that predates the nation-state, and the historical depth of the experience of dispersal is certainly definitive. I propose preserving the term "diaspora" for those groups without a nation of origin, for whom their "homeland" is either mythic or metaphoric.

The distinction between transnationalism and diaspora that I wish to assert is not predicated on degree of suffering. Those who have been forced to leave their homeland due to contemporary conflicts suffer their losses greatly; losses cannot be compared. Rather, I am advocating for a precision in terminology that allows for analytic specificity in relation to nations and nationalism. Whether Mexican migrants, second-generation Vietnamese refugees, or Cuban exiles, their transnational identity is constructed in relation to an existing nation-state.

Obviously, there are overlapping experiences and peoples whose experience does not clearly fit one concept more than another, making the conceptual distinctions difficult. The point here is not to police conceptual boundaries, but to preserve these distinctions as analytic tools for understanding the variety of experiences of dispersed peoples, however wide and deep their dispersal may be. What I would like to emphasize is that at the most basic level, "diaspora" and "transnationalism" refer to different *qualities* of displacement and belonging. Those groups who hold out the hope of return to their *nation* of origin, who send remittances "home" to family and friends, who have a *country* that will speak up for them in times of conflict, who imagine their identity in relation to a specific *modern state* experience being in the world in a fundamentally different way from those peoples for whom a diasporic existence—an ancient displacement from a mythic or unattainable point of origin—is a core part of their shared identity *as a people*.

This distinction is also helpful for thinking about the repeated dispersals that have punctuated Jewish history. Diaspora is part of the condition of Jewishness, and wandering is a core concept in Jewish identity. However, even in the case of Jews, I believe the term "diaspora" is misapplied when used to refer to most dispersals subsequent to the *galut* (the exile following the destruction of the Second Temple), and especially when it references the more recent dispersals of Jews from later homelands. Jews who left Eastern Europe during the pogroms, those who left Europe during the World Wars, and those who left Egypt in the 1950s were emigrants and refugees. They left nations of which they were a part and carried the languages and cultures of those nations with them to other nations. However distant from these homelands they may be now, however impossible or unlikely their return, for Russian, German, Polish, or Egyptian Jews, their homelands are specific nations. They are fonts of cultural practices and identities that emigrants have passed to subsequent generations. That these more recent experiences of displacement can be articulated with those of generations in the past is part of the *original* condition of displacement. That contemporary Jews are not only scattered across the globe but also maintain relationships with family in other nations reflects their experiences as *transnational* peoples in addition to living in diaspora. Like other transnationals, they may send remittances, not to the original, mythic homeland, but rather to family in a country of origin (or another point of emigration) which is a contemporary nation-state, including modern Israel.

With regard to identity, then, while the Diaspora and the transnational experiences both involve elements of practice and the imaginary, the imaginary infuses the practice of those in diaspora, whereas the practice of transnationals is much more specifically grounded in a particular set of places. The distinction I am drawing between diaspora and transnationalism is important for the central question of this book: what is the relationship between ethnic and national identity? It is a question about belonging, about "cultural citizenship,"[14] and about sources of identity for those who are "always from somewhere else" (Agosín 1998), and for whom that somewhere else does not exist in the contemporary geopolitical landscape. It is also a distinction that is important for the host nation that constructs itself in relation to the differences contained within it.

The tension between diaspora and transnationalism has contributed to Jews being seen as "cosmopolitan," as having commitments to other nations, a dangerous predisposition in times of rising nationalism. What I wish to show here is that where ethnicity and belonging are more flexible, as in Brazil, belonging need not demand exclusivity. The problem, then, is not one of people having too many identities or too many passports, but one of nations reifying borders and failing to acknowledge the increasingly common condition of dispersal and frequent movement that characterizes the contemporary world. The Brazilian context, with its fluid racial categories and inclusive notions of ethnic and national identity, sets the stage for examining the meaning of multiple identities, even those that are apparently contradictory.

Identity and Belonging in the Country of the Future

From a certain perspective, Brazil has been a kind of social-scientific laboratory for the analysis of race and ethnic relations, the subject of much research by both Brazilian and foreign scholars. The fluidity of racial and color designations in contemporary Brazil has stood as one of the starkest contrasts to the bipolar classificatory system characterized by hypodescent (or the "one-drop rule") predominant in the United States (Harris and Kottak 1963). According to the logic of hypodescent, a person with mixed racial heritage belongs to the socially inferior group, regardless of her physical appearance. Underlying this logic is a notion of racial purity that understands "mixing" as polluting and has roots in the practices of the U.S. slavery regime. Historically in the United States, a child born of illicit master-slave relations was considered black and a slave. In contrast, in Brazil, where master-slave relations were more readily acknowledged, a child born under the same circumstances did not inherit his mother's racial category or slave status and was considered "mulatto" and free, allowing for the early emergence of an intermediary racial category and a free black professional class well before abolition.

These historical practices reverberate in the contemporary period; whereas a person of mixed white-black ancestry in the United States is usually classified as black, in Brazil that same person would be considered part of the large intermediary category in which dozens of terms may be applied depending on that person's combination of skin color and other physical attributes, as well as behavior, personality, and class position. Two siblings of the same parentage and presumed mixed ancestry might be given different "racial" labels based on their particular physiognomy, emphasizing individual qualities over group characteristics or shared descent.

The struggle over how to conceptualize the intermingling of cultures (motivated by the necessary departure from racial miscegenation models) gave rise to intellectual engagement with these issues in Brazil long before the current Euro-American academic interest in hybridity. The modernist movement of the 1920s introduced the concept of "anthropophagy" as a central metaphor for this dynamic relationship. As film theorist Robert Stam points out in his analysis of race in Brazilian cinema, "[t]he currently fashionable talk of postcolonial 'hybridity' and 'syncretism' often elides the fact that artists and intellectuals in Brazil and the Caribbean were theorizing hybridity over half a century earlier. In two manifestos— 'Manifesto of Brazilwood Poetry' (1924) and 'Cannibalist Manifesto' (1928)—Oswald de Andrade pointed the way to an artistic practice at once nationalist and cosmopolitan, nativist and modern" (1997:70).

It is not surprising that such a manifesto for overcoming contradictions, such as that between the national and the cosmopolitan, would emerge out of Brazil. The powerful "Manifesto Antropofágico" [Cannibalist manifesto] (1972) is an enigmatic declaration in which de Andrade develops cannibalism as a central metaphor for the relationship between Brazilian and European cultures, not as one of imitation but of consumption, absorption, and transformation. This ethos of cultural cannibalism echoes the Brazilian racial ideology of mixing as well.

In Brazil race is social and metaphorical, whereby racial qualities may be attributed to a person regardless of her apparent physical features, based on interpretations of behavior and social position. In Brazilian parlance, anyone can "have race"; "*ter raça*" means to be strong, courageous, and dignified, to be a fighter. These are admired personal qualities and survival skills. More significantly, the intermediary "mixed-race" category is central to the definition of what it means to be Brazilian, and Brazilians claim an a priori "mixedness" when asserting their national identity, even when this mixing is more ideological than biological.

Brazilian identity emerged in the postcolonial period as a way to assert a source of national distinction and pride in contrast to the popular European racial determinism that saw racial mixing as "mongrelization," considered an insuperable problem for those concerned with building national identity.[15] Like intellectuals in other parts of Latin America who source their national identities to the encounter between Europeans and Native Americans, the Brazilian modernists of the 1920s sought to free themselves of the confines of a biological racial model by constructing a cultural model for Brazilian national identity.

Anthropologist Renato Ortiz credits modernist social historian Gilberto Freyre with successfully reinterpreting the reigning racial construct at the time. Drawing on Boas' theories actively discrediting the biological notion of race, Freyre shifted the focus in Brazil from biological race to culture. For Ortiz, this shift to the "myth of the three races" (in which race is actually understood in cultural rather than biological terms) is fundamental for understanding Brazil; it is "a cosmological myth [that] tells of the origin of the modern Brazilian State, [the] starting point for an entire cosmology that precedes its own reality" (1985:38). In other words, it is a stated desire yet to be attained that has become the ideological base for shared notions of Brazilianness. This sharing or blending is *both* biological and cultural. Rather than damage to be repaired, *mestiçagem* (miscegenation) and all that is *mestiço* (mixed, hybrid) is raised up as the ideal to be achieved. Following the abolition of slavery in 1888 (Brazil was the last country in the Americas to do so), and the proclamation of the republic in 1889, the new state oversaw the social transformations under way. "The myth of the three races then became plausible and could be expressed (*se atualizar*) as ritual. The ideology of *mestiçagem*, which was imprisoned by the ambiguities of racist theories, upon reinterpretation could be socially disseminated and become common sense, ritually celebrated in daily relations or in major events like *carnaval* and soccer. What was *mestiço* became national" (Ortiz 1985:41). Rather than a source of weakness, racial mixing came to be identified as a source of strength and a distinctive national identity. This positive ideology of *mestiçagem*, that is, of a nation forged out of racial mixing, does not escape the racial model, but transforms it into a hope for the future, a future in which mixing will break down the social hierarchies that are inconsistent with the ideal of a country without prejudice.

The evocation of the future entails the hope of escaping this origin in racial mixing, what Brazilian filmmaker and social critic Arnaldo Jabor (1999) sarcastically calls "the hereditary diseases of our *formação* [background]," and Brazilian sociologist Bernardo Sorj calls "the original sin" (1997:15).[16] The construct of Brazil as "the country of the future," with a clear basis in racial mixing, was in evidence by the 1940s.[17] For example, Stefan Zweig, Jewish refugee from Nazi-dominated Europe, found Edenic possibility in Brazil: "The allegedly destructive principle of race mixture, this horror, this 'sin against the blood' of our obsessed race theoreticians, is here consciously used as a process of cementing national culture" (1942:9). In his idealistic portrait of Brazil (he even manages to romanticize slavery and dictatorship), Zweig not only identifies racial mixing as the hope for *Brazil*'s future but also presents Brazil as a model to be emulated by the *entire world*, as if racial mixing could eliminate prejudice.

These are the roots of the ideal of Brazil as a "racial democracy" that has so dominated discourse in and about Brazil: the idea that there is no racial discrimination, and that state and society are color-blind. Historically, Brazilians have suggested that the extremes of wealth and poverty that are so plainly evident throughout the country are a consequence of the country's uneven development; the tautology that economic inequality is due to class differences is invoked by elite and impoverished Brazilians alike, perhaps in defense of the idea of racial democracy. The compelling ideology behind this discourse of class inequality has buoyed what Brazilian sociologist Florestan Fernandes (1969) called the "myth" of racial democracy against all evidence to the contrary, including ample research by Brazilian and foreign scholars alike, beginning in the 1950s, that has clearly demonstrated a correlation between race and socioeconomic status. While Brazil has never had the kind of codified racial segregation that characterized the Jim Crow South in the United States or South Africa under the apartheid regime, there is no need for elaborate statistical calculations to see that de facto segregation still exists, and that there are a disproportionate number of people of color among the poor and precious few among the well-to-do in Brazil (Skidmore 1993:216). Moreover, while Afro-Brazilians of all shades have been socially, economically, and politically excluded, indigenous Brazilians have been even further marginalized within the discourse on national identity (Ramos 1998, Warren 2001).

Into this mix stepped immigrants seeking new opportunities and escape from persecution. The late nineteenth and early twentieth centuries saw an explosion in Brazil's population with immigrants mostly from Europe, the Middle East, and Japan. Scholarly emphasis on race, specifically on populations of African and indigenous descent and their influence on Brazilian culture and society, has only recently been supplemented by research on these sizable immigrant populations (see, for example, Fausto 1999; Fausto et al. 1995; Grün 1992, 1998; Karam 2007; Lesser 1995, 1999, 2007; Reis 2000; Seyferth 1998, 2000; Topel 2008; Truzzi 1997). This new research has corresponded to a growing interest in understanding the heterogeneity of Brazilian society, partly stimulated by the five hundredth anniversary of the arrival of the first Europeans on the shores of what would become Brazil. In effect, Brazilians have had to jettison the "myth of the three races" in order to accommodate Jews, Arabs, and Asians into the racial system even as they hold fast to the underlying ideology of racial equality.[18] The limits of this accommodation are exposed when these communities continue to foreground their distinctive origins rather than meld with the general population (e.g., Karam 2007:95–104). If racial mixing is a key element of national ideology, then those groups who do not actively participate in this national practice (through marriage, for instance) force a consideration of the limits of belonging within a cultural worldview that seeks to accommodate and even appropriate difference.

Jewishness and Brazilianness

When U.S. scholars have studied Brazil they have tended to focus on powerless people, groups that have nevertheless formed the cultural pillars of the nation. This has meant that most North American anthropology on Brazil reproduces (implicitly, if not explicitly) the three-race model of

Brazilian identity.[19] Michael Herzfeld (1997) reminds us that anthropology tends to be interested in marginal populations, including those that are not always central to the construction of the nation where they reside. Insofar as this book focuses on a population that has not been recognized within North American anthropology as fundamental to the nation of Brazil, it embraces that anthropological tradition of returning to the margins to get another view of the center. Furthermore, while "[n]ationalist objections rest on the view that such groups are numerically insignificant and therefore atypical" (Herzfeld 1997:33), in this case, a new national interest in the tiny Jewish segment of the population has emerged that demands analysis as well.

It is not only North American anthropologists who struggle against typologies. The relatively new field of Latin American Jewish studies emerged out of a lack of conceptual space for the study of Jews in a region characterized by particular racial and ethnic constructs, on the one hand, and the lack of interest in "marginal" Jews (or "Jews in strange places," as they are sometimes jokingly referred to) on the part of scholars in mainstream Judaic studies (Elkin 1998, Lesser and Rein 2008). Both Latin American studies and Jewish studies, and, consequently, Latin American Jewish studies were dominated by the academic fields of history and literature, with few contributions from fields such as anthropology until the turn of the twenty-first century. In some ways, newer developments in Latin American ethnic studies are only "new" because of poor dialogue across disciplines, and paradigmatic differences mean that scholars might talk at cross-purposes because of lack of knowledge about the underlying assumptions of other disciplines.

For example, one question that has emerged in Latin American Jewish studies is whether the Jews who live in Latin America are Latin American Jews or Jewish Latin Americans. More than a question of semantics, or merely emphasis, the question hinges on the relationship between ethnic and national identity. Historians Jeff Lesser and Raanan Rein have asserted the importance of emphasizing national identity as the nominal aspect in the Brazilian and Argentinean contexts, respectively, and "Jewish" as the ethnic modifier. Their research points to the centrality of the national context for the construction of a Jewish ethnic identity in relation to other ethnic and national identities, and they insist on the importance of pulling Jewish studies out of its insular tendencies.

While I am in complete agreement, from an anthropological point of view, this perspective is a given. The idea that ethnic identity is culturally constructed, performed, and made meaningful within a particular cultural context and shifts according to a range of other identity constructs is so firmly established in anthropology as to hardly need explanation. Further, rather than there being a singular answer, that is, rather than declaring that Jews in Brazil are Brazilian Jews or Jewish Brazilians (thereby emphasizing their Brazilianness), it is important to highlight how fluid and situational ethnic identity is. The salience of one or another aspect of their complex, layered identities depends on a variety of factors, including the historical moment, the spatial and cultural/ethnic context, religious orientation (with more Orthodox denominations demanding stricter adherence to Judaism in contradistinction to "outside" influences), and economic resources and ability to participate in communal institutions. In other words, the relationship between ethnic and national identity depends on many of the themes developed in this book. As such, I have used these terms interchangeably according to which aspect is most salient, not along a "continuum" of "types," as suggested by Lesser and Rein (2008:25), but along a continuum of practices and meanings that is flexible at both the group and the individual levels.

If pushed to choose, however, I would offer my oversimplified (and slightly sarcastic) response when asked for my "conclusions": Brazilian Jews are Brazilian. Their community organization reflects their national context, and they explain themselves and their practices in terms of Brazilian values. So this study is as much about Brazil and Brazilianness as it is about Jews and Jewishness. By "returning the 'nation' to a prominent position," as Lesser and Rein advocate (2008:25), the focus can also shift to the significance of transnational identities and practices. In the same way that studies of nonrepresentative groups can shed light on the construction of national identity, transnational groups provide another point of contrast for understanding the processes of national definition. As Gupta and Ferguson have stated, "national identities need to be understood against subnational ones and against supranational identities—and perhaps even against forms of imagining community that are not territorially based" (1997:17). Thus, Jewish Brazilians offer unique opportunities to examine Brazilian national identity because they represent each of these "forms of imagining community," as a "subnational" ethnic group, a "supranational" (i.e., transnational) one, and one which is rooted in a shared (diasporic) imaginary.

The question of identity is always on the table for Brazilians, who are forever trying to characterize and describe what it means to be Brazilian. This attempt at an unattainable definition derives from the enormity of the country and its internal contrasts and inherent contradictions, as well as from a desire for recognition within the world system. For Jews, the question of definition is also always in discussion, and the endless debates about definition have produced philosophical treatises and religious conflicts.

I wish to be clear from the outset that this book is not an attempt to define Brazilianness or Jewishness, as each category is so heterogeneous and complex as to defy definition. It is, rather, an attempt to examine where these two spheres of experience overlap and interact. The friction from the contradictions of this overlap (especially interesting because each is so internally differentiated) indicates what is at stake, that is, what it means to be Brazilian and Jewish and how each seeks a kind of resolution by embracing the contradictions that are inherent in their multiple sources of identity. The heat generated by this friction is also the place where culture change is initiated, a central concern for anthropologists. Jews in Brazil therefore offer a particularly interesting opportunity to examine both national and ethnic identity and the way they articulate, since these questions are explicit and internal, native to the groups and not externally imposed by outside scholars. Ultimately, in this book I seek to understand the interrelationship of ethnic and national identity. By studying Jews, a tiny and heterogeneous minority, I am taking an oblique approach to understanding Brazil. By studying those who seem to fall outside the categories, we can better understand the categories and what is at stake in maintaining or dissolving them.

At various points in history, Jews have been defined according to differing concepts, including nation, religion, race, and culture, and vestiges of these categories manifest today under a variety of circumstances. The concept of ethnicity allows for the interrelation of all of these categories, and for this reason it is a fruitful approach to studying Jews and Jewishness. Likewise, through studying Jews and Jewishness we can better understand the concept of "ethnicity" in all its situational, flexible, positional complexity. In the many national contexts in which Jews live today, their ethnic distinctiveness can be found intertwined in multiple experiences of dispersal, and the concepts of "diaspora" and "transnationalism" help to disentangle these many strands. Ultimately, in a world increasingly characterized by population movements, studying Jews in Brazil can offer us a greater understanding about how ethnic and national identities can be mutually constitutive.

The Fieldwork Mosaic

Accounts of Jews in Brazil often begin with the history of the forced conversion of Jews in Portugal and the explorers and colonists who settled in what became Brazil, many of whom were "New Christians," as the forced converts were known, whether they were practicing Christians or secretly practicing Jews. Though impossible to document, there may be over one million New Christian descendants in Brazil, which would make Brazil home to the greatest number of people of Sephardi Jewish origin.[20] Some of these descendants have been investigating their roots, and some are even "returning" or converting to Judaism (Ramagem 1994).[21] However, most of these descendants do not know about their Jewish heritage and are therefore not a part of the Jewish community or directly involved in the questions being addressed in this book. Very little of this history is directly relevant to the present-day communities of Jews who now reside in Brazil except insofar as they are able to capitalize ideologically by making an argument that Jews have participated in the building of the nation since the arrival of the first Europeans in 1500.

For most of the first three hundred years of Brazil's history, immigration to the colony was restricted, at least officially, to avowed Catholics. Legal Jewish immigration began very slowly following Brazil's independence in 1822 and the imperial Constitution of 1824, which allowed for the practice of other religions in private. Some of the first openly Jewish immigrants were Moroccans who settled in the Amazon region from the mid-nineteenth to the early twentieth century. Whereas some intermingled with the local populations and did not retain much in the way of Jewish practices, others maintained a strong Jewish identity, including the language Haketia (North African Judeo-Spanish), and established communal institutions throughout the region. Most Jewish settlers in Belém and other northern Brazilian towns were from Morocco, and these were joined by small numbers of Sephardim from Europe and the Middle East, as well as Ashkenazim from Central and Eastern Europe (Benchimol 1998:73).

Initially working as itinerant peddlers, during the rubber boom in the late nineteenth century, Jews played a major role as middlemen (Miller 1996:196), enjoying great commercial success and sending their children to schools in Rio de Janeiro, then the nation's capital. The proclamation of the republic in 1889 brought the legal separation of church and state and established freedom of worship, setting the stage for a larger-scale Jewish immigration. In 1917, just prior to the major influx of Jewish immigrants, the majority of the 5,000 to 7,000 Jews in Brazil were Sephardim in the Amazon.

While mass immigration in Brazil began in the late nineteenth century, significant Jewish immigration to Brazil began slightly later. Largely driven by dire events and policy shifts elsewhere, Jewish immigration to Brazil peaked between the World Wars, immediately after World War II, and in the mid-1950s, resulting in a community that includes Jews from more than sixty countries of origin, including other Latin American nations. In contrast to the previous century, following several larger waves of immigration, by the mid-twentieth century the majority of Brazilian Jews were Ashkenazi. Though most of the Amazonian Jews had relocated to the cities of Rio de Janeiro and São Paulo (Benchimol 1998), as of the mid-1970s, only 14 percent of Jewish families in São Paulo were Sephardi (Rattner 1977:191).

Today's Jewish community in Brazil is descended mostly from twentieth-century immigrants. What these immigrants and their descendants share with the earlier waves of Jews is tremendous economic and social success that allowed the majority to create a solid sense of belonging within Brazilian society.

There are somewhere between 100,000 and 120,000 Jews in Brazil.[22] The great majority of these live in one of three cities: São Paulo, Rio de Janeiro, and Porto Alegre in the south. Of the three cities, the Jewish population in São Paulo is the largest, at approximately 60,000.

Although both Rio and Porto Alegre would have offered more pleasant fieldwork environments, I chose to conduct my research in the community in São Paulo for several significant reasons. In addition to having the largest population in absolute terms, São Paulo plays a central role in representing Jews in Brazil more broadly. Insofar as there is a Brazilian Jewish community beyond the bounds of each specific locale, it is coordinated through São Paulo, home to the national umbrella organization CONIB (Confederação Israelita Brasileira, the Jewish Brazilian Confederation), and to several periodicals with national distribution. São Paulo is also where two nationally broadcast Jewish weekly television programs are produced, one of which is the oldest and longest-running program on Brazilian television; *Mosaico* has been on the air for over forty years.[23]

Further, and most significantly, São Paulo is the setting for the world's largest Jewish social and athletic club. The Associação Brasileira "A Hebraica" de São Paulo (the Brazilian "Hebraic" Association of São Paulo) is an increasingly inclusive community center that brings together the most diverse segments of the São Paulo Jewish community.[24] As a physical place and an institution, the Hebraica is the hub of the city's Jewish community. For this reason, I chose to conduct research there. I began the research during the five years I was living in São Carlos, making multiple field trips from the interior to the city of São Paulo. Building on that initial research, I conducted seven months of full-time ethnographic research in 1999 and made an additional three return trips in 2002, 2003, and 2006. During full-time research I participated fully in community and club life, becoming involved in two choirs, assisting in the governing council elections, interpreting for a series of lectures on the medieval philosopher Maimonides given by a visiting Israeli scholar, and taking a photography class with a cross section of club members and employees.

Joining the choirs was never part of my research plan but came about when I was first introduced to Maestro León Halegua. His first question to me was, "Can you sing?" Before I knew it, my bashful assent had been taken to mean both that I could sing and that I was available to join both choruses, each of which was in preparation for major presentations. The liturgical choir sang during the Jewish High Holy Days, and the larger general choir performed a version of Gershwin's *Porgy and Bess* with the club's theater and dance departments and sang in a couple of choir "encounters" at major music halls in the city. These proved to be the richest sort of ethnographic experiences, in which I was able to truly participate as an active, contributing member to a collective effort.

I lived at a distance from the club, renting a room from an elderly Jewish woman in the neighborhood of Higienópolis in order to be in regular contact with other Jewish institutions in that region. Higienópolis is an upscale neighborhood with a concentration of Jewish institutions and businesses, including Brazil's only Jewish bookstore, Livraria Sêfer. In order to further expand my experiences and networks I visited Jewish schools, philanthropic institutions, community organizations, and cultural centers and attended services at different synagogues. I also went to people's homes, met their families and friends, shared meals, and, incredibly, ran into them on the street, something that would seem impossible in a city that size, until I understood more about how people inhabit the city.

I conducted informal interviews at every opportunity, with as many different kinds of people as I came in contact with, under the many circumstances that presented themselves through casual conversations, in social situations, in transit, and following events. In addition to Jews, I spoke with many of the people whose work brought them in contact with Jews, including employees at the club, as well as maids and manicurists, security guards and taxi drivers.

I conducted most of my formal interviews with individuals after we had already established a relationship through informal conversations and activities. In twenty-five formal, tape-recorded interviews, and well over seventy-five informal interviews, I spoke with people in a variety of positions within the community, from central to marginal, and from those in leadership roles to those with little formal connection to the core institutions.

Because the goal of the research was not to focus on the experience of a specific subgroup within the community, but rather to consider the overall concerns and practices within the community as a whole, I threw my net widely. I interviewed old and young, women and men, immigrants and third-generation Brazilians, those who were actively involved in the community and those who were more distant. Additionally, I tried to interview across a gradation of religious affiliation from orthodox to atheist.

In spite of trying to be inclusive, I recognize that all studies have their limits. As was the case with a survey of the São Paulo Jewish community conducted in 1968, my research focused primarily on "those Jews who are most identified with their communities, while practically ignoring 'marginal' Jews" (Rattner 1972a:9; all translations from Portuguese are mine unless otherwise noted). The danger is always in confusing one segment of a social world for the whole. Since it was not my goal to take a census of the community or to make a comprehensive description of the community's organization and services, these limitations also reflect the research question itself. While I am interested personally and politically in those more marginalized elements of the community, the questions driving the research have to do with those who identify, and are identified, as Jews, including in a wider arena. This was the motivation for selecting the Hebraica club as a primary research site, to have access to the part of the community that is most publicly identifiable as Jewish.

Throughout the research process, I was impressed by the level of co-operation, the genuine interest in the research questions, and the guidance that I received from so many people. In several cases during formal interviews, participants turned off the tape recorder to tell me things "off the record." In other cases, people told me personal secrets because they thought it was important for my understanding. As one young man explained while telling me a personal story, "I am telling you this because you need to know it, and because I know you won't write about it." I frequently found myself in conversations about what I would or would not write about and am grateful to have had the opportunity to openly discuss the ethical choices that always pose dilemmas in field research.

At the beginning of fieldwork, I was interviewed more than I conducted interviews, but that is quite common. As Myerhoff (1978) experienced at the beginning of her research with the elders in California, these questions included: How did you come to be among us? What will you do for us? Where does your family come from? and Are you the daughter of a Jewish mother? I was researching identity, but my identity was also up for discussion. When I explained that my maternal grandmother was the only one of my grandparents who was not Jewish, the curt response from one young man was, "Estragou tudo," she had "ruined everything."[25] Nevertheless, in spite of Orthodox definitions, and my unorthodox background, I was apparently "Jewish enough" to conduct the research, something that I was told directly and with surprising frequency. While I did not encounter situations that would have been obviously closed to a non-Jewish researcher, I will never know to what extent perceptions of my own identity figured into the relationships that I developed and still maintain with members of the community. That most of these relationships developed within the context of a "Jewish space" certainly ratified my presence.

A City Called Hebraica

From the balcony on the second floor of the main building at the club one looks over a set of pools and landscaped greenery, a cool clearing in the midst of the ubiquitous gray high-rises that block views in every direction in São Paulo. Referring to its physical as well as its social space, some called the club an "oasis," others, an "island." They expressed a physical and psychic relief they felt upon passing through its guarded gates into an attractive environment, buffered from the noise, pollution, and general ugliness of most of the rest of the city, apparently safe from the many dangers of the streets. The club also provided a "Jewish" space, a place within which the Christian predominance that characterizes the rest of Brazil faded into the background, a place where a different set of assumptions was in operation. A young professional whose work took him all over the city, Benjamin organized his social life around the club and made a point of stopping by at least once a day, even if only for fifteen minutes, to "recharge [his] Jewish batteries." Considering the effort it must have cost him to navigate traffic and inconstant schedules, this commitment spoke volumes about the importance of this institution in his life, a commitment shared by scores of others.

In planning my research, I chose to concentrate my fieldwork at the Hebraica because it also offered me a place to focus within the overly complex city. Furthermore, it is an institution by which the community defines itself and is defined by others, a space where Jewish activities are held and where many kinds of Jews meet and mingle, and where I could find a concentration of the Jewish community, which made up only about one-third of 1 percent of the city's 18 million people.

Somehow, the Hebraica manages to be both uniquely Jewish and uniquely Brazilian, existing as an expression of both of these seemingly contradictory identities and facilitating a bridge between them. Its uniqueness stems from several interrelated aspects of the club, including its size (the physical space it occupies, as well as its membership), the extent of its facilities, and the breadth of its activities. In promotional material, the club refers to itself as "a city . . . a city called Hebraica." Rather than emphasizing the club's separateness, as the island metaphor suggests, or its value as a refuge, as invoked by the oasis metaphor so commonly conjured up by members, presenting the club as a city within a city emphasizes the variety of resources offered and the possibilities of social encounter. The glossy full-color book that is presented to formal visitors to the club extends the metaphor: "The Hebraica should be thought of as a real city, or a world, a planet. And if we extend these reflections on the city, the Hebraica could even be imagined as a utopian city, a special space for discovery [*invenções*] and humanism . . . A model of respect for the citizen, in the classic sense of the word, where everyone has the right to culture, art, leisure, and pleasure—as well as the study and celebration [*culto*] of the time-honored [*milenar*] and sacred. All of this within the beautiful and foundational ideal of Jewish continuity" (Faerman and Gontow 1996). In typical Brazilian hyperbole, the club presents itself in idealized terms: not just a city, but a world unto itself! However, the Hebraica is not an isolated world, but an institution integrated into the city of São Paulo and Brazilian society at large.

Established as an elite club in 1953 by a small group of Jewish industrialists, fifty years later the club's membership of approximately 25,000 represented about 40 percent of São Paulo's Jewish community.[26] The club's promotional materials declare that the Hebraica is "the biggest Jewish institution in the world," a claim that has been made since the early 1980s (Cytrynowicz 2003:131). Skeptical of this assertion in part because of the *paulista* predilection for the superlative,[27] I confirmed this fact with demographer Sergio DellaPergola (personal communication). The Hebraica is indeed without peer in the Jewish world.

In the Brazilian context, however, it is not especially remarkable, at least not in terms of size and structure. Social and athletic clubs are prominent fixtures in the social landscape throughout Latin America and should not be confused with country clubs in the United States, for instance. Clubs in Brazil fulfill roughly similar social functions for different ethnic, occupational, and socioeconomic strata. Even small cities may have several clubs serving different segments of the population, each of which may be based on class interests or industry segment. For example, the Bank of Brazil has clubs all over the country for its employees, with pools, tennis courts, soccer fields, restaurants, and so on, and employees of SABESP, the Companhia de Saneamento Básico do Estado de São Paulo (the state sanitation company) have access to a statewide network of sport, leisure, and health facilities. These clubs vary in their focus and facilities according to the groups they represent, with consequent differences in activities and services.

There are other ethnic clubs in São Paulo as well, the most prominent being the Esporte Clube Sírio (Syrian Sports Club) and the Clube Atlético Monte Líbano (Mount Lebanon Athletic Club) (see Karam 2007). Though the Hebraica occupies an impressive area of 62,000 square meters, there are larger clubs in São Paulo, including the elite Pinheiros club next door, which is more than twice as big, with over 168,000 square meters of land.

In the United States, Jewish community centers that meet multiple needs of the community have historical roots in the "synagogue centers" that were known by the derisive term "shul with a pool" (*shul* being Yiddish for synagogue; see Kaufman 1999). However, comparisons with these familiar institutions would be misleading, as they do not begin to describe the Hebraica in either size or scope. It is not only size that makes a city, but also complexity, and the Hebraica club's deployment of the city metaphor can be attributed to the variety of spaces and distinct activities contained within its walls. Inside there are theaters, sports facilities, a spa, a synagogue, a library, a day-care center, plazas, restaurants, cafes, bank branches, and a newsstand. In a remarkable feat of design and efficiency, nearly every space serves multiple purposes and every building has multiple uses.[28] The tennis courts occupy the roof of the Youth Center, underneath the kosher restaurant is an industrial kosher kitchen producing meals for airplanes and hospitals, theaters become synagogues, ballrooms become markets, and the basketball gymnasium accommodates a stage for large events. The flexible uses of each space make the club seem even larger.

In addition to the regular daily activities, at any given moment there may be several major events happening within the club. For example, on one Tuesday evening in the late winter of 1999 members could choose between (1) a benefit concert of Sephardi music by the well-known singer Fortuna in support of Chaverim (Friends),[29] a group that organizes activities for people with "special needs"; (2) the joint opening of an exhibit by an Israeli photographer and a weeklong Israeli film festival; (3) an open discussion with a local politician for the 25–35-year-old crowd; and (4) Israeli folk dance rehearsal for about fifty adolescents. On Sunday mornings there is an ongoing series of lectures and other cultural events for elderly members of the community,[30] followed by a free concert of classical music at noon that is open to the public (i.e., not just for club members), and the afternoons are filled with lectures and live music. Many of the elderly people who frequent these events are not members of the club. The club not only provides space and organized activities for them, but also provides a free shuttle between the club and the neighborhood of Higienópolis. All told, the club sponsors 5,000 events per year (Canecchio 2003).

The Publicity Department hangs colorful banners at the club entrances to advertise events and distributes flyers throughout the club. In addition to the numerous daily activities, there is always some major event under way, usually without disturbing the discrete spaces within the club where people relax and meet friends and family. Many of these areas bear names with specific Jewish referents, ranging from geographic to cultural, and from international to local: the Israel Room, Jerusalem Plaza, Carmel Plaza, the Marc Chagall Ballroom, the Yitzhak Rabin Civic Center, the Arthur Rubinstein Theater, the Anne Frank Theater, and the Adolfo Bloch Hall, the last named after one of the community's prominent businessmen, owner of Abril, publisher of major national magazines. Other spaces as yet unnamed include the main building, library, synagogue, spa, art gallery, and day-care center, to name just a few.[31]

My introduction to the Hebraica occurred several years before my formal research, when I was just beginning to explore the possibilities of research in the Jewish community in São Paulo. I had taken a course on the history of Jewish immigration in Brazil offered by demographer René Decol through the Judaic Studies Program at the University of São Paulo. Early in the semester, I met Rosa, a boisterous woman in her mid-sixties who was also taking the class. She took an interest in my research, took me in, gave me food and shelter during my early ventures into the city, and made sure I understood the contours of the Jewish community and its major institutions. The first time she took me to the Hebraica was for Rosh Hashanah services in the Marc Chagall Ballroom, where there were roughly 2,000 worshippers. On another visit we were walking along one of the paths in the club when we ran into another pair of women. Rosa introduced me to her friend who in turn introduced us to the fourth woman, her son's mother-in-law, who had come from Greece to see her newborn grandchild. Among the four of us we spoke eight languages: Portuguese, Spanish, English, Greek, German, French, Yiddish, and Ladino.[32] In spite of this linguistic abundance, we did not share a common language with the Greek visitor, so she spoke Ladino while we communicated in Spanish, which allowed us to be mutually intelligible.

Many layers of dispersal were represented in that group of women, our languages signifying diverse points in the Diaspora, the Jewish languages

(Ladino and Yiddish) marking further dispersal. However, it was not just our condition as a people scattered many times over that was in evidence. We found ourselves conversing that afternoon in a private plaza in South America because of our shared condition as transnationals as well, as women actively engaged in social, professional, and familial networks across national boundaries. That afternoon was the first glimpse I had into the profound interrelationship between diasporic and transnational identities as they were lived in the metropolis of São Paulo and elaborated in Jewish spaces, and most especially in the Hebraica club.

Unique in the world, the Hebraica club presents a series of challenges and paradoxes with regard to ethnic and national identity. It is a cultural institution and a presence in the city's physical and social landscape. As a Jewish Brazilian institution it offers a key to understanding not only the particular blend of backgrounds and outlooks which contribute to the experience of being Jewish in São Paulo, but also a way to understand the meaning of being *paulistano* and being Brazilian beyond the familiar tropes of national identity.

2

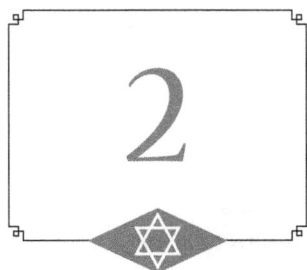

Braided Lives

A great many strands compose Jewish community in Brazil, and in São Paulo in particular. The most obvious strands are those derived from the dozens of different countries of origin and their concomitant cultural distinctions in language and practice. The distinctions of generation marked by distance from immigration also add complexity to the intertwined community. The histories of Brazil and the city of São Paulo further thicken the particular blending that distinguishes this Jewish community.

The history of how Jews from several continents found a home and created a community in a metropolis in South America is evident throughout the community. They were able to seize a moment of economic development, and in the main they rose above their impoverished and marginalized origins, as well as the abject poverty of the vast majority of Brazil's population, to attain a degree of social and economic comfort that the immigrant generation could hardly have imagined. Their economic success and the way in which the community formed key institutions that bridged internal differences have much to do with the way that race and ethnicity are conceived of in Brazil.

It is not my intent to give a full account of all of these intertwined histories, but rather to draw out the ways in which these historical trajectories are evidenced in the lives of Jews who now reside in the city of São Paulo, to effectively give an account of "the presence of the past," in Ruth Behar's words (1985), the ways in which the past is in evidence in the constitution of the community.

Gefilte Fish

The scene described by Rosa sounded like the setup to a joke: "Four elderly Jewish women were sitting around a table eating gefilte fish . . ." As it turned out, Rosa had observed the incident at the Lar Golda Meir, the Golda Meir Home for the Elderly, in the Vila Mariana neighborhood of São Paulo.

Rosa frequently visited the Lar to lead workshops. She took me with her once, a couple of years before I began full-time field research, a visit that left me sad. Without subsequent invitations I never returned to the Lar, hesitant to ask someone to take me, unwilling to go on my own, and not wanting to feel like a voyeur. It seemed particularly unfair to meet people only at the dénouement of their lives, after the loss of youth, family, work, independence, health, and well-being. During my visit with Rosa, I admired the pleasant surroundings, excellent facilities, and lovely green grounds as we passed before the glazed stares of elderly women and men, their worn bodies slumped in wheelchairs and unable to wave a greeting or crinkle the corners of their eyes in recognition as Rosa, who seemed to know everyone, gaily moved past as she took me on a whirlwind tour.

These were not the active and contentious elders of the center described by Barbara Myerhoff in *Number Our Days* (1978), feisty elders who still had their wits about them. These elders could not participate in the activities organized for the Third Age at Jewish institutions around the city, where elderly members of the community could participate in theater classes, Israeli folk dancing, afternoon musical performances, and lectures on topics of special interest for the elderly. There were activities and classes offered at the Lar as well, but not everyone was able to attend, and efforts often had to be considerably scaled down to accommodate the residents' physical restrictions and health problems. The ramps and wide doorways, the drone of television, the food trays with covered plates lining the hallways, and the hospital smell were all reminders of the institutional setting.

After our fast-paced tour, Rosa took me up to one of the rooms, where we visited with a nearly bed-bound friend of hers. As I tried to overcome the feeling of being an invader, Rosa introduced me to Sadie, who was propped up with pillows in her bed; I greeted her with a kiss on the cheek, aware of both her whiskers and her soft, tissue-thin skin as our cheeks touched. One of the things for which the Lar is frequently praised is that residents live in apartmentlike rooms. Though the spaces are small, their institutional qualities can be softened by the residents' personal belongings. As Rosa and Sadie caught up on events since they had last seen one another, I looked around the room at the artifacts of Sadie's life. Precious black-and-white portraits, posed for long ago by now-deceased parents and siblings, were displayed alongside faded color snapshots of children and grandchildren now grown and living their lives beyond the walls of the Lar. When I tuned back into the conversation, Rosa and Sadie were talking about what had happened to Sadie's belongings, how in the move from her old room to this one, the staff had broken and misplaced many of her records. I noted the disorderly stacks of LPs, recordings from the old country, a library of Yiddish songs and classical music. Sadie complained about the unresponsive employees, a mostly black staff working for minimum wage. As we left, Rosa whispered to me that Sadie did not have a record player, though clearly that was not the point. She had lost control of her material existence, and her music was an important part of her memory, even if she could not easily enjoy it. Once we were out of the room, Rosa added that Sadie always complained like that, often retelling the same stories as if the offenses had just occurred.

These memories of that visit to the Lar flooded back when Rosa told me about the incident that she had recently witnessed there. Four elderly Jewish women were sitting around a table eating gefilte fish: one Polish, one German, one Russian, and one Sephardi. In keeping with the jokelike structure of the story, the women were complaining about the gefilte fish. The Polish woman thought it was not sweet enough, the German woman thought it was not spicy enough, the Russian woman thought it was not salty enough, and the Sephardi woman did not want to eat it because she considered it poor-people's food. There are many ways of preparing gefilte fish, and twice as many ways of ruining it, but their complaints stemmed from the way gefilte fish was prepared in each of their countries of origin: in Poland it is sweet; in Germany it is spiced with black pepper; in Russia it is salty; an Ashkenazi dish, gefilte fish is not a part of the Sephardi diet. (Norman Stillman points out that Sephardi revulsion upon being served gefilte fish is a frequent joke in Israeli comedy [personal communication 2011].) In the story as told by Rosa, who was Ashkenazi of German origin, the Sephardi designation was undifferentiated by national origin. More than a cultural distinction, the differences between Sephardim and Ashkenazim had been conflated with class in São Paulo, where many Sephardi immigrant families were able to maintain the high standard of living they had enjoyed in their countries of origin, several prominent families had become wealthy as industrialists or bankers, and their fame eclipsed the more varied socioeconomic status of the community.

Each of the women in the story represents a different Jewish tradition, symbolized in the gefilte fish, an emblematic Jewish food. Gefilte fish is a dish of slightly oblong balls of cooked and spiced white fish frequently accompanied by *chrain*, grated horseradish. The dish is commonly eaten at the beginning of Jewish holiday meals, including Shabbat; since it is prepared ahead of time, people are spared the prohibited "labor" of separating flesh from bone. It is a staple for the Jewish New Year because the round shape is intended as a reminder of the cyclical nature of the year. Gefilte fish is a remarkably unattractive food, what many would consider an acquired taste: grayish in color, irregular in shape, and a bit slimy and smelly. Nevertheless, like many ethnic foods it has the power to evoke strong nostalgia among Ashkenazi Jews. Since it is associated with holidays, it evokes special, family times and carries the weight of the past, an especially poignant and powerful evocation for elderly Jewish immigrants, many of whom were survivors of pogroms, concentration camps, or wars. For the Sephardi woman in the story, the Eastern European referents of gefilte fish held none of that emotional appeal. Nevertheless, she found herself at a Jewish institution in Brazil, sharing a meal with other displaced Jewish women, being served "Jewish" food that was not her food.

Explanations always have a way of destroying the punch line of a joke. When told to Jews in São Paulo, this story draws the kind of immediate laughter that it cannot in settings where it requires an explanation. Nevertheless, it serves as a kind of parable of ethnic-group coalescence. How these four women came to pass their old age together in a metropolis in

South America and what this says about diaspora is part of the story I wish to tell. Another part of the story has to do with Brazil and the city of São Paulo: what does it mean that Jewish people have come from over sixty countries and remain to create a community? In so doing they have transformed the landscape of the city and have been transformed by it.

This is more than a two-part story that intertwines local and global registers of experience. This is a story of the multiple strands that make up the Jewish community in São Paulo, what Myerhoff calls the "histori-cal-geographic layers" (1978:109). Rather than constituting discrete layers superimposed on one another, local and national histories are interwoven with the multiple histories of people from many points on the globe whose condition of diaspora intertwines their various histories, braids within braids. It is in the encounter of these various trajectories that community is formed. The community that emerged in São Paulo is as much a product of that city's history as it is the result of the multiple histories contained within the Jewish community.

Concrete Jungle

Taken as a whole, São Paulo is a remarkably ugly city, a fact that even the most sympathetic poets cannot ignore. It certainly has little of the so-called colonial charm or natural beauty that attracts tourists and inspires the love songs to city and country that are a staple of popular Brazilian music. Even those who like São Paulo, and I count myself among them, are quick to recite a litany of its flaws even while finding a certain kind of beauty in them.

The bustle and growth and aesthetic challenges of the city have been noted by writers since the early days of the city's expansion in the first half of the twentieth century. In his ardent *Brazil: Land of the Future*, Austrian writer and cosmopolitan Stefan Zweig begins his chapter on São Paulo: "Just as only a painter could do full justice to Rio de Janeiro, so could a proper description of São Paulo be made only by a statistician or an economist. He would have to compile numbers and figures, compare them with each other, copy charts, and try to describe growth in words, because it is neither its past nor its present which makes São Paulo fascinating, but its almost visible growth and development, the speed of its transformation" (1942:211).

In contrast with the colonial capital city of Rio, with its stunning landscape and sophisticated centers of European arts, Zweig was enchanted with the technological developments and capitalist drive that he witnessed transforming a small town along the banks of the Tietê River into one of the world's largest metropolises. Zweig's admiration of explosive growth transforms the idea of conventional aesthetics into an aesthetic of potential. He described the dynamism of a city on the precipice of industrialization, a technological and economic expansion that brought money and immigrants from all over the country and all over the world.

Another prominent Jewish European intellectual, French anthropologist Claude Lévi-Strauss, depicted São Paulo in the mid-1930s, though in a far less idealized way than Zweig. Lévi-Strauss described the city as suffering from "architectural leprosy" and as having the quality of a cinematic forgery (1961:102, 1992:97). Nevertheless, he also found beauty in the "untamed" growth, which he explained by indulging in hyperbole: "São Paulo is growing so fast that you can't buy a map of it; there'd have to be a new edition every week" (1961:101). São Paulo has expanded even further in the decades since Zweig and Lévi-Strauss bore witness to its early growth.

Many of the qualities of São Paulo that Zweig identified in that first moment of explosive expansion have also been noted by contemporary writers and poets and have been further developed as themes and images. In Caetano Veloso's 1978 ode to São Paulo, "Sampa" (the city's nickname), he sings of how, as a recently arrived migrant from the northeastern state of Bahia, he did not understand anything "da dura poesia concreta de tuas esquinas" (of the hard concrete poetry of your corners). Challenging those who would be repulsed by the city's lack of conventional beauty, Veloso charges that "Narciso acha feio o que não é espelho" (Narcissus thinks that which is not a mirror is ugly). Like Zweig, Veloso anticipates that people will misunderstand what São Paulo has to offer and appreciates the city's positive and negative aspects, such as the manifestations of a tremendous concentration of capitalist enterprises. Among the many condensed images of the swirl of activity and social inequality in São Paulo that Veloso offers is "da força da grana que ergue e destrói coisas belas" (the power of money that erects and destroys beautiful things).

Another poetic treatment that emphasizes the harsh social relations in the city is offered by the rock band Titãs in their song "Homem primata" (Primate man). In their upbeat critique of "savage capitalism," which describes the city as a "concrete jungle" ("Eu me perdi na selva de pedra," I got lost in the stone forest), the Titãs equate city life with a primitive struggle for survival, inverting the association of city with civilization.

Paul Charosh (1968) has observed that songs about places people call "home" are social documents that shed light on the cultural milieu and reveal some of the social problems that characterize migration and urban life, in particular, those that might seem contrary to the more usual picturesque portraits of homelands. Considering the popularity of Veloso and the Titãs, their "home songs" offer more than a grounded perspective; they are also a means for transmitting their views and analyses to a wider audience, thereby having the potential to shape perceptions on a broad scale. While Veloso's ballad "Sampa" originated during the politically charged countercultural movement known as Tropicália (Dunn 2001), and the Titãs' ska hit, with its punctuating English cries of "Concrete jungle! Concrete jungle!" emerged during the nascent democracy and late capitalism of the end of the twentieth century, both belong to a line of writers' appreciations and critiques that embrace the contradictions of this vibrant and dissonant city.

*   *   *

One hundred years ago, at the turn of the twentieth century, São Paulo was a small city. The Avenida Paulista sported tree-lined promenades in front of the elegant new mansions belonging to the coffee barons. The belated end of slavery in 1888 accelerated a series of economic and political changes that transformed the social landscape of Brazil. The Proclamation of the Republic in the following year, followed by the growth of industry and the coffee boom in the southeast of the country, brought an infusion of money to the region and challenged leaders to imagine the nation and chart its course. Programs of mass immigration, especially from Europe, the Middle East, and Japan, were initiated to bolster industry. People and goods were funneled through the ports of Rio de Janeiro and Santos, on the São Paulo coast, and these two states received the largest portion of immigrants.

Looking at the city today, it is difficult to imagine the pastoral scene it presented so recently. The numbers tell a story of dramatic growth: in 1872, there were little more than 31,000 inhabitants in a half dozen parishes (Caldeira 2000:216). São Paulo was considerably smaller than the major cities in Brazil at the time, such as Rio (with 275,000 inhabitants) and the northeastern city of Salvador (129,000). By 1890, a mere eighteen years later, São Paulo's population had more than doubled, to 65,000. Three years later, the city had again doubled, to 129,000. By the turn of the century there were roughly a quarter of a million inhabitants, and by 1920, there were over half a million. By the mid-1930s, the city's population had surpassed one million and was the setting for the narratives that members of the Jewish community shared of their intertwining family histories, described below.

At the beginning of the twenty-first century, with approximately 18 million people living in the greater metropolitan area, São Paulo is home to approximately one-tenth of Brazil's total population. It is one of the world's largest cities in terms of population and has the dubious distinction of being one of the cities that grew the most in the twentieth century.

Vestiges of Immigration

Some six months after returning to California I had two visitors from São Paulo, the mother and brother of a dear friend and colleague. During our visit they brought me up to date on people and events since my departure. They had brought some music with them, and we were enjoying a tape of music by Antônio Moreira da Silva, known as Morengueira, who had died the week before their trip. Morengueira was famous for a style called *samba de breque* (from English "brake") in which the music would abruptly stop and he would interject rapid, spoken, usually humorous commentary before the rhythm resumed. Though his music was very popular among earlier generations, neither his music nor his wacky lyrics were well known among younger people. We were occasionally distracted from our conversation by some particularly playful singing, and more than once burst out laughing at his quirky humor and quick turns of phrase.

In the midst of the hilarity, one uncharacteristically plaintive song caught our attention. In contrast to his usual buoyant cleverness, and accompanied only by the melancholy strumming of the *cavaquinho*,[1] Morengueira sang of his love for a Jewish woman, likening his desire to a bee dancing around the red flower of her mouth.[2] The first lines of the song "Judia Rara" (Rare Jewess) evoke the early waves of Jewish immigration to Brazil:

A rosa não se compara
A essa judia rara
Criada no meu país

The rose cannot compare
To this rare Jewess
Raised in my country

One of the few examples of Jews appearing in popular music, the song echoes sentiments expressed nearly a hundred years before by the abolitionist poet Castro Alves. His love poem "Hebréia" is heavily laden with biblical imagery and drama:

Tu és, ó filha de Israel formosa . . .
Tu és, ó linda, sedutora Hebréia . . .
Pálida rosa da infeliz Judéia
Sem ter o orvalho, que do céu deriva!

You are, oh beautiful daughter of Israel . . .
You are, oh lovely Hebrew seductress . . .
Pale rose of unfortunate Judea
Without the dew that comes from heaven!

Written in Bahia in 1868, the poem is apparently about one of three sisters who lived next door (Gomes and Rocha 1971). These daughters of early Jewish immigrants, one of whom went on to marry the first rabbi of São Paulo (Veltman 1996:27–28), made a mark on Brazilian literature that is part of the record of early Jewish immigration.

The only other example of Jews in popular music that I have come across is "A Promessa de Jacó" (Jacob's promise), by the unstoppable Demônios da Garoa.[3] Unlike Morengueira's love song to a rare flower from another country, "Jacob's Promise" lampoons the speech patterns and business practices of the immigrant Jewish street peddler.[4] In the song, Jacó (Jacob, the standard Jewish man's name in Brazilian jokes) is a tie salesman who not only fails to deliver the promised product but also fails to dominate the language, as does the narrator, who speaks with a heavy Yiddish accent and grammatical mistakes, erring in the verb tense and gender agreement that are so difficult for non-native speakers to master.

Jacó, a senhor me prometeu
Uma gravata, até hoje ainda não deu.
Faz trinta anos que este se passar,
E até hoje o gravata não chegar.

Jacob, you promised me
A tie you still didn't give.
It's thirty years since this happen,
And until today the tie not arrive.

Specializing in comedic songs sung in the vernacular about the dramas of the "popular" classes, the Demônios have recorded several songs that mock the foibles of other immigrant groups, including Italians and Chinese; their "Tchum-tchim-tchum" from the same album as "Jacob's Promise" indulges in sexual stereotypes about Chinese men. Though these stereotypes would offend contemporary North American sensibilities, in the Brazilian context, where nicknames and jokes often play on racial and national stereotypes, they are not taken as seriously.

While these examples of songs and poems by well-known writers and performers are evidence of the presence of Jews in Brazil from their earliest immigration, and of their interaction with the host society, there is no evidence that these songs and poems have had any impact on the broader population's impressions of Jews in their midst. The concentration of Jewish immigration in time and space has meant that the idea of the Jew has remained very abstract for the majority of Brazilians, who have had little or no contact with real Jews.

For the most part, Jews arrived later than other immigrant groups (and later in Brazil than in the United States), following shortly after Brazil's enthusiastic industrialization. Additionally, their concentration in the southeast, where this industrialization was most extensive, also helped secure their position in the rapid economic growth of the country and the region. Through chain migration,[5] as immigrants settled they established community institutions (funeral societies, schools, and so on), as well as a variety of mutual-aid societies, so that newly arrived immigrants benefitted from the support of their community (Grin 1995). This assistance extended to providing work opportunities in specific economic activities where Jews had established niches, such as textiles and dry goods.

In the years following migration, without special training or resources, and with poor command of the language, becoming a *clientelchik*, a peddler, was one of the few options available, and the *gravatnik*, the tie hawker, was a subspecialization (see Scliar 2000). The immigrant peddler was a figure on the streets of big cities in Brazil during the period following immigration and appears in novels set during those times.[6] By the time the Demônios recorded "Jacob's Promise" in 1964, the immigrant Jewish street vendor was no longer a familiar part of the São Paulo landscape.

Part of the way that Jews have laid claim to a meaningful place in Brazilian history and culture is by taking note of Jewish influence on Brazilian practices. For example, they credit Jews with introducing the now standard practice of *prestações*, purchasing in parceled payments.[7] They also claim to have been influential in the settlement of the interior of the country by considerably increasing the circulation of manufactured goods by way of *mascates*, traveling salesmen, though earlier immigrants from Europe and the Middle East had also engaged in peddling (Truzzi 1997).

Nevertheless, Jews made use of these practices to carve out a place for themselves in the country. The combination of chain migration, mutual-aid societies and other assistance institutions, and professional favoritism for *patrícios* (fellow countrymen) allowed new immigrants to quickly get their economic and social bearings. An already-established *patrício* would give a newly immigrated man products (ties, shoes, cloth, and so on) to sell on the street or to take into the interior without his having to pay for the products up front. Over time, the accumulated capital from these sales might allow him to open a small textile, dry goods, or furniture shop in one of the small cities throughout the interior, or to purchase products outright, thereby increasing his profit margin, and possibly even to bring in other, more recent immigrants to work for him. Eventually, he might even begin to manufacture his own goods while helping out recent arrivals. Other "middle-man minorities" (Zenner 1991), such as Armenians, Syrians, and Lebanese, also followed similar patterns of immigration and socioeconomic integration in Brazil, occupying related but distinct niches in the industrializing economy. Armenians, for instance, still occupy the shoe niche, a major industry in Brazil for both internal consumption and export.[8]

Syrians and Lebanese are usually lumped together in the category "*sírio-libanês*,"[9] while Jews, Armenians, Lebanese, and Syrians together are popularly known as "*turcos*," a term used to refer to perceived shared physical types and business practices (Lesser 1998, 1999). It is an ironic fact of history that while there was never a significant Turkish immigration to Brazil, many of those who migrated to Brazil from the Ottoman Empire carried Turkish passports.

Immigration partly fueled the growth of the city, so much so that foreign-born residents made up over half of the urban population at the beginning of the twentieth century (Caldeira 2000:402). Even in the mid-1920s, 35 percent of the city's residents were foreign born, a proportion that would have been considerably greater if the Brazilian-born children of immigrants had been included (Fausto 1997:66). Brazilian historian Boris Fausto notes that "the *paulistano* environment was far from hostile to foreigners" (1997:66).

Immigration policy and the place of immigrants in Brazilian society were set against the backdrop of the concept of "whitening" (*branqueamento*), a long-standing social discourse that sought to mitigate the social effects of slavery by encouraging immigration of those "white" populations thought to have greater potential for assimilation.[10] The idea of *branqueamento* draws on folk biological conceptions of race in which phenotype is linked to a population's potential to become "civilized," and had its most explicit expression in popular eugenics, which gained traction in political discourse in Brazil in the 1920s (Lesser 1995:146). Although the Constitution of 1934 laid out a quota plan for controlling immigration, it was not until the beginning of the second Vargas regime, known as the Estado Novo (New State), that this discourse found anti-Jewish expression in secret documents that sought to prohibit the immigration of Jews, especially poor Jews, conflating religion, race, and class (Lesser 1995, Tucci Carneiro 1988).

Several organizations aided the immigration of Jews to Brazil beginning in the 1920s, including the rural settlement of Jews in the far south of Brazil sponsored by the Jewish Colonization Association.[11] However, the vast majority of Jewish immigrants settled in cities, specifically those of the southeast and south of the country, in a pattern that contrasted dramatically with that of other immigrants, who settled in rural areas (Decol 2009:100). Even most of those Jews, who initially settled in rural enclaves, relocated to urban centers; by 1940, nearly 75 percent of Brazilian Jews were living in one of the three cities where they are concentrated today (Decol 2009:105). One-sixth of the Jewish population in São Paulo is descended from the migrants during this period, and another one-quarter of São Paulo's Jewish population results from immigration during the 1930s (Elkin 1998:93).

The height of Jewish immigration in Brazil, which occurred between the two World Wars, was partly the result of systems of quotas imposed in the preferred American destinations of the United States and Argentina (Decol 1999:25), pushing emigrants to seek other nearby destinations with the hope of eventually reconnecting with family already established in "America." Even during the brief period in the mid-1930s during which Jewish immigration to Brazil was severely limited by quotas (as laid out in the 1934 Constitution), a moment when Brazil flirted with entering the war on the side of the Axis countries, Jewish immigration never entirely stopped, and the policies were inconsistently applied.[12] According to Lesser (1995), these policies were consistent with prevailing scientific racial theories and the nativist movement and did not necessarily represent an attempt by the Brazilian government to please the Nazi regime.

Another peak in immigration came after World War II, when Brazil, by then firmly on the side of the Allies, became one of the first countries to open its doors to Holocaust survivors. A final small rise in Jewish immigration to Brazil occurred in 1956, when Jews expelled from Egypt during the Suez Canal crisis chose Brazil as one of their preferred destinations. All told, 71,000 Jews immigrated to Brazil between 1840 and 1942, representing less than 3 percent of the total immigration to Brazil in this period (Decol 1999), and less than 2 percent of general immigration in the century between 1872 and 1972 (Decol 2009).

Data on the composition of the Jewish community are difficult to obtain, complicated by methodological inconsistencies and clouded by ideological motivations. One newspaper headline in 1940, in the midst of the debate about immigration policy, made the unsubstantiated claim that 400,000 Jews lived in Brazil, and that 150,000 had entered the country in the previous six months alone (Lesser 1995:129). The official Brazilian census only began counting Jews in 1940, at which time there were approximately 55,000. Decol (1999) suggests that while difficult to prove, anti-Semitic anxieties over the number of Jews in the country may have motivated the introduction of the category "Jewish" in the 1940 census.

Since the census includes "Jewish" as a category of religion, this appears on the questionnaire only for the 10 percent sampled for more indepth questions, and not on the full general census; those who consider themselves ethnically but not religiously Jewish would therefore not be counted. Nationally the trend is for increasing proportions of the population to define themselves as having no religion, a phenomenon found among the Jewish population as well (Decol 2009). An additional complication in accounting for the Jewish population is that, historically, Jews have been reluctant to identify themselves to census takers. As a consequence of these specific challenges, demographers of world Jewry have developed techniques for obtaining a more accurate estimate of Jewish populations based on the available data (DellaPergola 1993). Local Jewish federations and other organizations have conducted surveys of their communities of varying qualities and purposes, but a thorough census of the Brazilian Jewish population continues to be needed.

A survey of the São Paulo Jewish community conducted in 1968 by sociologist Henrique Rattner found that the community was composed of people from sixty-one countries (1972b:246): the greatest proportion (nearly 28 percent) came from Eastern Europe, nearly 8 percent from the Middle East, over 5 percent from Germany and Austria, a little over 2 percent from other countries in Latin America, and a similar percentage from Israel. These proportions were fairly consistent with national census data on the country of origins for Jews (Decol 2009). It can be assumed that Jews who migrated from other Latin American countries were the first or second generation and also brought with them the traditions of the countries of origin of their parents or grandparents. Today, many leadership positions in the São Paulo community are occupied by Jews from Argentina in particular, but also from Uruguay and Chile.

Two analytic points should be noted: (1) the many layers of diaspora are evident even in recent generations also characterized by dispersal; and (2) the concept of "generation" needs to be developed further, since it can refer to both chronological age and distance from migration. Two people of the same age can represent different generations regarding their families' immigration, and "generation" cannot describe situations where the parents may have emigrated from different places during different periods, such that an individual may have one immigrant parent and one fully integrated third-generation parent. If the concept is to help us understand cultural integration and ties to countries of origin, clearly, it needs to be made more complex to reflect reality.

In 1968, just over half the *paulistano* Jewish population had been born in Brazil, with almost 16 percent of the Jewish community born in other Brazilian states; Rattner's 1972 survey followed a period in which São

Paulo's Jewish community was the only one in Brazil that had grown. Like other Brazilians in that period of economic growth, Jews migrated to cities, especially those in the southeast, consolidating their communities. These scant data suggest some of the reasons that the São Paulo Jewish community incorporates such a tremendous variety of cultural influences. These many strands are interwoven to form a diverse community, one which manages to find points of encounter in communal institutions without erasing the many differences.

Ship Siblings

It was the first Shabbat after the High Holy Days, following what had been my immersion into Jewish liturgy through an intense rehearsal schedule with the Shir Hashirim (Hebrew for Song of Songs) choir. Informally known as the "*coral dos jovens*," the "youth's choir" had accompanied the *chazzan* (cantor) Moshe Stern during the Rosh Hashanah and Yom Kippur services in the Arthur Rubinstein Theater at the Hebraica club, marking the beginning of the year 5760 in the Hebrew calendar. It was the end of September 1999.

The sudden collapse of the Brazilian currency in January 1999 nearly doubled the cost of all foreign exchanges, a rude shock after the all-too-short purchasing frenzy stimulated by the economic opening and relative stability introduced by the Plano Real in 1994. The devaluation also doubled the cost of bringing Moshe Stern from Jerusalem, as had been done for the past twenty-two years, since his payment was negotiated in U.S. dollars. This was standard practice, as most foreign transactions through the many years of economic instability and rocketing inflation were conducted in dollars. A compromise was reached, and Stern received full pay but came alone, without the chorus of Russian men who had come with him in recent years. Instead, he was to be accompanied through the many hours of sung services by the fledgling liturgical choir. Although they had already been in rehearsal for months, slowly working their way through a thick book of sheet music and transliterated Hebrew prayers, my arrival in June corresponded to the intensification of the rehearsal schedule, which built up steadily until we were in all-day rehearsals just prior to Rosh Hashanah.

On that first Shabbat after Yom Kippur, I had been invited to attend the services at the Higienópolis branch of the Colégio Renascença, one of the oldest Jewish schools in São Paulo.[13] Originally established in the immigrant neighborhood of Bom Retiro, like many other Jewish institutions, the school opened a branch in a neighborhood where Jews had relocated. Unlike many of these institutions that had closed their doors in Bom Retiro, Renascença still operated in the old neighborhood, but most of the school's activities were concentrated in upscale Higienópolis, and the Shabbat services in the school's synagogue were well-attended. The invitation to attend the service had come from the school's music teacher, who had been one of the soloists with the choir. The invitation also facilitated my entrance onto school grounds, getting me past the stern, suit-wearing security guards outside the high walls. On the other side of those walls was a multistory concrete complex with internal courtyards for school and community activities.

As I waited for the services to begin, I looked around at the school decorations. There was a large installation in anticipation of the approaching five hundredth anniversary of the arrival of the first Europeans on the shores of what would become Brazil, the date still over six months away. The installation was a celebration of the immigrant groups that make up Brazilian society, part of a major revision under way that broke with the earlier canon that recognized only a tripartite basis for Brazilian society in the mixing of Brazilian native peoples, Africans, and Europeans. The shift in public discourse whereby Brazil is now understood as an immigrant country has been especially important for the inclusion and national identity of immigrant groups, Jews among them. Extending along the wall were photos and descriptions of immigrant groups and famous Brazilian immigrants. Protruding into the courtyard from the middle of the exhibit was an enormous diorama in the shape of a ship's prow. The two sides of the prow were topped on either side with six-foot-long enlargements of historical black-and-white photos, typical formal shipboard portraits of immigrants grouped around a lifesaver bearing the ship's name.

It took me a moment to realize that I recognized the second photo. Dona Ana,[14] my elderly landlady, had shown me a considerably smaller copy of that same photo a month earlier. Just to the left of the white ring in the middle of the photograph the slight girl of eight impishly looking back at the camera was none other than the young Ana sitting on the deck alongside her mother and four siblings as they made their way from Poland. Her father had left for Brazil ahead of the family and sent for them once he had established himself. More than seventy years later, those weeks on the ship remained vivid memories for Dona Ana. In the days following my happening upon this semipublic display of her family's shipboard photo, as we unraveled the mystery of how the school had obtained the picture, she recounted her experiences in great detail, the coincidence having stimulated her memory of those life-transforming weeks. She recalled how she and her siblings entertained themselves on the boat and their arrival at the port of Santos, all told in enormous detail, testament to the significance of her transformation from Polish to Brazilian.

Similarly, in describing his own family's multiple passages, Fausto recalls his mother's indelible memories of the boat from Turkey across the Atlantic: "The group's journey was not an ordinary incident. It was The Journey, in capital letters, a unique occurrence which would not be repeated and could not ever be compared to the trivial and rare trips taken into the interior of Turkey, or later into the interior of Brazil. So much so that my mother's family never forgot the details, the names of the ships, the storms, the nausea on the rough sea" (1997:44).

For immigrants, this momentous passage from the suffering of their old life to the hopes of a new life has many of the qualities of the liminal phase of both religious and secular rites of passage that has been described by anthropologists (e.g., Turner and Myerhoff). In the transitional phase, regular life is suspended and initiates are no longer in their earlier status, but have not yet attained their new social status. For being in between, this phase is fraught with danger, and is often marked by trials of endurance. The experience of the arduous travel across the ocean easily lends itself to an interpretation as the liminal phase of a secular rite of passage, by which the passengers enter a new life and new status as the residents of a new, and hopefully more tolerant, society. It is the drama of the transitional stage that makes it stand out so strongly in memory so many years later.

Dona Ana also told me about the other family in the photo, the one on the other side of the white lifesaver. They were *irmãos de navio*, ship brothers, whose lives were connected by the shared experience of crossing the Atlantic on the same boat, fleeing persecution, probably never again to see the people and places they were leaving behind, and full of fear and hope about what lay ahead in "America." The expression *"irmãos de navio"* encapsulates all these memories and also serves as the title for a documentary film that explores many of these themes. Additionally, Moacyr Scliar's historical novel, *A majestade do Xingu* (1997), based on the life of the well-known medical doctor Noel Nutels, takes as its premise the shipboard friendship between two young boys, Nutels and the fictional narrator. The intensity of the relationships established while crossing the Atlantic often carried over into immigrants' new lives in Brazil, institutionalized in this special form of fictive kinship.

When they stepped onto the boat, Dona Ana and her mother and brothers knew where they were headed because her father had gone ahead and prepared the way. The mass immigration around the turn of the century was driven by a desire to "*fazer a América*," to do America;[15] emigrants from all over Europe and the Middle East headed for the Americas to earn money and return home or to establish themselves in a new life. During early immigration, many bought passage to "America" without knowing where they were headed. Sometimes there was deliberate deceit as salesmen preyed on people's ignorance by selling them passages to "America," knowing full well that the emigrants desired to join family in North America, not in the South American destinations on their tickets. At other times, the need to flee quickly meant that people departed on any boat available that was headed to the Americas and assumed they would be able to rendezvous with family members later, once they had escaped immediate danger. Jews arriving in Cuba or Bolivia had no intention of staying and considered these temporary homes a mere "stepping stone to the United States" (Behar 2007:6; see also Spitzer 1998).

Serendipity further interfered in the form of illness or chance meetings, such that it was not uncommon for people to disembark or get left behind at the wrong port. Even the best-laid plans were foiled by seemingly capricious shifts in immigration policy (Lesser 1995), and ships were redirected to other ports in other countries. In some cases, it took families decades to reconnect after being scattered in these ways; one woman recounted how her father and his brother ended up separated at opposite ends of the Americas, and it took forty years for them to reunite. These stories have been amply documented in the research on immigration and oral histories and personal narratives.[16]

Similarly, the people with whom I spoke located their own origins in their varied immigration stories. Since the origins of the São Paulo community are so diverse, one individual might have several stories to tell, especially if the immigration occurred in the grandparents' generation and the grandparents came from different countries of origin, during distinct periods, and under varied conditions. These disparate immigration experiences set the stage for the establishment of a highly diverse, relatively integrated Jewish community in São Paulo.

*　*　*

Several months after first seeing the immigration exhibit with the boat diorama, I returned to the school and spoke to a high school class about my research and found that their own experiences illustrated the points I was making about the shared experiences of Jews in Brazil. Most of the students were at least minimally bilingual, with English being their most common second language; this is not terribly surprising for young people in Brazil who enjoy a comfortable socioeconomic standing and share familial expectations that they will attend college. As a result of these expectations, English was fully incorporated into the school's curriculum. Additionally, several students spoke French at home, something that is common among the more recent immigrant families from Egypt, Syria, and Lebanon. A few had lived abroad and had acquired proficiency in other languages. Further, as students in a Jewish school, they were also studying Hebrew, some having attained fluency. This tendency toward multilingualism is a reflection of their condition as transnationals. When I asked how many students had family in other countries, not only did most respond that they did, but some also had family in multiple countries, some in as many as six countries.

I was reminded of the incident of the four polyglot women several years before at the Hebraica. Being polyglot stems from this condition of dispersal, a means of maintaining connections spread out in many nations. It is also a strategy for those who know that mobility is key to survival, who have learned from experience to keep "um pé atrás," a foot behind them, as the Brazilian saying goes, always ready to leave if necessary.

"Shtetl" in the City

For most of the twentieth century, the neighborhood of Bom Retiro in the old center of the city was known as the Jewish neighborhood. Ashkenazi immigrants went there to find relatives, work, assistance, and love. Every Sunday the men convened at the corner of Rua da Graça and Rua Ribeiro, near old man Weltman's bookstore, next to the pharmacy, to talk about what was happening in the community. The language on the street was Yiddish. Known as the *plétzale*, the diminutive of *plátz*, Yiddish for "place," the corner re-created the village squares from the Old Country in the midst of the new city. In his short stories, author Samuel Reibscheid mourned the loss of the *plétzale* and the passing of that time, calling it the "ground zero of [his] memories" (1995:58).[17] For many, it was the starting point for a new life and a new identity as *paulistano* and as Brazilian, a familiar place within the vast and growing city.

Bom Retiro was not the only part of the city where Jews lived. Many Ashkenazi Jews also lived in Vila Mariana. Some of the earliest Jews to arrive in São Paulo were Sephardi and Mizrahi Jews (Middle Eastern Jews, known as *orientais*), who set down roots in the neighborhoods of Mooca and Brás and set up separate communities along the lines of countries and even cities of origin.[18] These neighborhoods have not stimulated the same literary reminiscences as the Bom Retiro of the first half of the twentieth century, possibly because of Bom Retiro's larger proportion of Ashkenazim, with their predilection for letters and the arts. Additionally, Sephardi and Mizrahi Jews integrated more quickly, partly facilitated by the Latinate roots of the Ladino or French spoken by many of these immigrants. Linguistic and cultural differences kept the Sephardi and Ashkenazi communities separate until, eventually, schools, clubs, and other shared institutions drew these Jews of different origins into an integrated community. With the incorporation of this community into the larger city largely through class mobility, Jews began to move out of the old neighborhoods into other parts of the city. In more recent decades Jews have tended to aggregate in the central-western region of the city, especially in neighborhoods along a southwesterly diagonal chain that runs from Bom Retiro at the old center of the city through Higienópolis, Jardins, Pinheiros (where the Hebraica is located), to the ultraelite Morumbi neighborhood on the other side of the river.

Upscale Higienópolis is especially well known for its concentration of Jewish residents. It is a centrally located neighborhood of high-rise apartment buildings, although it used to be a neighborhood of large single-family homes, and many old trees still line its streets. The high cost of maintenance and security has meant that many of the old houses have either been demolished or converted into businesses: English schools, insurance companies, banks, and shops. Similarly, few of the most elegant of the mansions of the coffee barons remain along the Avenida Paulista. The remnants of this "noble" past now house today's elite: BankBoston, a museum, and McDonald's. A handful of the mansions still serve as consulates, this having been the diplomatic region in the past. The Italian consulate flew its flags on the Avenida Higienópolis but recently moved to a more prominent location on the Avenida Paulista, where it serves the many Brazilians of Italian descent applying for Italian citizenship and passports in case they decide to try their luck in the European Union

The main conduit through Higienópolis is the Avenida Angélica, which slopes gently away at an oblique angle from the extreme northwestern end of the Avenida Paulista. This avenue is a high point in a city with few geographic features to help the disoriented, where the masses of tall buildings obscure any view that might help a person locate herself. The Paulista is the financial artery of São Paulo, Brazil's Wall Street. It is a cultural center as well, with museums, cinemas, and bookstores. The more desirable parts of Higienópolis are higher up the slope toward the Avenida Paulista, and closer to the Praça Buenos Aires, with better views and more trees. That part of the neighborhood, with streets named after Brazilian states, is where bank owners live and where then-President of the Republic Fernando Henrique Cardoso lived when he was not in Brasília.

I lived down at the bottom of the slope, technically just over the border into the Santa Cecília neighborhood, half a block away from the dreadful "Minhocão," the Big Worm, as the elevated thoroughfare is known. The Minhocão cuts a swath through what was formerly a middle-class neighborhood to connect distant parts of the city. Those whose homes were leveled were lucky; the Worm destroyed property values on either side and made *cortiços* (vertical slums) of the grimy buildings that, sadly, line its length. The freeway was just one of the sources of incessant noise that residents somehow grew accustomed to. The constant noise of cars, trucks, and buses throughout most of the city is punctuated by endless jackhammering. Radios, televisions, and loudspeakers add to the din. Trucks selling canisters of cooking gas blast distorted electronic versions of familiar melodies; Beethoven's "Für Elise" is forever ruined for me. I was not the only one who appreciated the antidote that the chorus provided; in rehearsals I could feel the muscles around my ears relax with the music.

Several people with whom I spoke claimed that the neighborhood of Higienópolis (literally, Hygiene City) got its name from the concentration of Jews living there. In contrast to the characterizations of Viennese Jews as the source of disease-bearing filth (Gilman 1991), non-Jewish Brazilians who are familiar with kosher practices understand them to be about cleanliness and health. Popular history notwithstanding, the name appears to have more to do with an early episode of the flight of the elite from proximity to the poor; the rapid growth of the city with its dense population in the center raised concerns about sanitation and disease, which were associated with poverty, leading to the kinds of geographic class segregation that drove the expansion of the city and now defines its spaces (Caldeira 2000:216–17).

* * *

Propaganda distributed by one of the many synagogues located in Higienópolis referred to the neighborhood as the "new Jewish center of South America." The glossy brochure opened out to a map of the neighborhood with numbered and color-coded dots marking the locations of kosher grocers and butchers and other Jewish businesses and institutions. The neighborhood's thirteen synagogues and four schools were listed on the map, but their locations were not identified, most likely for security reasons.[19] The only location specified was that of the synagogue that had produced the brochure and was soliciting members and funds.

Taking inspiration from the enormous Sephardi synagogue that had recently opened in the neighborhood, and in contrast to the very large, loosely conservative, often controversial, and mostly Ashkenazi Congregação Israelita Paulista (CIP) nearby, the newly relocated Sinagoga Knesset Israel claimed to be "affectionately known as 'the smallest major [*menor maior*] Ashkenazi synagogue in Higienópolis.'" Founded in 1916, the synagogue was originally located in Bom Retiro. Like so many others, this synagogue followed the exodus from the lower-class neighborhood, and the brochure justified the move. While a few institutions, such as the Colégio Renascença, maintained both their Bom Retiro and Higienópolis locations, without a sufficient population to support them, many of the foundational institutions in the old neighborhood had closed their doors. Though many people, for both practical and aesthetic reasons, preferred to attend services at the newer synagogues in their own neighborhoods, some made a concerted effort to attend services in Bom Retiro in order to maintain those historic institutions and buildings. Many in the community retained a sense of *saudades* (that peculiarly Portuguese sentiment that combines the pain of loss with the sweetness of memory) for the old neighborhood and a bygone way of life in the early days after immigration that mapped easily onto the collective nostalgia for *shtetl* life cultivated by Ashkenazi Jews.

Indeed, the parallel emotions were evident in the way in which the synagogue framed its move. However, the synagogue did not appeal to *saudades* for Jewish life in the old neighborhood, but rather to the earlier and more "authentic" Jewish experience of the Old Country. The synagogue's propaganda made an audacious claim that Jewish life in Higienópolis could be compared to *shtetl* life prior to immigration. In doing so, the synagogue was appealing to the small-town Eastern European origins of its congregation, and to the romantic longing with which stories of *shtetl* life are imbued. The brochure claimed that the many Jewish resources in the neighborhood, the "synagogues, schools, clubs, youth movements, bookstores, kosher butchers and grocers make Higienópolis a romantic, modern version of the *shtetl* where Jews remained united under the worst conditions. Today we are the result of many of them. Today, Higienópolis is living proof of the progress that a community can enjoy."

Drawing on contradictory class associations, the synagogue was making a sentimental appeal in claiming that an elite neighborhood in a metropolis should have anything in common with the largely impoverished Eastern European villages that have come to metonymically stand for authentic Jewish life. In this view, Ashkenazi Jews trace core cultural attributes to a time when, however marginalized in the host society, they lived in relative autonomy and in close contact with other Jews. These idealized enclave associations with *shtetl* life are pervasive, having been reproduced in fiction, film, and ethnography, most famously in the stories of Sholem Aleichem (including "Tevya the Dairyman," on which *Fiddler on the Roof* was based) and Zborowski and Herzog's controversial postmortem account, *Life Is with People* (1995[1952]). Zborowski and Herzog claim that Eastern European Jews lived in villages that were like "islands," influenced by the surrounding culture but largely autonomous (1995[1952]:214), representing this idealized existence as "the most authentic form of Jewish culture" by ignoring both the existence of urban Jews and the mobility of Jews among villages and cities (Kirshenblatt-Gimblett 1995:xvi). Much like the oversimplified and ahistorical representations of *shtetl* life, the synagogue's claim ignored the facts that Higienópolis was not exclusively Jewish and that the Jews who did live and work there came from a variety of backgrounds.

Like Kirshenblatt-Gimblett, Lederhendler warns against the idealization that comes from this composite of "*the shtetl*," "as if the collective singular noun 'shtetl' contained all the information required to describe an entire class or range of Jewish communities, spread across many provinces and political boundary lines" (1999:49). The desire for a coherent Jewish life has even given way to romanticization of impoverishment. To a certain extent, this coherence was reconstructed in the immigrant neighborhoods of the early part of the twentieth century.

However, as each successive wave established itself, the most successful members moved out into "better" neighborhoods and integrated into the larger society. Political, economic, and aesthetic shifts also brought other groups to previously more homogeneous parts of the city. While there are still many Jewish businesses in Bom Retiro, especially those related to textile production (sewing machines and wholesale fabrics) and food (delis, imports, and restaurants), as Jews have prospered in São Paulo and sought other neighborhoods in which to establish their residences and businesses, Bom Retiro is no longer an Ashkenazi Jewish neighborhood where Yiddish is spoken on the streets. Other waves of immigrants have settled into both the spaces and the economic niches previously occupied by Jewish immigrants. For instance, Korean is now heard on the streets of Bom Retiro, and the low-end retail and wholesale off-the-rack clothing businesses are owned and run by Korean immigrants and second- and third-generation Korean Brazilians.

It is not just that "the old neighborhood" is no longer the domain of a given immigrant group and its descendants. As they establish roots, immigrants integrate into the social and class structure of the host society and seek the associated comforts and other marks of distinction that help to distance them from the old ways and the poverty often associated with their immigrant forebears. They move with deliberation *away* from isolation, *away* from an ethnic neighborhood, and *toward* a place within the larger society.

So, even though there may be a concentration of Jews in Higienópolis, the neighborhood cannot be characterized as a "Jewish neighborhood" in the way that the old neighborhood could be. In the first place, in contrast to their separation following immigration, Ashkenazi, Sephardi, and Mizrahi Jews have all made their residences and established synagogues there, evidence of a community that no longer adheres to historical divisions along lines of origin. The local branch of the supermarket chain Pão de Açucar caters to the special needs of its Jewish clientele and makes a point of offering greetings for the Jewish holidays with banners outside selected locations of its stores and advertisements in Jewish publications; however, it is not a Jewish grocery store and satisfies its other customers' needs as well, by selling pork, for instance. Additionally, the presence of the (Catholic) Samaritano Hospital and the exuberant abundance of lights and other holiday decorations at Christmastime, including in front of apartment buildings where Jews live, are just a few examples that attest both to the strong presence of other groups and to the different character of this kind of neighborhood from those where immigrants lived in earlier generations.

The synagogue's appeal to a romanticized past is not unique; in the literature on Jews in cities, Lederhendler finds that rather than the polar opposites that shtetls and cities appear to be, "the shtetl metaphor has survived virtually intact within its urban counterpart . . . Neighborhood clearly and easily takes the iconic place of the shtetl" (1999:50). In the synagogue's use of the simile, the superposition of village onto urban enclave could refer to the greater ease with which one can be religiously observant and live a Jewish life with access to the necessary resources (for educating children, for equipping the home and kitchen, for maintaining kosher, and so on). Reminding potential congregants that Jews were "united under the worst conditions," the brochure also made parallels between the marginalization and poverty of the past and the dangers and stresses of urban living, in which Jewish spaces provide relief.

There is another way to think about the claim that Higienópolis should be considered a modern and romantic version of a *shtetl.* The "progress" to which the brochure referred was clearly economic progress, and the relocation of the core of the Jewish community to Higienópolis was an indication of how successful Jewish immigrants and their descendants have been. The mutual-aid societies of the past played an important role in advancing the integration of the new immigrants, who, as a group, caught the rising tide of economic development in Brazil, centered in São Paulo. As a result of this confluence of cultural, social, economic, and historical factors, Jews have enjoyed a disproportionately high standard of living, in contrast to the humble origins of most of their immigrant forebears. The impoverishment of the past lent legitimacy to the idea of struggle, while the reminder of the importance of remaining united in the face of difficulties made a connection between the "culture of fear" that is the condition of living in São Paulo and the role that living in community could play in minimizing the stress of urban living. The synagogue's propaganda seemed to suggest that by banding together, Jews could stave off the socioeconomic decline that had taken hold in the country. Perhaps it is reading too much into it, but the brochure may also have offered a veiled reminder that Jews ought not to confuse their socioeconomic successes with true integration and acceptance. The historical examples of Jews being scapegoated and expelled, even in national contexts where they had considered themselves nationals, such as in twentieth-century Germany and Egypt, seemed to be always at the front of people's minds.

The elderly people at the center in Venice Beach, California, studied by Myerhoff also referred to their urban neighborhood as a *shtetl*, though there were stronger continuities of poverty, marginalization, segregation, and internal orientation to justify the simile. Nevertheless, as Myerhoff points out, "this was clearly a nostalgic rather than a factual description" (1978:109). Further, the nostalgia of immigrants is qualitatively different from that of their second- or third-generation descendants. Whereas the children of immigrants may reject the nostalgia of their parents, sociologist Bila Sorj (1998) asserts that the longing for an idyllic past gains new meaning for later generations, who seek "authentic" sources of Jewish culture, which they feel have been lost through integration into Brazilian society.

Although the brochure came from a synagogue, and even though synagogues are obviously an important source of community affirmation, the synagogue roots its legitimacy in the neighborhood and the services and resources located there. Synagogues alone do not define Jewish community any more than religion defines Jewishness. Quite the contrary, when one looks at a community as a whole it could even be said that synagogues represent not points of unity but rather divisions within the community. Judaism is infamous for its many denominations and subdenominations, so much so that this is the subject of many jokes and a maxim: "Where there are two Jews there are three opinions"—never more true than where religion is concerned.

Different interpretations lead to different lines of religious practice within Judaism. Furthermore, for the many Jews who are not religious, synagogues are not points of contact with the community. By locating Jewishness in the conjunction of institutions and practices of daily life rather than religious life, the Knesset Israel synagogue situated itself within the community network, even while invoking a past model of communal organization to confront contemporary issues.

Communal institutions explore the juxtaposition of tradition and modernity that *shtetl* and city life would seem to present. The numerous groups who arrived over the course of several decades were integrated through these institutions, especially the clubs that provided a forum within which Jewishness could be negotiated and reconfigured to incorporate the many contrasting cultural elements that immigrants brought with them. Having come from so many countries of origin, with the accompanying cultural and linguistic differences exacerbating other internal distinctions among Jews, the apparent cohesion of this highly diverse collectivity demands explanation. One overly simple possibility is that this solidarity might result from the small size of the population, requiring the community to join forces with other Jews, ignoring the tremendous religious, political, and cultural differences that have tended to divide Jews in other locales of the Diaspora.

This explanation is inadequate, for it ignores historical and social factors affecting both the group and the receiving society that could create the conditions for a coalition that may be impossible or unnecessary under other conditions. People do not easily put aside ideology for the sake of convenience.[20] Judith Elkin, historian of Latin American Jewry, asserts that the historical moments of the Holocaust, the creation of the state of Israel, and the establishment of the second and third generations, who saw themselves "simply as Jews, without Old World modifiers," accounts for the breaking down of some of the inherited cultural barriers (1998:181). In Brazil, the dominant ideologies about race and ethnicity also had an effect on the development of an inclusive conceptualization of Jewishness that could have the power to transform ideological differences into shared ground for identity.

Fausto credits the clubs for bringing together different Jewish groups that had been "spatially and culturally separate for many centuries" (1997:72–73). Throughout Latin America, clubs provide an important form of socialization, and Elkin identifies the Jewish clubs found in every major community as "a hybrid between Jewish and Latin American institutions" (1998:189). She also credits them with being the primary vehicle for the creation of a secular Jewish identity, and one that facilitates the blending of Jews from different cultural backgrounds.

Jewish life in São Paulo cannot be understood according to either the ethnic-enclave model that typifies most descriptions of urban Jewish experiences, or the exceptional "Jewish city" model epitomized by New York (Lederhendler 1999:52); São Paulo is far too large and the community far too small for that. Jews in São Paulo live in the city and create a kind of "inner space/outer space dichotomy" (Lederhendler 1999:51) not through ethnic enclaves (though the neighborhoods provide an important part of the dynamic), but through the creation of Jewish space in the middle of the city. The Knesset Israel synagogue was seeking to create such a space, but the most successful of these urban Jewish spaces is the Hebraica social and athletic club.

The Biggest Jewish Club in the World

At the time of its establishment in the mid-1950s, the Hebraica club was located on the outskirts of São Paulo, a parceled plot of land on the banks of the Pinheiros River. Looking today at the stinking, stagnant waters of the Pinheiros and Tietê rivers, it hardly seems possible that in the lifetime of many of the city's residents the rivers contributed to their quality of life. São Paulo's unmanageable expansion outgrew all development plans, improbably stranding the Congonhas airport in the middle of the city, defiling the once-healthy waterways where citizens had enjoyed regattas just eighty years before, and situating the Hebraica in the midst of the vast metropolis.

There were other Jewish social and community centers at the time, but the founding of the Hebraica marked a turning point in the status of the city's Jewish community. The Círculo Israelita de São Paulo (Jewish Circle of São Paulo, established in 1928) was located in the Trocadero Palace (which also housed the Esplanada Hotel and the Jewish Federation), behind the splendid Art Nouveau Municipal Theater in the heart of the city (Sundfeld and Rodrigues 1996:48). Bom Retiro was near this city center, so young men and women gathered at the Círculo, where they created "friendships and groups of friends [turmas], romances and marriages" (Cytrynowicz 2003:23).

The Associação Brasileira "A Hebraica" de São Paulo was founded on January 1, 1953. The story recounted in the club's magazine every ten years or so is that a group of friends and community leaders, men of a certain

stature, gathered on New Year's Day after a particularly unsatisfying Rev-
eillon (New Year's Eve) at the Círculo Israelita.[21] The oft-told version of
the story only vaguely hints at the reasons for the dissatisfaction that led
to the establishment of a new club. In the postwar years, São Paulo was
enjoying rapid growth and the fruits of industrialization. The city's Jewish
community found itself firmly established, with its second and even third
generations fully integrated into the "liberal" professions and influential
in industry. An elite had formed that was interested in political leadership
both within the community and beyond.

There were already several elite clubs in the city, including the Pinheiros. The Esporte Clube Pinheiros, formerly the Sport Club Germania
(founded in 1899), was one of several clubs that were forced to change
their names during World War II when Brazil, after teetering on the edge,
entered the war on the side of the Allies. In 1942, the Brazilian government stipulated that all institutions with names associated with the Axis
countries had to be changed. This particularly affected the large Italian
population, though there were large numbers of immigrants from Germany and Japan as well. The Sport Club Germania was joined by another
German club, the Sociedade Gesellchaft Germania, and changed its name
to Esporte Clube Pinheiros. As part of this process of "nationalizing,"
these clubs also had to include a certain percentage of Brazilian nationals among their members.[22] It is unlikely, however, that there were Jews
among those first Brazilian elite club members.

What was not mentioned in the historical accounts in the club's magazine, but was brought up in numerous conversations, was that this group
of Jews originally sought to ally themselves with other elites in the city
and had attempted to join existing exclusive *paulistano* clubs. Unofficial
sources recounted that when members of this founding group attempted
to participate in the New Year's Eve party at one of the desired clubs, they
were turned away because they were Jews. Instead, the founders rang in
the New Year at the Círculo Israelita, and left "feeling quite discontented
[*desgostoso*]."[23]

By the early 1950s, the new elite had set in motion a series of changes
in the structure of the Jewish community. This was the period when well-
to-do families began to move out of Bom Retiro and establish themselves
in more desirable neighborhoods. They also began to differentiate themselves socially. When they were rejected by the elite *paulistano* clubs and

forced to celebrate New Year's at the Círculo, as one version of the story goes, they resolved to create an exclusive club for the Jewish elite of the city.

Indeed, the context was ripe for a change in the community. World War II was safely behind them, the state of Israel had been established, Eisenhower was president of the United States, and with the beginning of the Korean War, the Cold War had begun in earnest. Getúlio Vargas was enjoying his second administration as president (this time as part of a democratic government with populist appeal, in contrast to his earlier fascistic military regime), the plan for the new capital in Brasília was not yet complete, the population of Brazil and São Paulo had begun to grow exponentially, and international pressures and the need for increased industrialization and a developed infrastructure coincided with a significant increase in inflation—all harbingers of troubles to come. However, at this moment, the country was future oriented and developing rapidly, with São Paulo setting the pace, and this generation of Jews occupied increasingly important roles in the industrialization and professionalization of the workforce. The economic progress enjoyed by segments of the community was accompanied by substantive changes in lifestyle, especially for those who had left the *shtetls* and ghettos of the old countries. They found themselves in a rapidly developing city at just the right moment to take advantage of these changes.

The same economic expansion that facilitated the greater participation of Jews in *paulistano* and Brazilian society also contributed to a deepening integration within the community itself. The community was in a strong position to receive and support subsequent waves of immigrants. As but one example, the Egyptian Jews who arrived in Brazil (mostly in São Paulo) in the period following the Suez Canal crisis of 1956 found themselves easily absorbed into a well-established community with the cultural and financial means to enjoy a fully Jewish life provided by institutions ranging from the funeral society to synagogues to kosher butchers, with opportunities for enriching their Jewish life through schools and social institutions. Many of the Egyptians who arrived in São Paulo were well off and were absorbed into an economically comfortable Jewish society. Those refugees who arrived with few resources found that the community's institutions were able to provide assistance. For instance, Michel, whose penniless family came to São Paulo when he was a child, studied at one of the Jewish schools on scholarship, and he knew other Egyptian children who also studied there under similar circumstances. Though they were willing and able to help needy members of the community, some accounts of the founding of the club suggest that this group of elites sought to distance themselves from the poorer elements of the community.

According to the official version of the story, a group of friends, including Leon Feffer, a prominent businessman in the paper industry and then-honorary consul of Israel in Brazil, decided to bring together 300 members to found a club, and Feffer was named the first club president.[24] Recounting the history, the founders explained that the driving force in their decision to create a new club was concern over the need for an "adequate environment for the new generation. We even ran the risk of losing youths, who drew away from the heart [*seio*] of the collectivity in search of new spaces [*ambientes*] where they could satisfy their social, sport, and cultural needs."[25] "In view of the discrepancy [*defasagem*] between the existing institutions, which were adequate for the needs of an earlier generation, and new economic and social conditions, young people with different desires [*anseios*] distanced themselves from the Jewish environment" (*Revista "A Hebraica,"* January 1977:2). They feared that their children would be absorbed into the non-Jewish environments they frequented.

Although the initial motivations for establishing a new club may have been the creation of an exclusive space, ultimately, the rationale had to do with the continuity of the community, the raison d'être of many Jewish institutions.[26] The need to shed the association with the Old Country and an antiquated way of life was foremost in the minds of a "new generation," which saw itself as belonging to a different place and, most importantly, a different time.

The founders—after considering several central locations, including one in Higienópolis and another on the Avenida Paulista,[27] that were rejected at least in part because their central location would require "vertical construction," and having discarded the idea of a *clube de campo*, a country club outside the city because transportation difficulties would be prohibitive—settled on a 29,000 square meter piece of land belonging to the Canadian-owned São Paulo Light and Power Company. One of the founders described the location on the winding banks of the Pinheiros River as "sort of a swampy, remote place";[28] the river had not yet been "contained," nor had the Marginal Highway been constructed. In order to raise the money necessary to purchase the land, the founders sold club titles.[29]

As the planning proceeded, the founders foresaw a club of 500 families. However, interest grew once construction got under way, and the club began its rapid expansion. Although the Hebraica's first mandate was to be an elite institution, it quickly became evident that this exclusivity could not be sustained socially or financially. The mandate shifted toward a more inclusive ideology: "reunir a coletividade" (to bring the community together).[30]

As interest grew, plans were laid for an expanded club to accommodate a larger membership. "[W]e felt that the Hebraica could not be a closed club, and that we would have to open our doors to the collectivity," explained a founding member.[31] "Immediately, we felt the support from the youths who were distancing themselves from the community. Other older elements also drew near giving us their support." By the time of the club's inauguration in 1957, five years after the founding of the association, the vision of the club as well as the profile of its membership had changed considerably. There were 1,500 family memberships, accounting for approximately 8,000 people (Cytrynowicz 2003:43). By the early 1960s, 20,000 people frequented the club (Cytrynowicz 2003:45).

At the time of the founding of the Hebraica club, the well-established Círculo Israelita was the social center of the *paulistano* Jewish community, and there were some who were concerned that the growth and success of the Hebraica would threaten the continued existence of the Círculo.[32] Eventually, the Círculo Israelita and the other large Jewish club, the Macabi, joined forces and became the Círculo-Macabi, now located on the Avenida Angélica in Higienópolis. The Macabi, which was more oriented toward sports, still has a *clube de campo* in the far north of the city, so removed that even with urban expansion, the lack of adequate transportation continues to impede access. Consequently, many community members with whom I spoke had never so much as set foot in the Macabi's country club. Others who had been there reported that they found the club somewhat run down, in need of paint and repairs, making it a far less desirable weekend destination than the far more convenient Hebraica, with its pleasant environment and many activities. Furthermore, since it can take an hour or more by car to get to the Macabi, those who are willing to drive often prefer to drive a little farther and go to the beach (that favorite of Brazilian vacation destinations), or in the other direction, to one of the resort towns farther inland.

For some, there remains a tension between the Círculo-Macabi and the Hebraica, stemming in part from a historical competitiveness that was ultimately damaging to the older institutions, and in part from perceived differences in the membership along the lines of country of origin, socioeconomic class, and political orientation, but these perceptions are not borne out in fact, since the Hebraica is certainly frequented by the many groups who form the Jewish community in São Paulo. Nevertheless, it remains a point of pride for a passionate minority never to enter the Hebraica, and it is even a source of conflict within some families. One woman in her thirties explained that she was the first member of her family to join the Hebraica, and that her decision to join was met with hostility by her father. Her choice to become a member reflects the place of the Hebraica in the community today.

In spite of many programs aimed at including the entire Jewish community, the club is still widely perceived as elite and exclusive. This impression stems less from knowledge of the club's early mandate and more from a blend of factors including stereotypes of Jews as wealthy members of the social elite, the location of the club in what became the upscale neighborhood of Pinheiros, the social prominence of the club as a venue for high culture and as a place visited by local and national politicians. This impression is reinforced by the attractive and well-tended appearance of the club, and the obviously high security surrounding it.[33]

What is not obvious is that the club's modus operandi distinguishes it from that of other apparently similar clubs. Rather than serving a community defined exclusively by the ability to pay the initial cost of membership and the monthly fees, the Hebraica functions more like a community center, albeit a very large and complex one (consider the city simile favored in club propaganda). There are several programs that are intended to draw in segments of the community who are not members, such as those for the elderly that include transportation and food, or extending membership privileges to youths whose families cannot afford membership (discussed in Chapter 4), and which demonstrate that the club strives to be inclusive of the community as a whole. These programs also reflect the emphasis on Jewish continuity, as do the numerous accounts of members and leaders of the community who met their spouses in the club (see, e.g., Cytrynowicz 2003:69).

At its height, the Hebraica had 33,000 members (Cytrynowicz 2003: 159), and membership has hovered between 25,000 and 30,000 since the 1990s. As the institution continues to develop, the size of the membership has expanded and contracted as the community's fortunes have risen and fallen along with those of the rest of the country. By most estimates, just under half of the *paulistano* Jewish community belongs to the club, adding another dimension to what it means to be the biggest Jewish institution in the world.

3

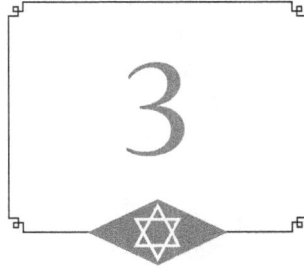

Kosher Feijoada

Drawing on its collective pasts, the Jewish community constitutes itself in ways that are particularly Brazilian. As James Holston says, "The past always leaks through the present" (2008:34). Jewish Brazilian identities are not made in the past but are continually in process, responding to the conditions offered at particular historical junctures, plucking meaning from the past to justify the present, and ultimately using the present to imagine and enact a different future, one in which Jewish belonging is not contingent upon sacrificing their meaningful pasts. Rather than being acted upon by a hostile history, these Jews are appropriating local and national ideologies, regardless of whether these are "mythic," and insisting on proceeding as if they are real. Even if these ideologies are utopic, they may still be the hopeful "beacon" that Brazil continues to offer (Sheriff 2001:224).

Jewish Brazilian identity poses a series of contradictions stemming from the paradox of being non-Christian in a Christian nation, even though sometimes the dominant expressions of Christianity are more cultural than religious. Other contradictions are internal to the Jewish community itself, rooted in what are often profound cultural and religious differences. Many *paulistano* Jews are willing to overlook differences of origin, religiosity, and even social class in the name of Jewish continuity, that is, making sure that young Jews marry other Jews. However, the emphasis on continuity is not sufficient to explain their flexibility. They locate the reasons for the acceptance of the sorts of differences that divide Jewish communities in other places in their Brazilianness, framing it in terms of Brazilian ideologies of race and tolerance. They even extend that explanation to a flexibility in religious practices, however much that might be part of the modern condition, and place great value on bridging difference as an expression of their national identity.

However, there are contradictions in community practices, as for example when some Orthodox families distance themselves from the non-Orthodox families who live in their same apartment building. The contrast with the celebrated tolerance in the context of shared institutions such as the Hebraica is just one of the ways that ethnic identity is exposed as a process rather than a fixed identity.

Jewish Continuity

"Where else could you see girls in 'dental floss' bikinis and Orthodox families side by side?" asked the maestro, with a mix of incredulity and admiration. (A professional conductor, formerly with the state symphony of Rio, and now responsible for the choruses at the Hebraica, he was frequently addressed by his title as a sign of respect.)[1] Although he claimed that the much smaller Jewish community in his native Uruguay integrated many kinds of Jews, Maestro León Halegua was nevertheless impressed by the unique synthesis of the São Paulo community that was in evidence that day at the Hebraica.

Indeed, weekends at the Hebraica club provide sometimes astonishing juxtapositions of the most apparently irreconcilable differences to be found within a Jewish community. Bands of bikini-clad adolescents sun themselves poolside while Orthodox women with long skirts and covered heads push strollers along nearby paths with a gradated set of children in tow. Hasidic men with their black garb, broad-brimmed hats, and full beards apprehend gangly boys sporting corporate logos on their oversized shorts and sneakers in order to remind them of their responsibility to pray; a few boys even accept help tying on the *tefillin* (phylacteries) right there in the club,[2] holding out their left arm to get wrapped by the leather strap while they balance a basketball with their right.

That all these Jews with different agendas and different relationships to Judaism and Jewishness frequent the same social institution presents more than intriguing visual contrasts. That they share the same social space speaks directly to the inherent contradictions as well as the possibilities offered by an institution that defines itself, through its membership and activities, according to something as variable as Jewishness. That neither the membership nor the activities are exclusively "Jewish" is just one of the many contradictions that make the Hebraica such a compelling space for understanding what it means to be Jewish in São Paulo.

The club provides infrastructure and activities for all ages, from a full-day preschool to weekly activities for elderly members of the community, from dance and martial arts classes to sports teams, and from lectures by prominent authors for young professionals to thematic evening parties for mature couples. However, the club's true emphasis is on the *jovens*, the youths of the community. The goal is for youths to transition from the dependence of childhood to a more independent young adulthood without distancing themselves from the community in the process.[3]

In order to accomplish this, that is, for the club to be seen as a "cool" place to be and be seen, activities are offered to attract young people, many of which are coordinated through the Youth Department, such as the Meidá group, which trains young people to be community leaders. The large Youth Department channels common youth activities into those that are meaningful for community identity and continuity. Its English-titled Adventure subdepartment draws on the growing popularity of outdoor sports such as hiking, camping, climbing, and scuba diving. The club also offers training in sports (including soccer, basketball, swimming, gymnastics, judo, and the Israeli martial art Krav Maga), and theater and dance activities. Many of these activities are offered elsewhere in the Jewish community as well as in the city at large. The point of offering everything in one place is to attract youths to this community center, to unify their social, athletic, and ethnic interests.

Each year culminates in the annual Carmel Festival, which draws Israeli folk dance groups from all over Brazil, as well as other Latin American countries and Israel, during which time the club is transformed into an enormous dance camp with bands of roaming, costumed kids. All of the club's stages are used, and additional temporary stages are set up in the Yitzhak Rabin Civic Center gymnasium, the covered Carmel Plaza, and outside in the grassy Jerusalem Plaza, while other areas of the club are used as refectories and dormitories. All festival activities are coordinated through the Youth Department as well.

The underlying logic of these many club activities for youths is that even if they attend non-Jewish schools, young people who socialize through the club are more likely to develop their strongest friendships within the community. In maintaining their involvement with the community they are more likely to continue as club members into adulthood, extending their community connections into business and employment networks. Most importantly, socializing through the club in young adulthood increases the likelihood that they will find Jewish spouses and have Jewish children, who will then attend the club, marry within the community, and so on. Their potential for social reproduction makes this age group centrally important for the continuity of the club, the community, and, indeed, Jewish identity.

In conversations with club members it became clear that Jewish continuity through brokering marriage was the real purpose of the club, the true mandate of this and other ethnic- and class-based clubs. Occasionally I heard thirdhand accounts of romances with non-Jews that began at the club. Non-Jews may join the club, and most of the staff and many of the instructors are not Jewish, so containing the majority of young people's activities within the walls of the club is no guarantee that these youths will develop romances only with Jews, though it increases the statistical odds.

While there are no reliable data on the rate of marriage between Jews and non-Jews in Brazil, exogamy has been sounded as the death knell for Judaism by demographers and rabbis for generations. The question of intermarriage is of particular interest to Jews concerned with the waning of Jewish communities around the world. Warnings about the demographic demise of Jewish communities are deployed to encourage participation in Jewish institutions. One Orthodox group launched an ad campaign in the Brazilian Jewish press that credited the superior fertility rates of Orthodox Jews for preventing this demise, appealing to the Jewish community to return to a deeper faith and its associated practices for the very survival of the Jewish people.

Sergio DellaPergola, famed demographer of international Jewry, has taken an unconventional and somewhat provocative approach to the question of intermarriage, juxtaposing the rates of exogamy among Jews in the United States with interethnic Jewish marriage in the Israeli context (i.e., marriage between Jews of different subethnic groups), suggesting that both result from the same processes of social integration that are part of national formation (DellaPergola 1999:43–48). Though the consequences for Jewish continuity are different in each case, DellaPergola draws our attention to the similar underlying social logic and practices.

Meanwhile, millennia of intermarriage and the incorporation of local culture within Jewish communities scattered around the world have resulted in tremendous cultural diversity as well as the paradox of continuity in spite of external pressures to assimilate and disappear. The largest groupings of these separated communities resulted in subethnic groups marked by major sociolinguistic differences: Ashkenazi Jews are descendants of those Jews who settled in Central and Eastern Europe and spoke Yiddish, while Sephardi Jews descend from the Jews of the Iberian Peninsula who spoke Ladino and were further scattered at the end of the fifteenth century, many to North Africa and the Middle East, where there were also Mizrahi Jews (pl., Mizrahim) whose ancestors had apparently never left the region. In contemporary immigrant societies, like the United States, Canada, South Africa, Australia, and certainly Israel, Jews from these dispersed groups have encountered one another once again and have had to reconcile their notions of what it means to be Jewish with other Jews whose practices are so different. Where Jews from different countries converge in many places throughout the Diaspora, they construct parallel institutions and communities that serve to maintain their differences. However, in Brazil, the Jewish community has embraced the Brazilian ideology of "racial democracy" and applied the concept to explain internal differences. *Paulistano* Jews have constructed a community that incorporates the many traditions and sources of identity that Jews have brought with them from dozens of countries of origin. For Jewish Brazilians, braiding many strands makes for a strong cord of continuity.

Mixed Marriages and Traditions

The first joke I heard at the Hebraica upon beginning formal fieldwork there got right to the heart of what drew me to study the heterodox Jewish community in São Paulo. In a playful reference to the newly remodeled spa in the club, I was asked the setup question: "Hey, did you hear that the

Hebraica now has a *sauna mista*?" A "mixed sauna" usually refers to one for both men and women, a rarity in Brazil. When I expressed surprise, I was hit with the punch line: "Yeah, Ashkenazim and Sephardim!" Instead of being about the social (especially sexual) mixing of the sexes, the joke hinged on the idea of a social venue that "mixed" races, mapping the idea of race onto Jewish subethnic difference. Although Jews as a group are at the "white" end of Brazil's socioracial spectrum, among Brazilian Jews the distinction between these two subethnic groups is often understood, albeit playfully, through a racial idiom. The differences between these broad social constructs are largely cultural (marked principally by linguistic and religious differences); however, in this context (and others), Yiddish-speaking Ashkenazi Jews with their European origins stand in for "white," while Ladino- and French-speaking Sephardi Jews with North African and Middle Eastern origins are considered "dark."

This idea of the social interaction between Ashkenazi and Sephardi Jews as being a kind of socially significant racial mixing was reiterated in the frequent, usually ironic, references to "*casamentos mistos*," mixed marriages, employing a term usually used to refer to marriages between Jews and non-Jews,[4] and between other incommensurable racial groups. That this concept should be used to describe mixing (or "miscegenation") between Sephardi and Ashkenazi Jews reflected a deeply internalized sense of difference. It also suggested some of the ways in which the Brazilian context influenced Jewish conceptions of difference and belonging.

On one occasion, I met with a woman in her spacious apartment in the upscale Jardins neighborhood while the nanny took care of her eighteen-month-old son. It turned out that the large apartment in a desirable neighborhood was part of her dowry, an attempt on the part of her parents to attract a good husband.[5] She explained that if she had not been able to marry a Jew, she would not have married. Brought up in an observant Ashkenazi family from Central Europe, she married a Sephardi man whose family was from Syria. In spite of their both being Jewish, the woman complained about the cultural differences between them, differences that she found alienating. Following patrilocal practices, she had married into his family, so she celebrated holidays with them and attended their synagogue. She was unaccustomed to the foods they ate, unfamiliar with the liturgy used in the synagogue services, and often unable to participate in conversations in their home, conducted in French.

The differences in practices were so great that it was as if she had moved to a different country. Little wonder, then, that such a marriage should be seen as "mixed." However, because both members of the couple were Jewish, no matter their differences, it was an acceptable form of mixing for families concerned with that kind of endogamy.

Other Jewish couples in similarly "mixed" relationships encountered other sorts of social challenges, including relationships between Sephardi and Ashkenazi Jews that had been actively discouraged if not completely prohibited by family members. Each case I heard about involved additional factors, especially economic class, such that no one could say for certain that the cultural or religious differences were the reason for familial disapproval. These stories of sabotaged marriages were told with considerable dismay; troublesome and symbolically potent, these examples violated key values espoused by the community, those that reiterated the purported Brazilian ability to overcome and accept difference.

Certainly not all "mixed" marriages posed problems, and the successful ones were held up as representing community values. I met numerous couples from different subethnic origins who navigated the cultural differences between them with remarkable ease, fusing traditions at home in a way that reflected the blending that is emblematic of Brazilian social relations. One such mixed family explicitly brought together the Ashkenazi traditions of the mother, Leah, and those of her Sephardi husband. It is in the religious realm that tradition and ritual are usually the most inflexible, and yet in Leah's home the family freely incorporated elements from both traditions as they observed Shabbat. Their ability to intertwine these differing traditions into a coherent whole reflected these tendencies within the community, whether within the home, within religious observance, or within community organizations. While there are many other cultural variations within the Jewish community, such as those tied to national origin, none of these differences carried the symbolic weight or social import of the racialized differences between Ashkenazim and Sephardim, which subsumed all cultural, linguistic, and religious differences under a single idiom.

The variety of cultural and religious traditions observed within the Jewish community is only partly reflected in the range of synagogues in the city. There are over thirty synagogues in São Paulo, a roster that includes freestanding congregations as well as those in schools, hospitals, and clubs. The reason for so many synagogues can be found in the combination of several key factors: denomination within Judaism; country or region of origin; and location within the city. In spite of a generally conservative approach to religion, the community in São Paulo tends to be fairly experimental, creating a religious mix-and-match from among the various Jewish movements, with little evidence of adherence to the denominations that are clearly demarcated in the U.S. context. As such, their expressions of Judaism are consistent with religious and other cultural practices in Brazil, where people often freely choose among multiple religions or combine elements that they do not see as mutually exclusive. Although they may adhere to a narrower range of synagogue options, even among Orthodox Jews Topel has found "a lack of rigid borders between the different Orthodox congregations" in São Paulo, such that they might attend "up to three different synagogues, each with a different vision of the Orthodox world . . . without seeing any inherent contradiction in doing so" (2008:165). There is even greater mobility and flexibility where Conservative congregations are concerned. The one Reform synagogue in the city, Shalom, also draws a select group based on its unique interpretation; with no Reconstructionist movement in Brazil, this is the only option for those seeking a more liberal form of Judaism in São Paulo.[6] Some of the synagogues are known for the national origins of their core membership rather than by their proper names, and are given nicknames that reflect cultural rather than religious affiliations (e.g., the "Syrian" synagogue discussed below). Synagogue location is significant because of traffic problems and the desire to avoid traversing great distances at the height of rush hour for Friday night services. Additionally, proximity is essential for more observant Jews who adhere to the prohibition on driving on the Sabbath. In selecting a congregation, people engage in a complicated social and practical calculus, one that also incorporates religious and personal preferences.

Some of the older synagogues in the immigrant neighborhood of Bom Retiro and one in the Lapa neighborhood struggled to survive as people moved to other parts of the city and sought other congregations. As the generation that sustained these congregations passed on, some of their children and grandchildren attempted to maintain the tradition, but many felt it was more practical to regroup closer to their homes, and in safer, more modern buildings. For sentimental reasons, there were a few attempts to revive ailing congregations and preserve historical buildings.

In other cases, people left a congregation because of changes in the synagogue itself, such as a new rabbi or a shift in religious or political orientation.

Certain regions of the city with a greater concentration of Jewish families, such as the neighborhood of Higienópolis, have numerous synagogues. Some of these synagogues are small and unobtrusive while others are large and ostentatious. For example, I attended services at two synagogues on the same street, just three blocks apart, which offered a meaningful contrast. One was little more than a room upstairs, invisible from the street (even the *mezuzah* was on the inside of the door frame), and attended by a core group of elderly Ashkenazi men (including the grandfather of Hannah, the young friend who brought me) who bickered over every detail of the service. The other service was at a Sephardi synagogue recently built by a Syrian banking family. It was so grandiose that it was known throughout the community as "the Third Temple," mocking its ostentation as if it were meant to signal the arrival of the messianic era.[7] My visit to the "Syrian" synagogue was formally arranged a week in advance by Michel, originally from Egypt, who occasionally attended services there. High walls and well-dressed, humorless guards were just part of the elaborate security system in evidence, the opposite of the invisibility of the upstairs synagogue down the street.

Because of the traditional orientation of these synagogues, both services were attended mostly by men, and in both, the few women in attendance sat separately, but the similarities ended there. In the first, Hannah and I sat on plastic chairs separated from the men by a low, wooden fence, more symbolic than providing true segregation, as we could clearly hear and see everything that transpired, even if we could not fully participate. In the large synagogue, Michel sat below with the other men, and I sat alone high above on the second floor on an ornately carved wooden chair, my head demurely covered by a lace kerchief, barely able to see the layout below, with its centrally located *bimah* (altar).[8] Without the aid of transliteration in the prayer books or the helpful announcements of page numbers common in less Orthodox services, I was unable to follow the service, which was sung entirely in Hebrew. The men below sang along with the *chazzan*, more or less, each following a slightly different pace, creating a low murmuring. I did not know the few women in attendance, all of whom were busy with small children, so I found myself alternating between being lulled into a meditative state by the drone from below and carefully making mental notations, trying to remember details until I could violate Shabbat by writing them down once I was outside the synagogue.

Even a bastion of traditionalism such as this Orthodox synagogue evinced unexpected flexibility and blending of traditions. For instance, the head rabbi was a well-known Hasidic rabbi from the Chabad movement (distinctively Ashkenazi in origin and practice), as were most of the junior rabbis. Apparently, the lack of available Orthodox rabbis trained in Sephardi traditions accounted for this flexibility. This is part of what Topel calls the "Brazilianization of Orthodoxy" (2008:160), in which even the construction and practices of the Orthodox community reflect the cultural milieu, even if expressed in a more insular way.

This cultural syncretism is certainly not limited to traditional Orthodoxy and the ferment of Orthodox renewal; there was considerable mingling of religious traditions throughout the community. For instance, Leah's son, from a blended Ashkenazi and Sephardi family, was in the process of becoming a Hasidic rabbi (and has since been ordained). Furthermore, I knew Sephardi and Mizrahi Jews who preferred the services at the large Congregação Israelita Paulista (CIP) founded by German Jews, and this same congregation had elected a Sephardi president (Lesser 1995:172).[9] Topel also notes that "Ashkenazi Jews . . . attend Sephardic synagogues, and vice-versa" and that non-Orthodox Jews frequently attend events and even Shabbat services in Orthodox synagogues without any intention of turning to Orthodoxy (2008:165). Still others regularly attended services at several different synagogues, depending on the week, sometimes for the sake of convenience and sometimes according to the sort of service they desired at the time, without any commitment to a particular line of religious interpretation.

With the exception of the most Orthodox among them, *paulistano* Jews generally took their religion *à moda brasileira*, very lightly. In fact, "*judaismo lite*" was frequently how *paulistano* Jews jokingly referred to Brazilian Judaism. While in many ways this "lighter" interpretive relationship to religion is a symptom of modernity, even as the flexibility of religious practices offered a window onto what it meant to be a *Brazilian* Jew, that is, how Jewish Brazilians saw being Jewish in Brazil as distinctively Brazilian, even within entirely Jewish contexts.

The "Brazil Effect"

The Brazilian concept of *convivência* (conviviality), meaning a friendly living together and sharing of social space, was extended in Jewish contexts to mean a companionability and intimacy among Jews of different backgrounds, and was a point of pride noted by many. Community members repeatedly made reference to shared aspects of Brazilian culture to explain the qualities of the Jewish community.

It was not always this way; in the period following immigration the Jewish community was much more like the divided Jewish communities that are common elsewhere. The roughly contemporaneous periods of immigration found recently arrived Jews from different regions and traditions with a simultaneous need to build communal services. Portuguese became their shared language. When the larger Ashkenazi faction tried to conduct the formative meetings in the 1920s in Yiddish, the Sephardi and Mizrahi contingents threatened to walk out. By the time the Egyptians arrived in the mid-1950s, the community was well structured and able to provide extensive services to those who came with nothing, while the established elite absorbed those who arrived with money. Several people suggested that since some Sephardi Jews did immigrate with money they were subsequently able to wield influence within the community. These historical factors are likely contributing but insufficient explanations for the *convivência* among Jews of such varied cultural backgrounds.

People in the *paulistano* community consider this ability to overcome the differences that separate Jews in other places to be a positive reflection of their *Brazilian* values. More than historical circumstances, the Jewish community reflects the local cultural context in the way it is structured and the ways in which Brazilian Jews understand and practice their Jewishness.[10] In order to explain their distinctive community integration, Brazilian Jews employ both racial and national idioms, drawing on familiar metaphors, stereotypes, and assumptions to interpret what they celebrate as their uniqueness within the Diaspora.

That secular and Orthodox Jews share the space within the Hebraica is iconic of this *convivência*, as evidenced by bikini-clad girls and basketball-toting boys, on the one hand, and long-skirted women with their heads covered and black-clad men in broad-brimmed hats, on the other. Successful mixed marriages are also held up as evidence of this ideal, and interference in mixed romances is seen by many as a violation of the Brazilian principle of equality across differences that is enacted through mixing. Further, in much the same way that Brazilians deny the existence of racism by claiming that "everyone is mixed," Brazilian Jews frequently racialize the differences between Sephardi and Ashkenazi Jews, even while denying their significance.

The way in which the community incorporated Brazilian values and racial ideologies was a frequent topic of conversation. Bernardo, a middle-aged doctor who was actively involved in numerous communal institutions, referred to this phenomenon as the "*efeito Brasil*," the Brazil effect. Key to this Brazil effect was the underlying logic of the country's vaunted racial democracy, which is rooted in the idea of miscegenation and insists that Brazilians of all races have equal access. This notion of equality is predicated on denying the significance of difference.

Having emphatically insisted that there was no longer a social separation between Sephardim and Ashkenazim, Bernardo turned the discussion into a joke using as a metaphor the insuperable differences between *torcidas* (fan bases) of two competing soccer teams in São Paulo: "Here in Brazil, if it exists it is '*very lite*' . . . *because of a characteristic of Brazil.*[11] Here, Japanese marry blacks. Corintianos and Palmeirenses marry. They're difficult marriages—we don't like them, but what are you going to do? I told my son,[12] you can marry a Sephardi, whomever you like, just not a Palmeirense" (emphasis added). Although Bernardo mocked the essentialisms that underlie ethnic and racial differences by way of the theatrics of soccer fan loyalty, the contradictions are implicit in his statement: Sephardim are almost as different from Ashkenazim as Afro-Brazilians are from Japanese Brazilians, but they are acceptable marriage partners. His is not a serious statement, and he does not say whether a non-Jew would be as unacceptable a partner for his son as a Palmeiras fan, but his use of the metaphor of mixed marriages reveals the moderating effects of intermarriage and other forms of social mixing. While noting the community's internal differences, Bernardo clearly favored the principle of intermingling, which he attributed to "Brazil."

Overcoming differences in this context does not mean erasing them. Though some people claimed that while growing up they were not aware of the differences between subethnic groups of Jews, they also, contradictorily, claimed to have had Jewish friends of different backgrounds. Others recalled being very aware of the cultural and putative racial differences.

Using a familiar example that often stands in for perceived cultural or biological difference, Miriam, an older Sephardi woman, recalled a social dance when she was a young woman, shortly after her arrival from Greece, when she had been struck by how poorly the Ashkenazi men danced. (It is worth noting that the event was "mixed.") Making use of another familiar trope of difference, Raquel, a middle-aged, second-generation Ashkenazi woman, also recalled these social events of her youth, and the sudden arrival of dark, handsome men. In the years immediately following the largest waves of immigration, Ashkenazi/Sephardi relations were "um horror," horrific, according to Raquel, who added that for her father the perceived differences were so great that "it was as if they [the Sephardim] weren't Jews." With time, she explained, alliances were built and families "assimilated"—then she caught herself and corrected: "mixed." The words *"assimilar"* and *"assimilação"* were frequently used as code to refer to marriage between Jews and non-Jews, as opposed to the usual meaning of cultural integration. Raquel's use of *"assimilar"* here reflects both the strong emphasis placed on Jewish endogamy as a primary means of guaranteeing Jewish continuity, and the beliefs held by her father and others of his generation that there were essential differences between Ashkenazi and Sephardi Jews. Eventually, even Raquel's father *pegou o jeito deles,* (picked up their ways). "Now we don't really know who is who." There was plenty to indicate that others had also lost track of how to tell different kinds of Jews apart.

There are some efforts today to teach about the cultural differences between Jews of different origins and to integrate these cultural traditions. This does not mean that all activities and spaces are equally shared. Several club members even suggested that a spatial analysis of the Hebraica club would reveal internal differentiation along subethnic lines; the elderly Egyptian men playing backgammon in the Carmel Plaza certainly represented one such ethnically defined space. Synagogues are, generally speaking, another space within which Jews of different subethnic groups are less likely to mix, though even there the boundaries are continually broken down as people choose to attend and even join synagogues for the variety of reasons discussed above. One man on the margins of the community, Felipe, explained: "Here an Ashkenazi talks with a Sephardi, they have coffee together, tell jokes together. They [just] might not go to the same synagogue." However, outside of a few circumscribed arenas, the community is notable for the way that subethnic differences are overlooked, if not completely overcome. Clearly, differences exist, but with *convivência* in the schools and social arenas, and growing distance from immigration, the tendency seems to be for these distinctions to diminish and for social worlds to blend.

The "Brazil effect" means that in the context of Brazil, Jewish practice and ideology explicitly reflect the national ideology of racial mixing and equality, however qualified and incomplete these may be. It means that Jewish Brazilians are Jewish in *Brazilian* ways. Jews have understood and constructed their community in ways that reflect the larger cultural milieu wherever they have lived in the world. What is unique here is that the particular ideology in question is one that these Jews celebrate as being especially favorable to the inclusion of Jews in the national landscape.

Symbolizing and Consuming Identities

When I first arrived in Brazil, I was surprised to see many people wearing a Star of David pendant and confused by those who also wore a cross on the same chain around their necks. My first thought, given the rise of Protestantism in Brazil, was that the evangelical group Jews for Jesus had made enormous inroads into Brazil. There was another, albeit less colorful, explanation. Though there is a growing messianic Christian movement in Brazil that deploys Jewish symbols, through frequent inquiry I found that most people who wore what they thought of as a pretty star were unaware of its symbolic significance. Similarly, I knew a woman in the interior of the state who wore a pendant with the Hebrew characters for *chai* (living) on it, but in spite of my telling her what it was more than once, without a larger frame of reference, she never retained the information. It was simply a pretty pendant her son had brought her from the capital. I also had occasion to stay in the home of a wealthy family in the Northeast where I was surprised to see a menorah displayed on a table in the entryway; curiously, it was placed on a table just below a painting of the Ascension of Mary. As with so many other instances when I came across Jewish symbols in Brazil, the family was entirely oblivious of the symbolism of their candelabrum. They did not recall any other visitor ever having mentioned it to them, nor were there family stories that might have suggested a crypto-Jewish origin. Sometimes a menorah is just a candleholder.

In other instances, the use of "Jewish" symbols was more conscious and even intentional. While some Jewish-owned businesses used Hebrew words in their names or Jewish symbols in their advertising as a signal to potentially sympathetic customers, even these signals were easily crossed. The salon in Higienópolis where I had my hair cut had a Hebrew-derived name, and the owners and their staff wore pendants with "Jewish" symbols (the Star of David, the word *chai*, the blue eye).[13] However, the salon was owned by two non-Jewish women (one of Japanese descent and the other Italian), and the symbol-laden jewelry turned out to have been gifts from their largely Jewish clientele. Rather than communicating the ethnic identity of the shop owners, these symbols signified the incorporation of the salon into a Jewish social world.

Though Hebrew writing is rarely visible on the street, one notable exception is illustrative: a blue-and-white sign in Portuguese and Hebrew on a building strategically located in the middle of Higienópolis advertises a messianic Christian congregation. Like Jews for Jesus, these congregations have the explicit goal of converting Jews to Christianity and deploy a series of symbols intended to confuse Jews: services on Friday night and Saturday morning, celebrations of Jewish holidays, the use of Hebrew in the services, and Jewish religious terminology.[14]

In Brazil, where groups are not proprietary about their ethnic markers, symbols that might serve to distinguish an ethnic group in another context may be appropriated without ulterior motives. However, sometimes symbols are co-opted for other purposes, and the symbol may come to represent something else entirely. Jewish symbols might be worn without any intention to signal ethnic affiliation on the one hand, while Jewish religious objects and linguistic gestures may also serve to represent a particular form of Christianity on the other. In this context of mixed and borrowed symbols, there are few Jewish symbols that can be counted on to retain their signifying power.

One of the most powerful sources of ethnic symbolism can be found in foodways, which may be so particular that they can serve to represent an entire nation, a far-flung ethnic group, or even the particularities of subgroups within a given ethnic group. Much has been written about the relationship between food and culture, and potent food symbolism permeates both Brazilian and Jewish folklore. In the rich expression of Brazilian national identity through food, there is considerable folklore about specific foods, their properties and symbolic significance (Câmara Cascudo 1972), and about eating.[15] Brazilian Portuguese is "peppered" with all manner of food metaphors (*abacaxi*, a pineapple, means a prickly problem, for instance) and food-related metaphors (to have *um pé na cozinha*, a foot in the kitchen, means a nonblack person has black slave or servant antecedents). The special cooking skills attributed to black women fuel a cycle of metaphors involving race, sexuality, and food, which appear in idiomatic speech, scholarly writing,[16] and popular music. Brazilian performer Gal Costa sings a recipe for the Afro-Brazilian dish *vatapá*, calling not only for *um pouquinho demais*, a little too much of everything from hot pepper to cashew nuts, but also for a *nega bahiana que saiba mexer*, a black woman from Bahia who knows how to stir (to move). The tradition of popular music about food traverses styles, periods, and regions, with emblematic songs including Luiz Gonzaga's need for "Ovos de Codorna" (quail eggs) to resolve his problem (understood to be impotency, quail eggs being a well-known folk remedy); Jackson do Pandeiro's "Chiclete com Banana" (gum with banana), representing the incongruous mixing of U.S. and Brazilian culture (now also the name of a popular band from Bahia; see Perrone and Dunn 2001); and Tim Maia's preference for "Chocolate." In their highly political song "Comida" (Food), the rock band Titãs employs the metaphor of food to critique the unequal social order, food being both necessary and insufficient. Each of these instances is thickened with double entendre.

Food provides a particularly rich symbolic medium, and the way it is altered and reinterpreted offers evidence of some of the central ethnic and national cultural contentions. As "both substance and symbol," food is a means to understanding the relationship between national and transnational cultures (Wilk 1999). Foodways have long been recognized by both scholars and laypeople as one of the most persistent domains of ethnic expression. With growing distance from immigration, and the blending of cultural influences from many origins in countries that have received immigrants from all over the world over the last century and a half, culinary conservatism has broken down. In the United States, food fads latch onto food elements from immigrant cultures and repackage them in ways that seem to emphasize their value as novelty or entertainment over what they might teach about cultural difference. Nevertheless, a certain degree of cross-cultural recognition, if not acceptance, is indicated by the inclusion of a given group's "ethnic" food on fast food or buffet menus.[17]

With its large immigrant populations, Brazil has also enjoyed the influences of foods from abroad. As in the United States, the extent of culinary integration varies considerably by region and class, in large part reflecting the local differences in immigrant populations. In the medium-sized cities of southeastern Brazil, local diet has been transformed to varying degrees by the Italian, Arab, and Japanese *colônias* (colonies, as settlements or communities are known). Pizza is ubiquitous (especially in creative Brazilian versions), as are *esfiha* and *kibe* and similar snack items of Arab origin introduced to Brazil by Syrian and Lebanese immigrants.[18] Additionally, though not evidently ethnic, the far greater variety of vegetables (such as broccoli and fresh mushrooms) available in the southeast of the country is owed to the presence of Japanese and Chinese farmers.

In the big cities, the immigrant influence on local food is even more apparent. One of the largest fast-food chains, Habib's, serves Arab food, and sushi is popular in São Paulo far beyond the limits of the Japanese immigrant neighborhood of Liberdade. Sharing in this regional food pattern, the Hebraica club has both a Middle Eastern restaurant serving falafel and a sushi bar, the latter being so popular that it expanded in 2002 to accommodate more customers.

The relatively small proportion of Jews in Brazil (especially compared to the more successfully integrated Arab and Japanese populations) and the general lack of knowledge about Jews and Jewish culture(s) in Brazil only partly account for the absence of identifiably Jewish foods in the Brazilian diet. The diversity of their origins and the lack of a strong shared national cuisine are equally significant. Because Jews have lived in so many different cultural contexts, their foodways are exceptionally diverse, reflecting these many influences, and have resulted in different interpretations and practices with regard to dietary laws. One of the better-known differences between Sephardi and Ashkenazi traditions is in the interpretations of the dietary laws for Passover: Sephardi Jews eat rice whereas rice is one of the foods avoided by Ashkenazi Jews during this celebration of the Israelites' flight from ancient Egypt. Furthermore, what counts as Jewish food is highly contextual and subject to interpretation. For instance, most of what are considered Jewish foods in the United States are Ashkenazi, and many of these are primarily New York phenomena and are not necessarily Jewish signifiers in other cultural contexts. They have acquired their Jewish significance through their association with a particular set of visible and influential Jewish immigrant groups.

The humble bagel serves as an interesting case in point: not only are most non-Jewish Brazilians unfamiliar with bagels; neither are they well known to Jewish Brazilians, including those from Eastern Europe, where the bagel had its origins. Instead, Brazilians who were familiar with bagels knew them from their travels in the United States. As further evidence that bagels are read as "American" and not "Jewish," there was a bagel shop next to the U.S. consulate (in the Jardim Paulista neighborhood) for a brief period in the 1990s, though it eventually closed for lack of business. Only a few places in the city prepared bagels; one shop in Bom Retiro made them twice a week. In Higienópolis, a gourmet Jewish deli that sold expensive imported foodstuffs regularly carried bagels, but they were certainly not an item that was broadly familiar or sought out.

For Jews in the United States, the wide acceptance of the bagel as standard fare, the incorporation of other Jewish foods in select regions of the country, and the availability of Jewish specialty foods in supermarkets (in the ethnic food aisle), on the one hand, indicate a large enough market to justify the availability of these items, but, on the other, also signify a certain level of recognition of Jewish cultural influences. This form of cultural integration, albeit particular and partial, begins to bridge the gap between strangeness and familiarity, initiating a process that is fundamental to intercultural communication, tolerance, and acceptance. There is no such familiarity with Jewish foods in Brazil in general, or in São Paulo in particular. It is only in neighborhoods with a concentration of Jews (Bom Retiro, Higienópolis, Jardins) that supermarkets carry specialty items and display them during Jewish holidays. Not surprisingly, the few Jewish restaurants in the city are also found in "Jewish" neighborhoods.

One such restaurant provides an excellent example of the way that the practices of the Jewish community are entirely consistent with those of the cultural milieu. In the old neighborhood of Bom Retiro, a restaurant that has offered "typical Jewish cooking since 1964" has the improbable name of Buraco da Sara, Sarah's Hole. The name partly refers to the fact that the restaurant is sunk a few steps below street level and partly to the odd location of the restaurant, nestled in the narrow point of a triangle where the sharply angled streets of Bom Retiro meet. It would be disingenuous to dismiss the name as purely descriptive and ignore the obvious sexual reference. The name was originally a nickname that became popularized and was eventually institutionalized. Even the restaurant's business card now bears the name Buraco da Sara.

This process is common in Brazil, where people and places are frequently known by their nicknames, often to the exclusion of their official or formal names. Other examples of establishments in São Paulo that have undergone similar processes include the well-known Bar das Putas, the Whores' Bar (also known, by extension, as Sujinho, Dirty Little One), and the bar known by the crude name of Cu do Padre, the Priest's Asshole, the latter apparently because it is located at the back of the Pinheiros church. It should be noted that both Buraco da Sara and Cu do Padre draw their sexual meaning from spatial metaphors, one at the crotch formed by the intersection of two streets and the other behind the church. As such, the renaming of Buraco da Sara reiterates a local process whereby even an ethnic restaurant in an ethnic neighborhood can become incorporated into the larger cultural landscape.

While there has been virtually no integration of Jewish foods into the Brazilian diet, it is certainly not surprising that Brazilian Jews eat Brazilian food; wherever Jews have lived in the world they have adopted and adapted local customs and foodways. "Local regional food becomes Jewish when it travels with Jews to new homelands" explains Jewish cookbook author Claudia Roden (1996:xx). In São Paulo, these processes are combined where, for example, there are several restaurants that offer kosher though not necessarily "Jewish" fare, including pizza and hamburgers, foods that have already undergone a process of "Brazilification." The only full-menu kosher restaurant in the city is at the Hebraica, which offers a buffet of Jewish, Brazilian, Italian, French, and Japanese food, underscoring that all of these national food traditions can be made "Jewish." The intertwining of the processes of adaptation of food to the Brazilian context, on the one hand, and accommodation of local food to Jewish dietary requirements, on the other, stands as yet another example of the braiding that characterizes Jewish Brazilian identity.

Of further interest is the way some members of the Jewish community have incorporated and adapted elements of Brazilian food, especially those that contradict Jewish dietary laws. Special symbolic significance can be found in the national dish, *feijoada*, which serves as a double example of the relationship between ethnic food and national identity. Folklorist Câmara Cascudo describes *feijoada* as "the most national and popular dish in Brazil, preferred by all classes throughout the year" (1972:388). A thick black bean stew served with rice, *feijoada* is usually made with a combination of dried, salted, and smoked meats or sausage. There are many variations, the most "authentic" of which reflect the widely known slave origins of the dish, specifically in the inclusion of meats that would have been discarded as undesirable by the masters, such as pig ears, feet, tails, and entrails. The composition and consumption of *feijoada* are symbolically loaded with national identity.

As a metaphor in popular speech, a *"feijoada"* means a confusion or tumult, associating the characteristics of the popular dish with those of the nation. Anthropologist Roberto DaMatta suggests that typical Brazilian food, such as rice and beans, can be seen as a metaphor for Brazilian culture in that what is consumed is a mixture of cooked elements, "such that the beans, which are black, are no longer black, and the rice, which is white, is also no longer white" (1991b:56). DaMatta asserts that it is the *intermediate* category that Brazilians value, whether in food or in other aspects of social experience (see also DaMatta 1995). Both Peter Fry (1982) and Renato Ortiz (1985) provide critical anthropological analyses of the appropriation of Afro-Brazilian ethnic symbols as national symbols. Ortiz suggests that this appropriation is a double-edged sword, diffusing the potency of symbols around which marginalized ethnic groups can rally while permitting their incorporation in national identification. By claiming a national affinity with Afro-Brazilian culture, the ability of Brazilians of African descent to effectively redress their exclusion is diminished.

For Jews in Brazil, this relationship between ethnic and national symbols is inverted. Rather than their distinctive foods being appropriated for national purposes, as has occurred for Afro-Brazilians, blending Brazilian and Jewish foodways serves to confirm both their ethnic and national belonging. Because of its national significance and the contradictions it poses for Jewish Brazilians, *feijoada* offers an especially compellling example of the relationship between ethnic and national identity.

For observant Jews, *feijoada*, with its heavy pork component, violates the most elementary of Jewish dietary restrictions, at least in its traditional forms. In a treatment of the symbolic significance of the pork prohibition, Mary Douglas explained that "pork avoidance and Friday abstinence [for Catholics] gain significance as symbols of allegiance simply by their lack of meaning for other cultures" (1970:62). As significant a symbol of Jewishness as pork avoidance has become over the millennia, it neither defines Judaism as a religion nor Jewishness as an ethnic identity. However, because the pork prohibition is so basic among Jewish precepts, and because it has become emblematic of Jewishness at various points in history, even minimally observant and nonobservant Jews may avoid pork for its symbolic significance, such that for some it may be more an issue of cultural identity than of religious practice. For those who are religiously observant, pork avoidance is the sine qua non of Jewish practice, while those Jews who are not strictly observant take a much more individual approach to interpreting the array of practices available to them in the performance of their identity, fully aware of the contradictions as they must appear to others, even as they are reinforcing their identities within their own understanding.

It should come as no surprise that some Brazilian Jews eat pork, even if it remains a contentious issue, discussed by community members as an example of the strains in negotiating their Jewish identities. Pork consumption can operate as a condensed symbol of the tensions between Jewish identity and religiosity and as a source of contention between Jews even within a single family. Although she was tremendously active in the community, Raquel was minimally observant and not much concerned with following Jewish dietary laws. Raquel described the tensions in her home as her children grew and wrestled with their own Jewish identities and recalled an incident when her then-adolescent daughter denounced her to the rabbi for eating ham.

Beyond particular foods, certain practices also come into conflict, even among those who are at least somewhat observant. For instance, although Felipe spent Saturdays in synagogue, he was nevertheless selective about which elements of Judaism he observed. He turned his defiance into a joke on himself and the clash between Jewish and Brazilian practices: "One [Jew] runs into another and says, 'Are you going to eat pork now, you bum [*vagabundo*]?' I said, 'Yeah, today is Saturday, the day for *feijoada*! I love it!' Yeah, I say it. And I go eat *feijoada*. It's delicious in the winter." It is the symbolic significance of the consumption of *feijoada* by Brazilians with a strong Jewish identity that demands attention here. The blending of Jewish and Brazilian practices, in spite of the contradictions, is especially potent in the consumption of *feijoada*, all the more so because it is traditionally eaten on Saturday, the Jewish Sabbath, further adding to the tension between Jewish and Brazilian expressions of identity.

On one occasion, my close friend Miriam invited me to her family's home for Saturday *feijoada*. Though the family had a strong and expressive Jewish identity, with several of the family members heavily involved in activities in the community, they did not observe religious precepts or dietary restrictions. A complete *feijoada* was served, accompanied by rice, collard greens (*couve*), and oranges, and was enjoyed by all three generations present without incident (or threats of denunciation).

However, because *feijoada* has been reinterpreted in many contexts to appeal to the sensibilities of the upper classes and tourists alike, it lends itself to other adaptations. For example, I enjoyed a variation of *feijoada* in another Jewish home, that of Ephraim and Sarah, where chicken products had replaced the pork and beef components. In this case, the alterations were not motivated by kosher prohibitions but were instead a health concession because of concerns about Ephraim's high cholesterol, since traditional *feijoada* can be very fatty and salty. It did not taste the same, but was a reasonable approximation. Of interest here is that rather than preparing another dish, the family celebrated its strong Brazilian identity through sharing a modified *feijoada*.

In finding a balance of identities, Jewish identity extends beyond the religious, and for many it is cultural and not religious. While there are clear proscriptions for behavior and consumption for Jews who follow the lines of Orthodoxy, those who follow more liberal lines within Judaism may be highly idiosyncratic in their relationship to the religion. In each of the instances of *feijoada* consumption, when their two sources of identity collided, Jewish individuals and families enacted their Brazilian identity, sometimes in concert with (by making accommodations) and sometimes in apparent contradiction to their Jewish identity.

There may be a more subtle dynamic involved in the apparent favoring of Brazilianness over Jewishness in these examples, demonstrating how Jewish Brazilians live comfortably with contradictions. Felipe, who defiantly ate *feijoada* with pork, also attended synagogue on Saturday and found that for him one set of observances did not preclude the other. Ephraim and Sarah, who served chicken *feijoada*, had a very particularistic religious expression, almost entirely rejecting formal religion while having exceptionally strong ties to the community and expressing both their Jewish and their Brazilian identities with unwavering conviction. Their chicken *feijoada*, while explained in health terms, certainly allowed for them to enact their family's Brazilianness without directly violating the commandments of Judaism. In serving a traditional *feijoada* on Saturday and bringing the entire family together for a large meal on the day of rest, Miriam's secular family was reinforcing a set of values that were both Brazilian and Jewish, that of family coherence and unity. That none of these individuals or families chose to serve *cholent* (or *hamin*, the Sephardi version), a slow-cooked meat stew made especially for the Jewish Sabbath, in place of *feijoada* is further confirmation of the way that their Brazilian identity figured centrally in their decision to serve the national dish.

This deliberate consumption of the national dish parallels the way Brazilians immigrants abroad "eat Brazil—. . . engage in the self-conscious reaffirmation and reformulation of their identities" (Linger 2001:75), though in the case of Jewish Brazilians in Brazil, they are not "displaced" in relation to Brazil, but continually reaffirming their national identity. As transnationals, their need to enact their national identity is similar to that of Brazilians abroad precisely because their identity as Brazilians is *not* taken for granted (Margolis 2007:213–14). Whereas for Brazilians abroad, their national identity becomes ethnic, for some ethnic groups, Jews among them, their ethnic distinctiveness demands that they perform their national identity in a self-conscious way to confirm their commitment to the nation.

Lest this discussion of nonkosher *feijoada* be dismissed as merely another instance of the cultural chasm between Orthodox and other Jews, the development of kosher *feijoada* at a São Paulo restaurant clearly illustrates the interpenetration of Jews and Brazilian culture. According to journalist Bill Hinchberger (2005), the Bolinha restaurant in São Paulo accepted a rabbi's challenge to make their famous dish edible for the Orthodox congregants at the O Shil synagogue next door, for whom *cholent* was apparently not an adequate substitute.[19] The cooks at the restaurant developed a kosher version of the national dish by replacing pork with beef and experimenting with seasoning until it was acceptable even to experienced *feijoada* chefs. The spreading appeal of the Beit Chabad movement was evident when the restaurant owner recognized former (pork-consuming) customers among the newly Orthodox Jews trying out his first kosher *feijoada*.[20]

The availability of kosher *feijoada* may ease the transition to Orthodoxy for less observant Jews by allowing them to enjoy this national dish. While the restaurateur considered his invention a conversion of the Orthodox to a Brazilian practice, the Chabad rabbi claimed a conquest of his own when he was able to "kosherize" part of the restaurant's kitchen, "the pinnacle of pork" (Hinchberger 2005). Perhaps the most significant pinnacle attained was the blending of Jewish and Brazilian cultural elements in the creation of a Jewish version of this emblematic national dish.

Not all such tensions are so creatively resolved. Differences in interpretation of laws and precepts are what distinguish the divergent religious lines within Judaism and are the principal source of tension between Jews of different orientations. Whereas non-Orthodox Jews operate within far-ranging interpretations of the religious laws and customs as handed down in the Torah and Talmud, for those who are strictly observant there is no question of interpretation but only of degree, with the goal being to continually deepen one's practice. Within this understanding, certain aspects of observance are essential, including keeping kosher and observing the Sabbath. Clearly, navigating contradictory sources of identity through food is more treacherous for non-Orthodox Jews, for whom the flexibility of interpretation leaves open a greater range of possibilities and pitfalls.

In conversations about relations between Orthodox and non-Orthodox members of the community, nonobservant Jews claimed that their strictly Orthodox neighbors maintained distance from them and considered them non-Jews. Offended by the lack of solidarity between Jews, several complained, "They treat me like a goy," a slight felt all the more acutely in the context of a country in which deliberate distancing between peoples violates strong sensibilities. However, the Brazilian context has little to do with the response of Orthodox Jews to their less-observant neighbors. As Topel notes, one of "Orthodox Judaism's way[s] of excluding others is reflected in . . . its dismissing of other ways of being Jewish . . . [T]here is no place for tolerance and relativism in a revelatory religion" (2008:163). Nonobservance by Jews is offensive to those for whom observance is not optional but a fulfillment of God's will and commandment and seen as turning one's back on God and tradition.

There is no singular Jewish Brazilian identity any more than there is a singular Brazilian or Jewish one. The differences within the Jewish community are in many cases more significant than between secular Jewish Brazilians and their Catholic counterparts, for instance. As Boyarin remarks, "Jews' 'external others' . . . may also be other Jews" (1996:56). It will be interesting to see whether the tolerance that is a core Brazilian value moderates the tension between the budding Orthodox segments and the more deeply rooted secular pragmatists of the community.

Being Brazilian

Whereas food practices indicate one level of conflicting interpretations to be navigated, the way Brazilian Jews deploy terms to refer to themselves and others reveals deeper contradictions at the source of their identity. Most Brazil-born Jews with whom I spoke took their Brazilianness for granted, at least at the level of citizenship and formal belonging. However, many were inconsistent in their use of the term "*brasileiro*," referring to themselves as "Brazilian" and then setting themselves apart from other Brazilians by using this same designation as a code for non-Jews. In this usage, "*brasileiro*" was a euphemism for "goy," a term that many understood to have pejorative undertones and which refers only to someone's status as a non-Jew. This usage of "*brasileiro*" sets up a distinction between Jews and Brazilians that contradicts much of what these same individuals said about feeling Brazilian and belonging to the nation.

This and other contradictions were frequently explained in terms of the cultural complexity of Brazil: "Mas, isso é o Brasil" (but, this is Brazil) was the frequent rhetorical response, as if contradiction was to be expected. Similarly, Felipe explained this view of Brazil by listing some contradictions at the nation's founding: "If you want to do well here, you can't take [Brazil] seriously. It's like they say: a Portuguese [man] discovered Brazil. A Portuguese, no, a *cristão-novo* [New Christian].[21] The first emperor of Brazil was king of Portugal. The first president of the republic was a committed monarchist . . . [22] The most beautiful woman in Brazil was a man.[23] And you want this to be a serious country? Here he echoed a controversial but oft-cited statement attributed to French president Charles de Gaulle, claiming that Brazil was not a "serious" country and listing some of the most frequently cited absurdities about the nation.

The first error, as many Brazilians see it, was the "discovery" and conquest by the Portuguese, who are the primary butt of jokes in Brazil. That the "discovery" of what became the world's largest Catholic country may have been aided by a Jew (*cristão-novo*) is an added irony.[24] Greater ironies are found in Brazil's gaining independence not by an autochthonous group but under the leadership of Portuguese royalty, while the dubious commitment to republican process gave Brazil a weak foundation for establishing a democracy. Culturally, the acceptance of bending the categories is evident in the fame and admiration accorded the transsexual

Brazilian model Roberta Close. These fundamental contradictions are part of what makes Brazil unique, often summarized simply as "only in Brazil."

However sarcastic Felipe's comments may have been, there was also pride in his voice. He went on to praise Brazil: "Brasil é um país que não existe no mundo [There is no country in the world like Brazil]. Here, everyone lives side-by-side [*convive*] with everyone else." This *convivência* frequently noted in the Jewish community was clearly an expression of the national ethos, one which was also welcoming of Jews.

Felipe was not alone in his admiration for Brazil. While many spoke warmly of Brazil and praised the tolerance and acceptance they felt, immigrants offered the strongest statements about the welcoming safety that they felt in Brazil, in contrast to their premigration experiences. After more than thirty years, Ephraim still held a foreign passport, but explained that he felt Brazilian "because my children were born here and my parents are buried here." Addressing me as a fellow sympathetic outsider, as if this accorded us greater objectivity, he elaborated: "I live in Brazil, in a marvelous country.[25] There is no other country like Brazil. You're a foreigner, I'm a foreigner, we can tell the truth. A welcoming [*acolhedor*] country like no other, with the Brazilian people, a marvelous people . . . who do not discriminate against minorities. Brazilians discriminate among themselves, among populations of various regions.[26] [But] the foreigner feels very comfortable in Brazil." This contrast between the acceptance of foreigners and minorities and the racial, regional, and class discrimination within the Brazilian population is one more instance of the contradictions that underpin Brazilian society. It is the national *ideology* of acceptance that immigrants recognized and embraced, however far from this ideal reality may fall.

Afro-Ashkenazim and Other Identity Experiments

The ideology of racial democracy and adamant antidiscrimination is embraced so fiercely by members of the community that it softens their own experiences of discrimination. Nevertheless, in contrast to preimmigration experiences of anti-Semitism and their knowledge of the persecution of Jews in other countries, the occasional and largely unorganized spasms of anti-Semitism in Brazil are frequently minimized. In both formal interviews and informal conversations, *paulistano* Jews frequently insisted that there was no developed anti-Jewish sentiment in Brazil, and certainly no history of active anti-Semitism. This is not to say that there is no prejudice in Brazil, as many also reported being told: "You're okay for a Jew," or "You're cool; you don't even seem Jewish." They also cited the common usages of "Jew" and "Jewish" as examples of negative associations with Jews: in Brazilian Portuguese "*judiar*" (v.) and "*judiação*" (n.) mean to abuse, torment, mistreat, and mock, and to call someone "*judeu*" (Jew, n. masc.) is an insult.[27]

Esther, a middle-aged community activist who had grown up in a small city outside of São Paulo, recalled returning home crying when she was a little girl because the neighbor had called her "*judia*" (n. fem.). Her father sat her down to explain that *judeu* was not an insult (*xingamento*), though of course the neighbor may have intended it as such. These verbal insults are not to be compared to the consequential prejudice and marginalization experienced by the majority of Brazilians of color, which is nevertheless dismissed as being "so subtle and mild as to be practically meaningless" within the framework of the ideology of racial democracy (Sheriff 2001:219). In this context, denying anti-Semitism becomes an important part of lauding this ideology, as it justifies Jewish belonging.

São Paulo Jews counteracted their ambivalence about the negative valence of the word "*judeu*" in popular Brazilian Portuguese through the deployment of many alternative terms. Many preferred the euphemism "*israelita*" (Israelite), its more positive meaning drawn from the ancient peoples of the Bible.[28] This term, too, can be problematic, as it is frequently confused with "*israelense*" (Israeli). Another term, "*iídiche*" (Yiddish),[29] was used by many in the São Paulo community as a generic term for Jews.[30] Not only did Ashkenazim use this as an inclusive term to refer to all Jews, but when I asked some Sephardim about the terms they also confirmed using "*iídiche*" as a blanket term instead of "*judeu*," extending its usage beyond its specific cultural referents. Using alternate terms, they explained, was a code, a form of ethnic signaling (Plotnicov and Silverman 1978). These terms were a way for Jews to identify each other and a means of talking in public about Jewish topics without being detected, since most non-Jewish Brazilians were unlikely to be familiar with words like "*iídiche*."

While hiding behind obscure terms is one successful survival strategy, publicly embracing one's distinctiveness is another, albeit riskier, one. At one of the many weekly meetings for young people held in private homes in São Paulo,[31] a charismatic Chabad rabbi reminded the assembled young people to never forget that they were Jewish and proceeded to deliver a litany of terms used to refer to Jews from several languages, many of which have acquired pejorative overtones: *judeu, judio, juden*, Yid, Jew. When the rabbi paused for dramatic effect, one of the more outspoken young men joked: " . . . member of the Hebraica . . . ," and the assembled young people laughed at this very local iteration of Jewish identity. This group of youths exploring a more religious expression of their Jewish identity was dismissive of anyone for whom Hebraica membership was the limit of their participation in Jewish life, though I had certainly seen most if not all of those in the room at secular social events at the club. Joking aside, the rabbi was attempting to redirect negative associations into empowerment, not unlike the way oppressed groups in the United States have "reclaimed" derogatory terms in order to defuse their injurious power.

In a serious discussion with Bernardo about linguistic revision, he explained that Brazilians had not yet embraced the fashion of "political correctness," which he dismissed as merely having to choose one's words carefully. After listening to my overly earnest explanation about the way negative terms condition how we think about people, Bernardo perked up: "But here things are starting to improve. You know, some words here in Brazil have already changed." Such as? I asked. "For '*Sephardi*,' we're going to begin saying 'Afro-Ashkenazi.'"[32] Noting my perplexed silence, he cracked up: "É uma piada," he said with a laugh, and repeated in English, "It's a joke!"

This deceptively simple and spontaneous "joke" trades on assumptions about racial and ethnic categorizations. On one level, Bernardo was mocking a perceived obsession in the United States with sometimes cumbersome terminology and linguistic militancy, where categories are rigidly circumscribed and labels are taken very seriously. While there is little evidence of a similar verbal vigilance in Brazil, many among the educated population are aware of these efforts in the United States and have difficulty understanding them. Arguments about the way language conditions thought hold less sway in a country where racial and color terminology is so fluid, and where nicknames that play with social categories and evident physical traits are commonplace.[33]

At a deeper level, Bernardo's joke drew on both the racialization of Jews by non-Jews and the racialized differences that Jews assert between Ashkenazim and Sephardim. While Sephardi Jews are not necessarily of

African descent, Bernardo's use of "Afro" stood in for "black" as a politicized ethnic construct in simplified contrast to the incomplete "whiteness" of Ashkenazi Jews. In certain contexts, Jews (as a group, without regard for internal differentiation) may be considered white insofar as they can *pass* as white, or at least as not markedly Jewish (Brodkin 1998, E. Goldstein 2006).[34] Historically, in U.S. and Brazilian immigration policies of the 1920s and 1930s, racial reclassification served nationalist agendas expressed through the idiom of national whitening, or *branqueamento* (also, *embranquecimento*).[35] Bernardo's nod toward the slippery categories of race when describing the place of Jews in Brazilian society clashes with the nationalist agenda that would have white ethnics disappear into majority society.

As neither white nor black, Jews (and other nonwhite/nonblack ethnics, such as Japanese, Armenians, Syrians, and Lebanese) threaten to disrupt the tripartite racial scheme that has been used to understand Brazil for most of the twentieth century (Lesser 1999, 2001). Even as the presence of Jews disrupts this scheme, Jews themselves deploy Brazilian mythologies of fluid racial constructs and egalitarianism to claim uniqueness for their community. By playing with race and then claiming that the differences do not matter, Brazilian Jews reproduce the ideology and social organization of the surrounding society.

Another example of how Jews organize their communities in ways that reflect the surrounding society comes from Mandelbaum's work in the city of Cochin, India (1975). Although the castelike system that divided the Jews in Cochin was beginning to change by the time Mandelbaum arrived in 1937, it was still very much in effect. Interestingly, the two historically derived castes were distinguished by color terms, "white" and "black" (the latter also known as Malabar Jews), though there was no correlation between skin color and caste. Mandelbaum explained that these two castes were similar to Hindu castes in their socioeconomic separation and hierarchy, in having distinct kinds of origin stories (one cosmological and one social), and in their concern with purity and pollution (which is part of the logic that maintains castes separate). Once they settled in Israel, the caste stratification of Cochin Jews gave way to other forms of factionalism, ones that reflected those found in Israeli society. Through an analysis of Cochin Jews, Mandelbaum was able to draw out some of the most salient aspects of the caste system in India and to understand national culture through the lens of one of its least representative minorities.

Mandelbaum's analytic purpose was similar to the point being made here: because of the many ways Jews intersect race and culture, they provide an especially useful lens for studying the societies in which they live. Mandelbaum was able to dissociate Jewish identity from some of its presumed conditioning factors (such as "the cohesive force of religious oppression" or organized anti-Semitism), which were not present in India. Most importantly, Mandelbaum argued for the integrated study of Jews and "their non-Jewish neighbors" (1975:203), referring to the "legitimating ideology" (1975:201) which "form[s] the matrix" within which Jews live and organize themselves (1975:200). In other words, it is only through an examination of the larger cultural context in which Jews reside that we can understand local Jewish practices, whether in India, Brazil, or elsewhere. Similarly, the ways that national cultures interpret and incorporate the Jews in their midst tell us about how race, ethnicity, caste, and national identity are constructed and disseminated.

Jews in Brazil enthusiastically reproduce the widely disseminated rhetoric about Brazil being a nation without prejudice, even while acknowledging the existence of and participating in discrimination and exclusion. They employ racial idioms to talk about themselves and others and proudly interpret their own community organization as being in keeping with the reigning myth of Brazilian inclusiveness, even while they are fully conscious of the contradictions that are everywhere evident. It is not necessarily an evaluation of the present situation that they report, but a desired goal: to live in a place where they do not suffer prejudice for who they are. It is a desire compatible with that of other Brazilians. In practice, however, the insidious politics of class and exclusion continually operate.

4

The High Cost of Jewish Living

Although a majority of Jews in Brazil arrived in the first half of the twentieth century as impoverished immigrants and refugees, within a generation most enjoyed economic and occupational success that located them in "the elite 5%" of Brazilian society (Rattner 1987:199). Economically, Jewish Brazilians of all subethnic groups have enjoyed a privileged position, having made major contributions in business, politics, law, medicine, academia, literature, journalism, and film and television. Their privilege is evident by any measure, but all the more so in the context of Brazil, globally infamous for extremes of wealth and poverty. Their high levels of education contrast sharply with the multitudes of the functionally illiterate, in spite of the success of programs to address this and other basic needs. The comparative comfort and ease of the lives of most Jewish Brazilians relative to the everyday violence of grinding poverty and inequality experienced by millions of other Brazilians heightens the perception of their universal privilege. This perception is further reinforced by the high profile of institutions such as the Hebraica, presumed to operate like other elite clubs in the city, and elitist and exclusionary practices such as private schooling and residential preferences.

While there is more to these institutions and practices than is readily apparent, it is also the case that not all Jews enjoy this level of privilege. Those without sufficient means may be forced to choose whether and how to participate in Jewish community and religious practices. Where there are conflicts between their economic status and their ethnic participation, some Jewish Brazilians may identify more strongly with their national identity than with their religious or ethnic identity.

The Kit for Jewish Living

The English word "kit" and the associated marketing gimmick are used by Brazilian retailers to sell functionally or thematically related items as a single unit, such as kits for making fondue or *churrasco* (Brazilian barbecue), with all of the ingredients included, or kits for watching the World Cup. Extending the idea of a kit into the metaphoric realm, in Brazilian Portuguese a *kit* (pronounced "keetche") can also refer to the requisite items for a way of life. So I knew what Bernardo meant when he joked about "*o kit completo*," the complete kit for Jewish living.

Bernardo was active in several of the Jewish community's institutions and drew on his experiences and observations as he enumerated the emblematic components of the *paulistano* Jewish "way of life" (as he called it in English): the right neighborhood; the Jewish school; the club membership; the vacation house in the right location and/or vacations abroad to the right destination. The children's kit also included studying at the right private English school (with mostly Jewish students) and participation in the right sport at the club or school (soccer for boys and Israeli dancing for girls). More than a simple list, Bernardo's playful descriptions had a bit of an edge. Bernardo was not merely pointing the finger at others; he was citing his own participation in this game of cultural capital one-upmanship and offered as additional pieces of the kit his own involvement in communal institutions and having a grandfather living in Bom Retiro (presumably a marker of legitimacy).

When Bernardo spoke of "*o custo da vida judaica*" (the cost of Jewish living) or "*o custo de ser judeu*" (the cost of being Jewish) he was referring to the cumulative costs associated with maintaining a Jewish *social* existence. (He left unexplored the double meaning of "cost" in the sense of an emotional toll.) While each of the elements he cited (neighborhood, school, club, vacation destination) implies a certain level of economic comfort, each also increases social contact, builds connections, and facilitates future alliances of all sorts, including potential business partnerships and marriages within the community, thereby guaranteeing the maintenance of that economic standing. In other words, they are perceived as a socially necessary set of expenses. In fact, non-Jewish Brazilians list an almost identical set of middle-class markers, though without the Jewish ethnic accent, and with a similar goal of maintaining class and ethnic distinction (O'Dougherty 2002).

Although completely consistent with the aspirations and practices of other middle-class Brazilians, Jews framed these in terms of the practices of the Jewish community. Bernardo's list of the kit's primary components was reiterated by others in discussions about normative Jewish *paulistano* life: living in Higienópolis; membership at the Hebraica; vacations at Disney World.[1] "Custa caro ser judeu" (it is expensive being a Jew), stated Raquel, before contrasting contemporary priorities with her experiences growing up. The daughter of a tailor, she explained economic difference in terms of clothing; as a teenager in the early 1960s she had a pleated skirt and two "twin set" sweaters in different colors. "Quem tinha três era rei" (literally, "the one with three was king," that is, privileged). Today, she noted, not only did everyone have more clothing, they also had to have brand-name fashions, which she dismissed as "sloppy but expensive." She reminisced about dances every Saturday during her youth, and *carnaval* spent in the coastal city of Santos or at the Macabi club; in those days her family could not afford the Hebraica. On the occasions when she was able to go to the Hebraica with a friend she was not allowed to use the pool because she was not a member. Leah, who worked in garment production in Bom Retiro from the time she was a child, recalled using a friend's membership card to enter the Hebraica and giving someone else's number to get into the pool. "Tem que ser cara-de-pau" (you have to be shameless), she explained.[2] In spite of the earlier barriers, as adults, both women were actively involved in the Hebraica. "I've made the Hebraica my home," said Raquel, who visited the club nearly every day.

At first glance, concentrating field research in a club might appear to be selecting based on class. This would be true if only well-to-do community members belonged to the Hebraica or participated in the events it sponsors. However, the original connection between class status and club participation was disrupted long ago. Officially, the club is still exclusive and expensive. Like most Brazilian clubs, potential members need to be recommended by current members, and a title must be bought and monthly dues paid to maintain the membership. In May 2002, a family membership cost R$9500 (approximately U.S.$3877, equivalent to nearly four times the Brazilian monthly minimum wage at the time),[3] which could be paid in twelve equal installments. A special price of R$6500 was being offered for a short time to the adult children of existing members in an attempt to maintain family continuity. Monthly dues vary according to the size of the family, with couples paying R$210, and another R$50 per minor child (well over the 2002 monthly minimum wage for a family of four). Clearly, the initial outlay and ongoing expenses associated with club membership mean that it is out of reach for all but the most solidly upper-middle and upper classes.

However, there is another logic at work. Since Jewish continuity is the true mandate of the club, this guiding principle is reflected in a lesser-known policy, that of extending membership privileges to the adolescent children of Jews who are unable to afford club titles. This is the critical age at which individuals are either integrated into the community (socially and romantically, if not religiously) or alienated from it. As Brazil's flagging economy hits the middle classes the hardest, parents who are unable to maintain their membership, or who cannot afford to join, can approach the club and arrange for their children to obtain membership cards and fully participate. While not a formal policy, neither is this practice a *jeitinho*, one of the myriad little ways that Brazilians get around barriers (Barbosa 1992, 1995); instead, there are channels within the club that direct families who ask for assistance to an in-house social worker for evaluation. The club's Director of Jewish Culture, José Luiz Goldfarb, explained, "I wouldn't say that it is a '*jeitinho*,' but rather an informal practice with the goal of not leaving anyone out" (personal communication 2011).[4] According to Goldfarb, the club is able to help with most requests for assistance; in April 2011 the club's president announced that there were approximately 1,000 people receiving such assistance (Goldfarb personal communication 2011).

In fact, this is not a new practice, but one that was first introduced in 1958 as part of the original expansion of the club to serve the larger community (Cytrynowicz 2003:59–61). Policies such as this that extend access to those in the community who are unable to pay what for many are prohibitive rates are an underappreciated expression of the club's unofficial mandate, and a significant way that the Hebraica distinguishes itself from similar clubs.

Although the club is certainly not a philanthropic organization, in some aspects it assumes the roles played by the mutual-aid societies and other charity organizations that were common during the immigration period. Opening its doors to the community's elders, and providing free activities (followed by a meal that for some participants may be the only meal of the day), is also part of preserving the memory and continuity of the community. More than once I found myself in the awkward position of trying to explain to the club's non-Jewish maintenance staff why these elderly people would descend on a table of food as if they were starving, devouring the snacks, slipping some into their bags in spite of admonishments from activity directors, and leaving only when there was nothing left. In an even more awkward instance I explained to a staff member why elderly Jews would steal the toilet paper from the club's bathrooms. For these employees, who belonged to the country's vast salaried poor, their luxurious workplace was likely their only source of information about Jews. With minimal formal education, these employees could hardly imagine the extremes of destitution and suffering that many of these elderly had survived during the war, or how this might explain the hoarding they witnessed in the midst of abundance. Neither did these employees know that some of the elderly who attended these events were not club members, but were themselves impoverished and the beneficiaries of a variety of community charities.

It has been the club's unpublicized policy to seek ways of including more of the marginalized elements of the community, to become more of a center serving the broadest possible range within the Jewish community. Additionally, many in the community also see club participation as central to their own continuing involvement in Jewish life in São Paulo. Families may seek to establish or maintain membership even if this proves to be a financial hardship. This is but one example of the ways in which a purely economic logic is defied by the stronger pull of participation and belonging.

I came to understand this hierarchy of priorities through several families who could not afford a complete Jewish kit. For example, Ephraim and Sarah drove an old car, lived near but not in a preferred neighborhood, and sent their children to study in a Catholic school. The primary locus of the family's activities was the Hebraica, where Ephraim and Sarah assumed organizational responsibilities. Similarly, Leah's family did not have a complete kit for Jewish living. They did not live in the "right" neighborhood or drive the "right" kind of car, and although Leah's children attended Jewish schools, this was possible only because they received scholarships. She and her husband worked hard at multiple jobs and engaged in creative economics to make ends meet, though I never heard anyone in their family complain about financial difficulties. A family with a relatively low level of formal religious activity, their considerable involvement in the Jewish community was channeled through secular activities. Their focused involvement at the Hebraica guaranteed them access to their community, including regular social contact with members of their extended families. Each of these families prioritized long-range social contact within the community over other elements of the *kit*, indicating that Hebraica membership and participation represents more than a status marker.

In order to make sense of what clearly falls outside of standard pragmatic economics, the club must also be understood beyond its capacity as a space of social and athletic activities, and even its function as a space of identity formation and maintenance. Individual economic decisions must be set in a broader cultural context, since these decisions are not made on the basis of a narrow financial calculus, or on some abstract notion of a universal hierarchy of priorities. For Leah's family, in addition to the abstract value of maintaining identity through participation in community institutions, there are also solid if not immediately obvious long-term economic reasons for maintaining associations that do not make financial sense at first glance. Through an active presence and participation in community institutions, opportunities may present themselves for her and her husband in the form of jobs and mutual patronage. The children's future prospects may be also considerably enhanced through community involvement, whereby these ties can develop into extended personal networks that can lead to marriage, employment, and career opportunities.

Awareness of the density of Jews in select locales has given rise to joking names for these preferred places. Since Higienópolis is the neighborhood of choice, I heard people in the community jokingly refer to Higienópolis as "Iidichenópolis" (Yiddishopolis, or Jewtown, though without the pejorative tone that the English translation suggests). Likewise, the preferred beach town on the São Paulo coast, Guarujá, is known as "Guarujalém," combining the town's indigenous Tupi-Guaraní name with Jerusalem.[5] According to Bernardo, the concentration of Jews in Higienópolis is not a question of convenience, or even of group solidarity. The preference for a "good" neighborhood is of course more than a choice to live in a region with relatively less crime; an address in Higienópolis indicates the resident's socioeconomic standing and is thereby a code for high status. In this, Jews are no different from other Brazilians of their class (O'Dougherty 2002). Brazilian sociologist Bila Sorj describes it as constructing "their ethnic culture in interaction with their new class culture" (1998).

While familiar and culturally consistent, for some in the community this upper-middle-class tendency toward materialism posed a serious problem. As a second-generation Brazilian, Felipe had enjoyed the benefits of financial security in the past and subsequently fell into poverty and alienation from family and former friends. From his perspective on the margins, Felipe had especially biting critiques of what he saw as a shift in values in the Jewish community: "The part that the Jewish community here in São Paulo absorbed was this material side of the Brazilian community . . . It is the affliction [*mal*] of the end of the century of the whole society. It's just that the Jewish community knew how to absorb it with exuberance, with the refinement [*requintes*] of graduate studies at Harvard." In other words, they studied and excelled at absorbing and implementing the values of the broader society, especially those of the privileged classes. Felipe's analysis paralleled that of sociologist Henrique Rattner, who attributed Jewish "identification with the political ideas and values of the dominant oligarchies" to the marked social mobility they enjoyed following immigration, though Rattner points out that this tendency toward a shift in values and practices correlating with socioeconomic mobility is not unique to Jews (1987:197).

It is not surprising that the sharpest criticisms of this absorption of values came from those who were in some way excluded from participation in the community's "exuberance." Michel also discussed at length his feelings of stigmatization and alienation from the community in light of its materialist values. He made a sharp contrast between the Jewish *community* (the collectivity of Jews) and Jewish *society* (the exclusive elite), in which he saw the latter as driven by material concerns and status. Still others pointed out the tensions generated by participation in the extreme class hierarchy for which Brazil is infamous, and the contradiction this participation posed for Jewish values as they understood them. Some of these tensions existed between social layers within the community, and some were played out in relations with non-Jews, most especially household employees. Again, in this Jews do not distinguish themselves from other Brazilians, although the contradictions with explicitly held values are more acute.

Domestic Servants and Social Elevators

Most households in Brazil with a minimally middle-class standard of living have some kind of hired domestic help. With the weakening economy, it was becoming more common for households to hire *faxineiras* to come periodically to do general cleaning, as a less expensive alternative to live-in or full-time maids. Nevertheless, the *empregada doméstica* (domestic employee, or maid) is so ubiquitous as to be reflected in architectural design, new and old. The layouts for new apartment buildings in newspaper and magazine ads nearly always show maid's quarters: a tiny bedroom and bathroom tucked behind the utility area just off the kitchen, the entire service area accessed by a second entrance, a second elevator, a back door. It does not take much of a leap of imagination to see the continuities with the kind of social spatial division described by Freyre in *The Masters and the Slaves* (1986a). The Portuguese title, *Casa-grande e senzala*, makes direct reference to this separation between the plantation owner's house, literally, the "big house," and the slave quarters. The simultaneous physical proximity and social distance are plainly evident in the structures of former slave-based plantations. The separation of social, intimate, and service areas that is a standard Brazilian architectural feature not only serves to separate functions, but also reflects the more penetrating principle of separating classes (Holston 1989:178). In spite of political and social changes since the colonial and slave eras, key elements of these architectural features persist in even the newest high-rise apartment complexes in São Paulo. The social relations that these physical arrangements helped to reinforce were so entrenched that they were reproduced by descendants of Jewish immigrants, people who had no part in the history that shaped the social world in which they participated.

In addition to maid's quarters, apartment buildings have double entrances, usually one more formal and welcoming, and a second service elevator used by people making deliveries or walking dogs, as well as by maids. In some buildings, the two elevators are side by side and barely distinguishable, while in others they are entirely separate and distinct. This difference is likely due to economy in construction, with middle-class apartment buildings usually having side-by-side elevators and upper-class buildings nearly always having separate entrances (Holston 1989:178). Although this separation is a normalized aspect of city life, it was not until I actually lived in one of these buildings that I began to understand the nature of the social constraints that these architectural features reflected and reinforced. In the small building where I lived in Higienópolis, the two elevators were not accessible from the same entrance, neither at the ground level nor from the apartment. When the main elevator was out of order, if I wanted to leave the building I would have to reenter the ninth-floor apartment and pass through the kitchen and then to depart again through the service entrance, which also provided the only access to the stairway.

More profoundly, on an everyday basis the separate elevators bolstered a deeply rooted social problem that new legislation had done little to ameliorate: service personnel, including those who resided in the building, continued to enter and exit the building almost exclusively through the service entrance and elevator. Most of these service personnel were brown skinned, but this pattern is often overlooked because of a denial of racism in favor of explanations about class segregation; the presumed association of Afro-descended people with the working classes has meant that "discrimination by elevator" can be justified in terms of function, ignoring the ways in which Afro-Brazilians have been differentially sent to service elevators regardless of class standing or profession (Schemo 1995).

National legislation prohibits segregation for any reason, and racism is a federal crime punishable by imprisonment.[6] Some of the discrimination has been ameliorated since 1996, with the passage of a municipal law in São Paulo that specifically prohibits elevator segregation, an injunction reiterated on small plaques affixed outside elevators: "Any form of discrimination in access to the elevators of this building on the basis of race, sex, color, origin, social condition [class], age, disability, or disease that is not contagious through social contact is prohibited under penalty of fine. Municipal Law 11,995, January 16, 1996."

The law is clear, but practice is quite another matter. While "habit" may account for some of the continued separation, in some instances the law is actively contested. For instance, when I was not able to find the text of this plaque in my notes I asked a friend in São Paulo to send it to me. Along with the text she reported that she had retrieved the wording from the plaque outside the elevator in her daughter's building since she had "discovered that my building does not have one. I think an annoying guy [*chato*] who lives here had it removed." She added as an explanatory aside that "he does not allow his maid to go up the elevator with him."

Individuals resist the law, and not only those who wish to preserve their social superiority. Those with limited opportunities to exercise power may exert a modicum of agency by refusing to go along with the appearance of breaking down boundaries that they know very well exist; in other words, it is a form of resistance to refuse to pretend there is social equality. I watched in silence as Dona Ana and her maid, Maria, would leave in the mornings to do the shopping in the neighborhood together, simultaneously exiting through separate doors and descending separate elevators, only to reunite outside to conduct the household errands. However, on the few occasions when Maria left the apartment with me, she joined me in the social elevator. I never learned whether it was she or Dona Ana who initiated or insisted on using separate elevators, but clearly a blanket restriction had not been imposed on Maria, and she did not insist on her right to share a confined space with her *patroa* (boss), even for a few moments.

This social order extended to other areas of interaction, including the small pool at the back of the building. On a particularly hot day, I could not hide my astonishment from Maria upon learning that she could not make use of the pool, not even on her days off, although she lived in the building. Noting my consternation, Maria responded with an astute analysis of the class discrimination which kept her separate and unequal, noting that the children who lived in the building had more rights than she did. Her analysis parallels the distinction between the two kinds of Brazilian citizenship described by Holston (2008), in which *formal* citizenship does not necessarily confer *substantive* citizenship in terms of rights of access and distribution. Even though Maria resided in the building, her position as a domestic servant meant that she was not considered a resident and was not entitled to the rights accorded *substantive* (real?) residents, as determined by their ability to purchase an apartment. Though she was *mulata*, she did not address race or color, but consistent with Brazilian discourse about discrimination, she kept her analysis to issues of class and occupation.

I was additionally disconcerted by the coincidence between some of Maria's preferences and a well-known character in Brazilian literature, a coincidence that heightened my awareness of the tremendous inequalities dwelling in the apartment. Although she was in her early twenties, Maria was unschooled, and she often asked me to explain things that she had heard on the radio. To keep herself company, Maria listened to the radio constantly and at high volume. We teased about our different music tastes, but not about what really troubled me. One of her favorite radio stations was Rádio Relógio (Clock Radio), a radio station that continually reports the time, interspersed with random facts (such as the number of times a fly beats its wings per minute) and advertisements for products targeting a gullible audience. The honey-voiced radio announcer regularly intoned: "You really should buy this product. And do you know why? Porque é muito bom (because it's really good)." In part, what was disturbing was having to explain why a given product would not, could not possibly do what Maria hoped it would. She was painfully naïve. What I found additionally disconcerting was the fact that this same radio station, with its smooth-talking announcers and inane factoids, provides the backdrop for a novella by one of Brazil's premier (Jewish) authors, Clarice Lispector: *A hora da estrela* (1977) (The Hour of the Star, 1986). Like Maria, Lispector's protagonist, Macabéa,[7] an illiterate migrant from the Northeast to Rio de Janeiro, listened to the constant drone of the radio as a source of company. Throughout the excruciating, tiny novel, the radio intones, "*Você sabia*...? [did you know...?], to introduce many of the very same useless facts that were regularly imparted with such seriousness from the radio behind the kitchen in my São Paulo home. This parallel between fiction and reality was painful to observe because it signaled a parallel trajectory in the tragic lives of the fictional Macabéa and the very real Maria with whom I shared a residence.

My experiences with maids in Brazil have never ceased to be disconcerting.[8] One of the difficult things about living in Brazil for foreigners unaccustomed to such extremes of wealth and poverty is the structured dependence on domestic help, and the collusion in inequality that this implies. Affluent Brazilians often refer to the *mordomia*, the material comforts afforded those with enough resources to be able to pay others, albeit poorly, to do menial tasks. Social inequalities are structured into these relationships that confuse race, class, and status and make for a disturbing blend.

It is a relationship that also muddies the boundaries of privacy and intimacy, where someone who is employed in the family's service can sometimes be incorporated into the family structure, accompany the family on vacations, and participate in family crises. While some middle- and upper-class people genuinely enjoy a special familiarity with their maids (who might be in the family's service for decades), others are forever complaining about their inadequacies, and the tension can be palpable. Most of the troubles with maids are typical of the very problematic relationship that layers intimacy and aggravated class differences.

Although federal labor laws have vastly improved the lot of those who work in menial jobs (who now have rudimentary forms of health care and social security, as well as some fairly strong legislation protecting them in case of conflict with employers), implementation and reinforcement of these laws depend on benevolent employers and sufficiently informed employees. The extremes of poverty as well as the intimate and dependent nature of the relationship of domestic employees with their employers conspire to undermine the strength of these legal interventions.

The tensions related to service elevators and personnel are an instance of the contradictions within which Brazilians live and operate. Middle- and upper-class Jews are no different from other Brazilians occupying a similar place in the socioeconomic hierarchy. The contradictions arise in the inconsistencies between the values of equality and lack of prejudice espoused broadly by both Brazilians and Jews and the practices engaged in by members of the privileged classes (O'Dougherty 2002).

Some of these same segregation practices have been the source of considerable controversy over the years at the Hebraica, where at various points in time the maids or nannies accompanying families to care for small children have been required to wear uniforms to indicate that they were working, or were not allowed to enter the pools or use the other facilities.[9] The humiliation of being subjected to marked exclusion, on the one hand, and the impracticality of separating primary caretakers from their charges, on the other, exacerbate the status tension that resides in middle- and upper-class Brazilian homes and are not unique to the Jewish context.

When a *paulistana* Jew refers to the woman working in her home as "*minha shikse*" (my shikse), she is deploying a Jewish term within the context of a Brazilian social (and linguistic) construct, one that reflects both distance and intimacy. "Shikse" is a Yiddish term for a non-Jewish woman and is generally understood to be derogatory, though as with other such terms, context and intent can considerably modify the degree of negativity.[10] This term was frequently used among Jews in São Paulo without its strongly negative meaning, more as an ethnic marker among Jewish speakers than a judgment of the object of their speech. Once, when leaving a gathering, I heard a woman tell her friends that it would not be a burden for her if they brought their kids over to her house because, she explained, "I've got a shikse at home." In this context, "shikse" stands in for "*empregada*," though it could hardly be considered a euphemism. In non-Jewish parlance, the usual Brazilian euphemism for maid is "*menina*" or "*moça*," both meaning "girl." In the Jewish context, while the choice of term to refer to domestic help is specific to Jews, the general structure is not.

Beyond the contradictions inherent in Brazilian class relations, Jews experience another layer of class contradiction, something they share with other Latin American Jews. Sociologist Irving Louis Horowitz critiques the "bourgeois perspective" of Latin American Jews as a distortion of "Jewish aspirations for a just society." "Membership in athletic clubs, private banking societies, and generally well-heeled life styles was a bourgeois expression of this same aspiration. Thus when the political crunch has come, Jews—whether as open or closed middle-class members—face a crisis of class membership" (Horowitz 1974:122). The humanist values that permit the acceptance of Jews into Brazilian society and are embraced by Jews as part of their shared legacy come into conflict with the social hierarchies that structure Brazilian society. In a desire to fulfill the Enlightenment promise, Jewish class interests enter into conflict with these humanist values.

The Cost of Jewish Education

While place of residence speaks directly to economic position, schooling brings up another set of concerns that bear on Jewish Brazilian identity. Jewish families have several options when deciding where to send their children to school: the collapsing public school system; one of the increasing number of for-profit secular private schools; a parochial (usually Catholic) school; or a Jewish school. Beyond the usual concerns regarding the scope and quality of the education provided by a given institution, each option presents a set of social, religious, and economic considerations.

In order to understand what is at stake in the decision to send a child to a Jewish school, it is first necessary to understand a bit about the Brazilian educational system and the state of public and private schooling. Primary school in Brazil is roughly equivalent to elementary school in the United States, whereas secondary education is split between technical schools and academic schools. High school lasts three years, until students are about sixteen years of age. In order to enter university, candidates have to take a set of comprehensive exams called the "*vestibular*." Each university has its own assessment so that a student applying to multiple institutions has to take a set of examinations for each school. (Public university systems, such as the Federal University, use one exam for multiple campuses.) Although this approach to student evaluation is being reconsidered, at this point college entrance is decided entirely on the basis of the *vestibular* exams. Interested students apply to a particular program (there is no such thing as an undeclared major), and acceptance is based on their exam scores relative to those of the other students competing for the same program. Rather than selecting a program based on interest or vocation, some potential students select their programs of study based on the ratio of spaces-to-applicants in order to increase their chances of acceptance. If a student wishes to change her field of study, she must start over again with the *vestibular* and basic course work for her new major; there are no transferable courses. Adding to the pressures surrounding acceptance to desirable programs, many fields that are the focus of graduate programs in the United States are taught in professionalizing undergraduate programs in Brazil (for example, medicine, dentistry, law). Though some students apply right out of high school, the difficulty of the exam and the unfavorable ratio for desirable programs mean they are rarely successful. A profitable industry of private, postsecondary schools called "*cursinhos*" (literally, little courses) offers intensive exam preparation, exacerbating the already extreme economic inequality between those with resources and those who cannot afford these preparatory programs for the exams, giving the former a considerable edge in being accepted to college.

A major teacher strike in the state of São Paulo in the early 1990s was the watershed moment after which even those committed to the ideal of public education felt they could no longer afford to sacrifice their children's education. This was immediately followed by an explosion of private high schools. Franchises that formerly offered only the *cursinho* began offering high school programs, and some of these new for-profit school chains now also offer middle- and elementary-school education. Academic high schools are increasingly oriented toward college entrance exam preparation, and the rate of their students' success has become one of the criteria parents consider when evaluating potential schools for their children. Increasingly, even elementary schools are evaluated less on their educational philosophy than on their preparation of students in fields such as information science and English, areas that have become essential to the economic well-being of individuals and the nation.

Private schools are obviously an added expense, and private Jewish schools tend to be even more expensive than their secular or Catholic counterparts. The higher fees are due in large part to the high cost associated with teaching Hebrew, which Bernardo called "*o custo hebraico*" (the cost of Hebrew). Hebrew is frequently taught by specially trained teachers from abroad (especially from Israel and Argentina) who are paid in U.S. dollars. Materials for teaching Hebrew are also imported. These expenses skyrocketed with the faltering Brazilian currency, thereby raising the overhead for Jewish schools. In Orthodox families there is little dilemma about whether to send their children to one of the five religious Jewish schools in São Paulo, since the religious content and structure of these schools are consummate. However, the city's four "traditional" Jewish schools (whose Jewish content is more cultural than religious) face the task of providing the kind of superior education that is available at competitive non-Jewish private schools, in addition to providing Jewish education (i.e., culture and history).[11] These added subjects demand additional teaching and material resources, driving up the cost of the schools.

When parents in the community weigh cost against college entrance, they often opt out of sending their children to a Jewish high school, and Jewish primary schools also suffer. Drawing on his involvement in the "traditional" school where his children were studying, Bernardo guessed that the school was losing 5–10 percent of its students per year. Although Bernardo's estimate was probably inflated, there has been an overall reduction of nearly 13 percent in enrollment at Jewish schools from 1969 to the present, a figure that is more significant when taking into consideration that the community is slightly larger now than it was in 1969 (Milkewitz Trzonowicz 2006). Additionally, the total number of schools has dropped, from eleven to nine. In 2006, there were nearly 4,400 students attending Jewish schools in São Paulo (Milkewitz Trzonowicz 2006).[12]

The cost of this special education is certainly a factor in the dropping enrollment and school closings. In 1999, for two children in primary school Bernardo was paying R$1388 per month, for thirteen months of the year,[13] which we calculated to be roughly equivalent to ten times the monthly minimum wage, five minimum wages per child.[14]

Given the high cost associated with Jewish education, in order to retain students Jewish schools have had to invest in the areas emphasized by their competitors, something that at a certain point transforms a Jewish school into a secular school. The point of a Jewish school, Bernardo explained, was *formação* (training, shaping) not just *informação* (information). He elaborated on the importance of this difference in terms of a day-to-day Jewish *clima* (environment). As is the case with the club, the social ties that students make in school have repercussions for their future social and employment networks, and for the continuity of the community. The survival of Jewish schools, therefore, has far-reaching implications for the shape of the community as a whole.

The expense of private school is a long-standing issue in the community, and *paulistano* Jews of all ages (from the second generation after immigration) have attended public schools and even Catholic schools for both financial and educational reasons. One solution to the loss of students has been the availability of a limited number of scholarships (*bolsas de estudo*) at the Jewish schools. Some adults who had received these scholarships were happy to have had the opportunity to study at Jewish schools, while others complained that the scholarships were partial and insufficient, or worse, that as children they had been stigmatized because everyone knew who received assistance.

In order to provide scholarships, the schools must receive donations earmarked for that purpose. Large donations tend to be made for libraries and other important infrastructural features that then bear the donors' names rather than for scholarships whose recipients are, ideally, anonymous. Bernardo criticized potential investors who did not want to pay for scholarships because they wanted their investments to be memorialized with plaques, though, he added, they would deny it.

All of these issues were aggravated by the economic decline of the community, a theme that was under constant discussion in relation to all aspects of Jewish life in the city. As the pool of community members who could afford to pay for Jewish schools, clubs, and other communal institutions shrank, these institutions came to rely even more on donors in order to guarantee the continuity of the institutions and the community as a whole.

Poor People Can't Afford to Keep Kosher

The costs of maintaining a Jewish life are those associated not only with social ties, but also with being able to fulfill the numerous *mitzvot* (pl. of *mitzvah*), or commandments, for a religious life. With the weakened Brazilian economy, these commitments also became more difficult to meet for a growing proportion of the community. A brief look at each of the cornerstones of Jewish religious practice (studying Hebrew and the Torah, placing a *mezuzah* on the doorframe, keeping kosher, Jewish burial, and even attending religious services) reveals that the expenses associated with the special skills and personnel involved (teachers, scribes, butchers, and so on) drive up the costs of observance. The financial difficulty encountered in meeting religious obligations created resentment among those who felt forced to make religious decisions based on economic constraints.

One of the *mitzvot* commands that a *mezuzah* be placed on the doorpost of every Jewish home. In observant homes a *mezuzah* is placed on every doorframe within the home, except bathrooms and closets. For example, in addition to the *mezuzah* at the front door of the apartment where I lived, the doorframes to each of the three bedrooms had a *mezuzah*, though the doors to the bathrooms, kitchen, and maid's quarters did not. In a gesture typical of observant Jews, whenever she entered or left the apartment, Dona Ana touched the *mezuzah* three times, kissing her fingertips between each touch.[15]

A *mezuzah* is a case containing a parchment on which the passage of the commandment to "write [these words] upon the door-posts of thy house, and upon thy gates" is written. The passage begins with the prayer known as "the Shema," one of the most widely known prayers in Judaism: "Shema Yisrael, Adonai Elohenu, Adonai Echad" (Hear, o Israel, the Lord is our God, the Lord is one). The case containing the parchment may be made of metal, ceramic, glass, wood, or combinations of these materials. Whether industrially produced or handmade, simple or ornate, it is often decorated with Jewish symbols.

Although the cost of the case can vary considerably according to the materials used and the degree of embellishment, the basic cost of the *mezuzah* is tied to the price of the production of the parchment scroll, written by a specially trained scribe. In the United States, where there are trained scribes, the parchment alone costs approximately $50. In Brazil, where there were no trained scribes (though last time I checked there were scribes in training), the parchments had to be imported from either the United States or Israel. Like all imported items, *mezuzah* parchments are bought and sold according to their dollar value. Once again, what was already expensive suddenly nearly doubled in price with the dramatic fall in the value of the Brazilian currency on the world market in January 1999. This meant that at the end of 1999, at U.S.$50, the inscribed parchment cost R$80, equal to more than half of the official minimum monthly wage at the time. Two years later, in October 2001, Livraria Sêfer, the Jewish bookstore in São Paulo, was selling the parchments for U.S.$30–35. At the exchange rate of 2.73, that was equivalent to about R$95, still half of the monthly minimum wage, in spite of the increase in the minimum salary.[16] Subsequent changes in both the exchange rate and the minimum wage have brought about greater fluctuations in price. The minimum salary has been increased to R$350/month, and the parchment price has dropped again to R$80. Although this represents a smaller proportional expenditure, the price still represents nearly 23 percent of a monthly minimum wage, making the purchase of a single *mezuzah* (let alone one for each door) impossible for families living on a limited income.

One of the solutions to this high cost has been for Jewish philanthropic organizations to give the parchments to low-income families so that their limited financial means are not an impediment to religious observance. While the translation of "*mitzvah*" is "commandment," the fulfillment of any of the 613 commandments is understood to be a good deed or blessing as well. As such, giving parchments, that is, helping others observe a commandment, is also a *mitzvah*. For observant Jews, fulfilling a *mitzvah* is itself a strong motivation and does not require public recognition.

Similarly, financial considerations interfere in the observance of several other *mitzvot*, as well as other forms of observance and participation, including keeping kosher, celebrating a boy's Bar Mitzvah,[17] and attending services during the Jewish New Year.[18] Several philanthropic organizations in São Paulo assist those who do not have the financial means to meet their religious obligations. Where the primary purpose is social assistance, those who receive donations from the charities with more

Orthodox orientations may also be encouraged to "return" to a deeper religious observation.

Keeping kosher also has high costs associated with it. While the commandments regarding *kashrut* are quite specific,[19] in practice there are degrees of observance of these dietary laws. The difference in degree is only partly attributable to cost, as the complicated laws and associated inconveniences also play determining roles in the extent to which an individual or family follows the restrictions and practices of *kashrut*. In effect and meaning, these practices can range from an affirmation of Jewish identity (for those who are less observant) to the transformation of all activities related to food into a meditation on the nature of God's universe (for those who are strictly observant). Only those animals that conform to the general order of the world are edible: animals that chew cud and have cloven hooves; fish with fins and scales; and fowl that are not carnivorous. Rabbis also interpreted one passage to mean that meat and milk may not be eaten together. The injunction to separate meat and milk also applies to food preparation, storage, and presentation. It is common for this separation to be maintained by means of double sets of dishes and utensils, and some households have separate refrigerators and ovens to avoid inadvertent contact. With the added cost associated with dishes, utensils, appliances, and spatial separation, setting up a kitchen that meets kosher guidelines demands an outlay of nearly twice the amount of money as for a nonkosher kitchen. Once the kitchen has been set up, the effort involved in maintaining the separation is lessened by systematization and mnemonic devices such as distinct flatware and dish patterns.

After I moved into her apartment, Dona Ana informed me that I would not be allowed to cook. Highest among her concerns was that I might inadvertently disrupt the system of *kashrut* in her kitchen. Her apprehension was justified when my attempt to fry an egg, an apparently simple operation, turned into an incident. The difficulty hinged on which frying pan I could use if I wanted to use margarine instead of oil because of my incorrect assumption that margarine was a purely vegetable product.[20] At that point I gave up trying to feed myself anything other than cereal at home. On the few occasions when I was home at dinnertime (a small meal in most Brazilian households, where lunch is the main meal), I preferred to eat at a restaurant in the neighborhood rather than take my other option and have Maria prepare something for me. By eating outside the apartment, I all but eliminated the risk of disrupting the system of *kashrut* while reducing my participation in the system of inequality and servitude.

On the occasions when I ate lunch with Dona Ana, I learned that Maria was well trained in kosher practices and adept at making some traditional Ashkenazi dishes, including delicious and labor-intensive potato *varenikes*, pasta dumplings with crisp onions on top. Maria's cooking earned her the recognition of "almost Jewish" that is bestowed upon adept maids in Jewish households. This honorific hints at the importance of food in Jewish identity, but does nothing to break down the social barriers that keep maids in their place (and out of pools and social elevators). It also allows the "lady of the house" to take credit for the cooking (since the recipes are hers, as the logic goes), something I have observed in many Brazilian households, not just Jewish homes. The added layer of "conversion" of Brazilian maids is merely discursive, never ritualized or complete, and is confined to the realm of the kitchen.[21] She remained a *shikse*.

Although most of the costs associated with keeping kosher are accrued at the time the kitchen is established, there are ongoing costs associated with maintaining a kosher diet. Kosher varieties of common items are generally more difficult to produce and more difficult to find, making them, consequently, more expensive. In addition to the well-known dietary restrictions on the animals considered edible, many standard cuts of meat are not allowable: only the front part of the animal may be eaten (nothing from the hinter parts). To be kosher, meat must also be specially slaughtered; the involvement of a *shochet* (ritual butcher) and rabbinical supervision are also part of what makes kosher meat considerably more expensive.

A price comparison I conducted in July 2006 at the Pão de Açucar supermarket in Higienópolis confirmed that, where comparable, the prices of kosher varieties averaged three to four times higher than those of nonkosher varieties of meat. For example, whereas a frozen chicken cost R\$2.19/kilo, a kosher frozen chicken cost R\$8.95/kilo. Where chicken sausage cost R\$6.22/kilo, the kosher variety cost R\$20.90/kilo. The same held true for kosher cheese and milk. These price differentials are consistent at kosher butcher shops, and are even more extreme if compared to the prices for nonkosher meat and dairy products outside of the elite neighborhoods.

While some might choose a vegetarian diet for strictly economic reasons, there is growing interest in vegetarianism based on Jewish scripture and principles that may or may not be reinforced by economic pressures.[22] Though I did not meet anyone within the Jewish community in São Paulo who pursued vegetarianism as an expression of their Judaism, there were books on the subject in the Livraria Sêfer in Higienópolis. In spite of a national passion for meat, especially beef, and a large and powerful meat industry which promotes meat-centered parties (*churrascos*) and restaurants (*churrascarias*), there is a solid and growing interest in vegetarianism and natural foods (*comida integral*, whole foods) in urban centers in the southeast of the country. In keeping with this interest, the food concession at the Hebraica that serves fresh juices and salads maintains a solid following. Nevertheless, the high value placed on meat consumption does not make vegetarianism a widely attractive option.

The costs of setting up a kosher kitchen and maintaining a kosher diet mean that the decision to keep kosher has economic consequences in addition to religious motivations. Those with limited income see their ability to follow religious precepts as being financially constrained, a painful dilemma with consequences for their identity. People on limited income who wanted to keep kosher spoke with resentment about the high price of kosher meats and of being forced to make economic decisions with regard to keeping kosher. As I heard on numerous occasions: "Pobre não pode comer casher" (poor people cannot [afford to] keep kosher).

In addition to the expenses associated with keeping kosher at home, those who maintain a kosher diet must make major lifestyle accommodations, since the prohibitions significantly curtail not only what can be eaten and how, but also where, because of the strict guidelines for food preparation. Depending on the extent to which someone maintains kosher (i.e., whether he limits his observance to his own home or keeps kosher under all circumstances, to the point of carrying his own food), there may be limits on his social life. One woman explained that the surge in religiosity among many Jews in São Paulo was a response to the improved conditions for maintaining kosher (availability of products and services). With a critical mass living in proximity, rather than being spread out in tiny towns in the interior, these businesses can thrive. For example, spurred by increased interest in Orthodoxy among youths in the community, kosher fast food restaurants offer pizza and hamburgers. This targeting of youths is an attempt to keep them within or bring them back to Jewish practices by facilitating the maintenance of kosher (as one of the paths to deeper observance) within a lifestyle that is typical for Brazilian youths of the middle and upper classes (Topel 2008).

The Hebraica club has the only full-service kosher restaurant in the city, though many of the other food services at the club do not even remotely meet kosher standards. One offers cheeseburgers, for instance, mixing meat and milk. The *churrascaria* that opened to great fanfare in the club in the final weeks of 1999 (and closed within two years) served an abundance of meat that was not kosher.

However, certain precepts are never breached: none of the food concessions at the club serve pork. Other adjustments and accommodations have been made so as not to offend the sensibilities of the more observant members of the club. For instance, the sushi bar (located immediately next to the entrance to the kosher restaurant) does not offer any shellfish or shrimp,[23] and McDonald's was allowed to open an ice cream stand, though not a full operation.[24] Though the latter may have been more out of respect for an existing concessioner than for reasons of *kashrut*, I was told (but not able to confirm) that the reason for limiting the service was so that the ice cream could be consumed by those who kept strictly kosher without fear of employees inadvertently contaminating the milk products by contact with meat products.

These restaurants serve a population that (for the most part) enjoys financial security and help them maintain a lifestyle commensurate with a certain socioeconomic class without having to sacrifice religious precepts. For those in the community with more limited financial means, the culinary innovations do little to help them meet religious obligations, forcing a different set of choices based on economics rather than convenience.

Another *mitzvah*, Jewish burial, was also repeatedly cited as a source of economic strain in the community.[25] The importance of burial in Jewish life is so central to the functioning of a Jewish community that the *chevra kadisha* (funeral society) was one of the first Jewish institutions to be established in São Paulo. Burial practices are also an area where the satisfaction of *mitzvot* intersects with community cohesion in the form of *tzedakah*, or charity. Community members complained about the high cost of burial in the Jewish cemetery and about the humiliation suffered by those with limited means who had to rely on philanthropic organizations to make sure their loved ones were properly buried.

Bernardo claimed that burial in the Jewish cemetery cost thirty times more than in other cemeteries. He broke this down further by explaining that in the less desirable "corners" of the cemetery, he estimated that burial cost R$5,000–R$8,000, whereas "a hole in the 'Morumbi' of the cemetery" cost R$50,000. At the time of the interview, these prices were equivalent to roughly U.S.$2,800–U.S.$4,500 and U.S.$28,000, respectively. Felipe, who was considerably less comfortable economically and far less integrated into the community, gave similar estimates for the lower end of the scale, although he emphasized that the prices were in dollars, indicating that the external economy was at work in even this intimate practice. He said that it cost U.S.$2,000 to bury someone in the Jewish cemetery, plus another U.S.$9,000–U.S.$12,000 for a headstone.

According to the *chevra kadisha*, the minimum cost for a funeral was R$1,800, which included transportation, washing of the body, coffin and shroud, the opening and closing of the grave, a box of candles, and registration of the death. Religious practices come into conflict with local legislation; according to scripture the body is to be wrapped in a simple shroud, regardless of an individual's socioeconomic status, while municipal law requires all bodies to be buried in a coffin. The compromise has been to bury everyone in identical simple black boxes, each decorated with a Star of David.

Death is an equalizer, at least ideologically. The differences in funeral services, preferred regions in the cemetery, and headstones show that practice is quite another matter. The least expensive of the cemetery plots costs R$5500, while the most expensive can reach as high as R$60,000–70,000. The gravestone, unveiled on the one-year anniversary of the death, can cost between R$3,000 and R$15,000. All told, in 2006 the minimum cost for a burial was R$10,000, or roughly U.S.$4,600.

Built into the price differentials is a system of redistribution; those willing to pay R$60,000 are helping to pay for the burial of the poor, among other things. The *chevra kadisha* is in constant contact with social workers from the other charitable organizations in the community to make sure that Jews are buried in the Jewish cemetery, a *mitzvah* made possible by this added income, though the philanthropic organization UNIBES (União Brasileiro-Israelita do Bem-Estar Social, Jewish-Brazilian Social Welfare Association) covers burial expenses for the families under its care. By way of explaining the exorbitant costs, Bernardo added that the expenses associated with Jewish burial served as "a forced tax" on the community, providing funds that were then reinvested in synagogues, Jewish schools, and other communal institutions, especially those that were suffering with the impoverishment of the community. "*Chevra kadisha* is the biggest donor of all the entities" in the community, he explained. The costs associated with the fulfillment of the *mitzvah* of a religiously proper (and socially appropriate) Jewish burial cycle back to support the life of the community.

Although the estimates provided by Bernardo and Felipe were not too far from the figures provided by the funeral society, they differed in interpretation, even where charity was concerned. Their perspective revealed their relative positions as donor versus beneficiary of philanthropy. Felipe's account of how the cemetery staff did not treat the families aided by UNIBES with the same respect afforded others had the sting of recent experience. While Bernardo also commented on the humiliation of family members who had to ask for assistance to bury their loved ones in the less expensive areas of the cemetery, he emphasized the good that was done by the organization. For those dependent on the charity of others, it is the perceived marginalization, the experience of being slighted, that lingers, not only the fact of assistance. This shared perception of economic exclusion, these experiences of marginalization, are "social facts," highly subjective perspectives on social reality upon which individuals act (Rabinow 1996). Although Felipe was highly opinionated and prone to exaggeration, he supported his assertions with compelling evidence from his personal experience.

A View from the Margins

Felipe and I met at a Shabbat gathering at the home of someone I did not know, in a pocket of the community that I had not yet come in contact with. In spite of months of participation in community life, that evening almost felt as if I were starting fieldwork all over again. The people who brought me introduced me around the room and then left me to explain myself and make conversation for the rest of the evening. Felipe was happy to have an audience, and as he spoke it became clear that he offered a perspective that I had had some difficulty finding, the importance of which was becoming increasingly evident. So many people had talked about the *empobrecimento da comunidade* (impoverishment of the community), and I had grown close to a number of people who were struggling to make ends meet, but few could articulate the consequences of poverty for Jewish identity. Felipe needed no prompting; this was the theme of his life.

What I learned that evening was that Felipe had been part of the elite, of Jewish "society," but had suffered a series of losses and found himself without a safety net. Falling on hard times, he had withdrawn from the community and had only recently begun to make his way back to peripheral participation, with assistance from UNIBES. Felipe agreed to an interview; we exchanged phone numbers and arranged to meet.

My interview with Felipe was an exception in many ways. He offered a view from the margins of the community, that of someone who had experienced the community both from the center and from being completely outside. He was not integrated into the network of people whom I already knew, so he offered a fresh perspective, as well as uncensored criticism.

Additionally, because I rarely conducted in-depth interviews with people I did not already know, and because the Hebraica offered a common meeting ground (except in the cases of working professionals who asked to be interviewed in their offices), I rarely faced logistical problems in arranging interviews. Felipe was no longer a member of the club, so that would not have been convenient. Although we lived relatively near each other, on opposite sides of the great rift created by the Minhocão, it would have been unseemly for me to go to his house, and it would have been impractical to conduct an interview where I lived, either in my tiny room with the door closed or in the living room with Dona Ana nervously pacing and interrupting with plates of her delicious guava paste cookies. Ultimately, we agreed to meet in a bar (*choperia*) not a half a block from my apartment, the only interview I conducted in a public establishment.

In the heat of the coming summer, we sat at a sticky table about halfway back and talked while the TV blared in the background, punctuated by occasional outbursts from the men playing a round of the boisterous card game *truco* out front. We chose Diet Cokes rather than beer to wash down the *mandioca frita* (fried manioc root) that we ordered to sustain us through the interview. While I knew other *paulistano* Jews who drank moderately, Felipe was the only one who openly discussed drinking to get drunk. He indulged in a bit of hyperbole about drinking to make a point about class differences, acknowledging that what he said was not actually true: "Depression is an indulgence of the rich [*frescura de rico*]. Poor people don't have time for depression. So, since I can't allow myself the luxury of getting sad, I can allow myself the luxury of getting drunk. And then the next day I have to work twice as hard because of the hangover." Felipe was not worried about decorum. In rather colorful language, his Portuguese liberally sprinkled with Yiddish obscenities, Felipe needed little prompting; he knew the story he wanted to tell and did not care who knew it.

As someone who had enjoyed the benefits of financial security in the past and subsequently fallen into poverty and alienation from former friends, Felipe was especially critical of what he saw as a shift in values in the Jewish community. "I was part of the elite of the community and now I'm part of the community that the elite wants to hide," he began, before we had even settled in, before I even had a chance to ask a question. In spite of the constant noise and the movement of waiters and customers around us, Felipe's concentration was unbroken for the next three hours. He wove his personal story into a stinging critique of the community, its institutions, and the values they reflected. "Today we live in the age of materialism," Felipe asserted, offering a mocking version of the kit for Jewish living: "Who are you? Meaning, what does your father do? How much does he earn? What family does your mother come from? What do you do? Who are you going to marry? What family are you from? What kind of car do you have? Where do you live? *These* are the values you find today in [the Jewish community]."

When I asked in what way these materialistic values that he disparaged differed from those of the Brazilian upper middle class, he confirmed that they were "absolutely identical" and referred to Brazilian culture as "*our* culture." Rather than set himself apart from Brazilians, Felipe shared in the larger middle-class discourse, described by O'Dougherty (2002), that is critical of crass consumption as a reflection of shallow values. In doing so, he embraced the ambivalence inherent in his contradictory identity.

Indeed, Felipe's critique of these values is keenly felt in the broader Brazilian society as well, where class is such an acute marker. The conspicuous consumption of the middle classes and the pretensions of those who aspire to greater *poder aquisitivo* (purchasing power) are reproached in common idioms. To accuse someone of "*comer mortadela, arrotar peru*," eating bologna (cheap food) but burping turkey (expensive food), means that someone claims to be something they are not. To accuse someone of excessive pride one might say "*tem um rei na barriga*," he has a king in his belly. Derived from the full saying that he ate a deck of cards and forgot to "pass" the king, the expression suggests that someone aspires to higher status than is rightfully his. Felipe's humorous critique of the Jewish community resonated well with this broader appraisal.

Acknowledging the apparent discrepancy between his criticisms and his pride in and willingness to defend Judaism in any context, Felipe explained: "I separate them. Judaism is the religion. The community is something else . . . The community only remembers Judaism when there's a Hitler, when a bomb explodes. Then everyone holds hands . . . And this is what I see here in Brazil in the Jewish community. They feel superior . . . untouchable, and *forget* the values. Because here you don't have war, because here you don't have fights, because here you don't have that thing they have in the United States with neighborhoods of just blacks, of I-don't-know-what. Here everyone is everyone." He seemed to be suggesting that Jewish absorption of Brazilian values and the acceptance Jews enjoy in Brazilian society has allowed them to be complacent.

Felipe touched on many of the same themes that Bernardo did in his description of the "Jewish kit"—the status symbols of family, neighborhood, and material goods. Though both men were critical, the bitterness with which Felipe deployed his critique gave it an edge that Bernardo, from the comfort of his home in the right neighborhood with his children in the right schools, could not. Rubbing his fingers and thumb together in the gesture for money, Felipe explained, "I changed political ideology," reinforcing just how much class position has to do with economic prospects and perspective (Rattner 1987:197).

His tone changed dramatically when he came around to talking about UNIBES, which he called "the jewel of the community." Given Felipe's personal history, it is not surprising that he was most admiring of this charitable organization that has done so much to help him and other impoverished citizens, Jews and non-Jews alike.

Tzedakah and *Cidadania*

Enduring stereotypes about Jews being wealthy, reinforced by the evidence of Jewish clubs, schools, synagogues, and banks in "noble" areas of the city,[26] lead many to assume that all Jews are well off. While there is no denying that as a group Jews enjoy a higher standard of living than many other ethnic groups in Brazil, upon closer examination it is also evident that this pattern is not as absolute as it might seem. The prominence of international banking families like the Safras overshadows the struggles of middle-class and poor Jews. With increased integration into Brazilian society, the networks and mutual-aid societies that provided a safety net for new immigrants are no longer there to catch second- and third-generation Brazilian Jews. They have been replaced by important charitable organizations, but shame and assumptions about the status of the Jewish community mean that Jews may hide their need because they think it is an indication of personal failure rather than part of a larger social pattern. The resulting invisibility of poor Jews contributes to their difficulties getting back on their feet.

The ironic flip side of the successful social and cultural integration of Jews into every level of Brazilian society can be seen in the fact that the families of impoverished Jews with whom I spoke were not impoverished a generation ago. The continued existence of the various charitable organizations that help members of the community is the strongest evidence of an ongoing need, one that has grown during times of national economic instability; this too is further evidence of the economic integration of Brazilian Jews. At least some of the Jews who seek assistance from these organizations have fallen on hard times more recently, and their difficulties are connected to the economic difficulties of the country. While some poor Jews come from families that never gained a toehold in the Brazilian economy, others are not able to work due to disabilities, and still others have run into financial difficulties, like so many others in the middle classes.

With the return of economic instability in Brazil at the turn of the twenty-first century and the greater integration of Jews at all levels of Brazilian society, Jews experienced the national and local socioeconomic fluctuations more than ever before. More and more Jews were faced with having to make economically motivated choices about the extent of their involvement in Jewish communal institutions and religious practices. This does not necessarily mean that families with lower incomes drop out of the community and lose their religion. The mutual-aid societies and business networks that helped immigrants in earlier generations get established in the new country have given way to numerous philanthropic organizations that assist Jewish families and individuals (as well as non-Jews).

As the community grew aware of its collective risk, it began to reach out to Jews who had already fallen through the cracks. A 1998 exposé by the Jewish cable television program *Shalom Brasil* showed Jews living in *favelas* (the shantytowns in the interstices of Brazilian cities), barely able to eke out a living. In an extension of the charitable aspects of the club, I learned that one of the men interviewed for the program subsequently secured a job at the Hebraica as the synagogue's caretaker. In its charitable efforts, the Jewish community reaches out first to "its own," offering them advantages over the vast majority of the population, which is barely able to make a living and is subject to the extreme violence for which Brazil has become famous. However, this comparative privilege in no way negates the tremendous suffering and shame that these impoverished Jews endure, and it is clear that many Jews have become so alienated from the community that they may never be reached by these charities.

Prominent among the local community initiatives in São Paulo are the Albert Einstein Hospital, the OAT (Oficina Abrigada de Trabalho, roughly, Sheltered Workshop), Chaverim, the Lar Golda Meir, Ten Yad, and UNIBES. With slightly overlapping objectives, each of these institutions reaches a different segment of the community. The Albert Einstein Hospital is one of the country's most respected hospitals and charities. While not functionally a *Jewish* institution, it serves and represents the community and extends its philanthropic activities to residents of the *favela* nearby. Both the OAT and Chaverim provide services and activities for disabled members of the community; OAT is an occupational development school with an international base that is locally run by the Reform synagogue Comunidade Shalom to train and employ individuals with disabilities, and Chaverim is an organization with a base at the Hebraica that teaches Jewish culture and religion to developmentally disabled individuals and incorporates them into communal life. The community's elderly are cared for in the Golda Meir Home for the Elderly, while Ten Yad (Hebrew for "helping hand") provides food (and clothing and household goods) for impoverished elderly and disabled members of the community through its center in Bom Retiro, and through kosher meal delivery to homebound individuals. An organization run by Hasidic Jews, Ten Yad's religious mandate extends to providing reading materials to Jewish prisoners and assisting them with fulfilling their prayer *mitzvot* by tying the *tefillin*.

UNIBES is unique among these organizations in that it provides a full range of social services for all ages. The bazaar raises funds by selling donated clothing and household goods, but also provides the families that receive assistance with coupons for use in the bazaar. In addition to child care, after-school activities, training for adolescents, and activities and occupational therapy for the elderly, UNIBES has a pharmacy and medical assistants, provides help with rent and utility payments, offers legal assistance, and assigns social workers to look after over 1,000 needy families. In 1999, 1,180 families were receiving assistance from UNIBES. By July 2001, the total had reached 1,400 families, or 6,000 individuals. The organization's Web site reiterated the impact of the economic crisis (in English): "Due to the economic situation prevailing in Brazil, this department is faced with a new destituted [sic] group. Caught by surprise, these middle-class families are not emotionally prepared for crises [sic] situations."

UNIBES is also one of the few Jewish charitable organizations that assist non-Jews and is visible beyond the Jewish community. Large electronic billboards in the city advertise the organization's services and events. Big names in popular Brazilian music regularly play concerts in major venues to raise funds for the organization, including Roberto Carlos, Daniela Mercury, and Leonardo. Among its many awards, in 1999, UNIBES received national recognition with the Human Rights Award from the Brazilian Ministry of Justice.

As an indication of the need for the services of these organizations, there are always more individuals requesting basic assistance than can be accommodated. Esther, a friend in São Paulo, sent me an update in October 2001. After filling me in on the increasingly central role of the Hebraica in the cohesion of the community, and the political and social shifts at the CIP synagogue, she discussed community changes rooted in the weakening economy: "Ten Yad . . . has been receiving more and more people who need help, and UNIBES too. In other words, our middle class is going down the tubes [pro beleléu], and there is a growing gap between the richest and the poorest." Although the fragility of the middle class in Brazil was not news, the visibility of these changes in the Jewish community certainly indicated a shift in their position.

In spite of increasing numbers of people seeking help from these institutions, there were many others who did not. Ignorance of existing solutions was one reason some Jews did not seek assistance, and this contributed to the distancing of individuals from the community. However, shame has also played a role in keeping people from requesting assistance from these charitable organizations. Based on his own experience, Felipe explained that Jews were very "proud" and that humiliation kept them from asking for help. His own initial lack of success at getting help from family and friends and the embarrassment of failure resulted in his distancing himself from the community, a scenario repeated by others. More than a decade after losing everything, motivated by his wish for a better life for his then-adolescent children, he eventually found his way to UNIBES and slowly began to reverse his fortunes a few years before our interview. Rejecting one set of values that he associated with the Jewish community distanced him from his social world, and embracing another set allowed him to draw near again and reorient his life.

Another of the clashes between materialism and charity has come in the form of a recent custom, Rosh Hashanah gifts. I learned about this during my interview with Bernardo in his medical office on the day of the eve (*erev*) of Rosh Hashanah. As our conversation shifted from the particular concerns regarding Jewish education to other components of the *custo judaico*, the cost of Jewish living, Bernardo illustrated the problem with the cards and gifts he had received from colleagues and patients in the weeks leading up to the High Holy Days. Whereas ten years earlier nothing more than a card and perhaps some chocolate had been exchanged, within certain circles a simple greeting card was no longer sufficient. Not only had recent years seen a spiraling of social obligations tied to gift giving, he explained, but this was occurring simultaneously with the impoverishment of the community. He showed me one particularly nice gift from a patient who he knew was suffering financially, but who would not want the embarrassment of not giving him an adequate present. In addition to putting pressure on those who cannot afford to keep pace, Bernardo suggested that this new practice of elaborate gift giving had also negatively affected communal organizations. Instead of making needed charitable donations during the High Holy Days, people in the community were engaging in Christmas-like gift exchanges, even when they could ill afford to do so. As a result, the charities were suffering under the double pressure of increased need and decreased income. Of course, these contradictions are not unique to the Jewish community or to Brazil, as seen every year in the tension between the extreme materialism of Christmas contrasted with the appeals for charitable giving that supposedly characterize the season.

The intersection of the Jewish concept of charity with the Brazilian concept of citizenship makes for a potent sense of responsibility and belonging. The Hebrew word for charity is *tzedakah*, meaning "righteous-ness," another *mitzvah*. For Jews, degrees of righteousness are derived from the selflessness of the giver and the lack of shame or humiliation for the receiver, the highest form of which is when both are anonymous. In Brazil, charity is couched in terms of *cidadania* (citizenship), understood broadly to refer to contributions to one's community. This use of "*cidadania*" differs somewhat from both the political and the "substantive" senses of citizenship explored by Holston (2008), which emphasize formal and practical rights, and from Rosaldo's notion of "cultural citizenship" (1994a, 1994b), which emphasizes differentiated belonging through participation in the national collective. Both Holston and Rosaldo consider the ways in which different conceptions of citizenship encompass the inequalities that characterize Brazil and the United States, respectively. However, in this context the use of "*cidadania*" seems to be a way of enacting Jewish belonging through participation in the nation. This kind of participation acknowledges systemic inequality as a starting place, whereby those who are actively participating, that is, middle- and upper-class Jews, are in a position to distribute resources to those in need, rather than being the ones to receive them. In doing so, and by framing it in terms of *cidadania*, they are actively demonstrating their belonging out of a need to prove their commitment to the nation. Their problem is different from that of the vast majority of Brazilian citizens who have formal rights, but not substantive rights because of insufficient education, racial inequalities, and class hierarchies (Holston 2008). In spite of having legal citizenship, as transnationals they need to continually assert their belonging by par-ticipating in and meeting the needs of the larger society, and couching it in terms of *cidadania*.

In the São Paulo Jewish community, the concepts of *tzedakah* and *ci-dadania* merge into a coherent whole. For instance, the Hebraica's an-nual winter *campanha do agasalho* (coat drive), when donations of warm clothes are solicited and distributed to needy families, is categorized un-der "*cidadania*" in the club's literature, framing it in terms of responsibil-ity to the larger community in the context of Brazil, rather than in terms of *tzedakah*, which would carry a more exclusively Jewish meaning in this context. The combined ideals of *cidadania* and *tzedakah* are expressed in a growing profile of Jewish philanthropic organizations directed to-ward both the needy segments of the Jewish community and the society at large.

Of course, this dovetailing of ideals is not necessarily reflected in the practices of members of the community, as both Bernardo and Felipe made clear, each from his own point of view. Felipe's unqualified assertions invited debate, and I challenged him on the apparent inconsistency between his criticisms of the community's materialism—of which he had been both a participant and a casualty—and his praise for the community's charitable organizations—of which he had been a beneficiary. He explained that only a minority of people in the community got actively involved in philanthropy and volunteering, and then added that the majority of these volunteered at places like the sports programs at the Hebraica. He explained that when a friend told him she was volunteering at the Hebraica pool, he sarcastically responded, "You'll go straight to heaven." In a caustic mix of English and Yiddish, he grumbled, "Kiss my *tuchis*," then added, "Go volunteer at places where they can't afford to pay you." Helping out at a private club is hardly an example of the kind of volunteerism and charity that is meant by either *tzedakah* or *cidadania*.

Tying the righteousness of *tzedakah* with the grounded sense of belonging of *cidadania*, where these concepts meaningfully unify these two sources of identity for Jewish Brazilians, class position poses barriers, favoring one identity over another. The linking of core Jewish and Brazilian values, of parallel notions of participation and *tikkun olam*, healing the world, may well serve to deepen Jewish belonging in Brazil. It is hardly a coincidence that this should happen alongside, perhaps even as a consequence of, the fragmentation of the Jewish community along the familiar Brazilian class divisions. Where wealthier Jews express their Jewishness in ways that are reflective of their class position, those of the more disadvantaged classes and who have grown distant from the community because of lack of access and shame also strengthen their sense of Brazilianness, but because of an inability to sustain their Jewishness. Regardless of class position, the tension between economic status and ethnic identity forces a deepening of identification with the nation, albeit in dramatically different ways.

5

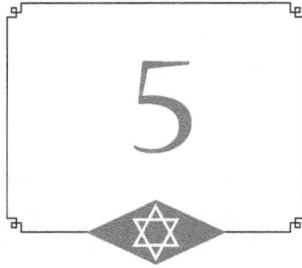

Inscribing Jews into the Nation

Indicators of Jewish integration into Brazilian society sometimes take surprising forms. For example, a century ago, when most Jews in Brazil were Sephardim and lived in the north of the country along the Amazon, they struggled to establish Jewish institutions. In 1908, Rabbi Shalom Emanuel Muyal immigrated and joined other Moroccans in the region, but he died two years later during an epidemic. Manaus did not have a Jewish cemetery yet, so the rabbi was buried in the municipal cemetery. In what must surely fall under the category of "only in Brazil," Rabbi Muyal has been credited with posthumous "miracles" by local Catholics, and his tomb has become a *Christian* pilgrimage site (Hinchberger 1999). Curiously, not only do visitors light candles, but some leave stones on his grave in accordance with Jewish tradition. Now that he is a popular saint known as the Santo Judeu Milagreiro de Manaus (Holy Jewish Miracle Worker of Manaus), the local Jewish community cannot relocate his grave to the Jewish cemetery, let alone to Israel, as requested by his nephew, a member of Israel's Knesset (Hinchberger 1999). Though especially colorful because of the way it intertwines traces of Brazilian history, syncretic elements of folk Catholicism, and interfaith tolerance, the incorporation of Rabbi Muyal into local culture is one of many examples of the broad acceptance that has allowed Jews to establish a home in Brazil.

Jewish Brazilians have become thoroughly enmeshed in national culture and society. They have attained a symbolic value that far exceeds their numerical significance, especially in light of recent anniversaries that have stimulated examinations of national history and identity. At the federal and municipal levels, agencies of the state have made deliberate, public gestures signaling the importance of Jews within the Brazilian nation. Institutions of popular culture have also joined in this celebration of Jews as part of this multicultural nation by incorporating Jewish themes and working with the Jewish community to promote a vision of a shared Jewish-Brazilian trajectory and set of values. The Jewish community has embraced these moments as opportunities to consolidate its place within the nation.

Rediscovering Jews

At the dawn of the twenty-first century, 500 years after Europeans "discovered" Brazil, Brazil discovered Jews. This discovery entailed a rewriting of the past and a new reading of the present, both in the service of reconfiguring the nation as more than a former colonial dependency, more than a Catholic country, and more than the product of the idea of the "three races" that has dominated national mythology. As the evidence mounts of Jewish contributions to Brazil throughout its 500-year history, Jews have come to be seen as collaborators in the national project rather than as recent arrivals. It is as if Brazilians' discovery of Jews in their midst sheds a new and positive light on the whole of Brazil.

In April 2000, Brazil marked the 500th anniversary of the arrival of Portuguese explorers at the protrusion of the coast now occupied by the northeastern city of Olinda, the formative moment in the creation of the new nation. To remind the citizenry of the approaching quincentenary, the Globo television network sponsored an oversized countdown clock on the Avenida Faria Lima in São Paulo. The preparations for the anniversary celebration were extensive and involved all levels of government, education, and news and entertainment media in the production of representations of Brazil for both internal consumption and export. Most endeavors reinterpreted the past, while a few took a look at the future.

Flavio Pinheiro begins his introduction to the edited volume on the "next 500 years" of Brazil, stating: "In the year 2000, emblem of the future, Brazil returned to the past. Five hundred years to try to explain the country spit out by the metabolism of colonization, by the cauldron of races, by the original sin of exclusion" (Pinheiro 2000:5).

As is typical of major anniversaries, this one presented an opportunity for revisiting Brazilian history. It also afforded an opportunity to revise that history, to reinterpret and salvage (*resgatar*) moments from the past in such a way as to redefine Brazilianness. In a country which seems to be continually examining what it means to be Brazilian, a major mark like the quincentenary was a rare opportunity to rewrite history in support of a new image of the nation.[1]

Set in motion in anticipation of this anniversary, there appears to be a major reorientation under way in how Brazil is conceived, one that reconfigures Brazil so as to include the many immigrant groups that have contributed to the nation. This constitutes a shift from the reigning tripartite social race concept toward an inclusive nation-based notion of culture. In preparation for the anniversary, government and public institutions promoted this multicultural model by sponsoring publications, conferences, museum exhibits, and celebratory events. Apparently, not every issue was up for reexamination, as Brazil's indigenous populations were infamously left out of these celebrations, marginalized yet again.

By celebrating the contributions of immigrant groups, this reorientation is an attempt to shake off the colonial past and put the emphasis on Brazilian history since the establishment of the republic (1889). This formal reinscription has been reinforced by efforts on the part of immigrant-descended groups, who have concurred with this revised history and added their own evidence and perspectives—all in the name of celebrating the inclusive, multiethnic Brazilian nation that they call home.

Jews were a part of this revision, as both objects and participants, increasingly included in representations of Brazilianness, and they are a salient example of the tenor of the change under way. Jewish institutions have sponsored revisionist exhibits and publications of their own to complement the official versions. This collaborative rewriting of national history positions Jews as participants in a shared trajectory from the first moments of European presence. This shift gives evidence to a process of mutual identity formation: of Brazilian Jews, on the one hand, and of Brazil through Jews, on the other. Indeed, this tiny minority offers the ideal foil for a Brazilianness that is substantively Catholic. It is for their symbolic potency, and certainly not for any sort of statistical or political significance, that Jews in Brazil are taking on a cultural weight far beyond their numerical importance.

As but one example of this revisionist history, a weekly calendar distributed by the Keren Kayemet organization in September 1999 (for the Jewish year 5760) included a dual timeline that drew parallels between Brazilian history and the Jewish presence in Brazil.[2] The timeline began in 1492—or 5252 in the Jewish calendar—which saw the expulsion of Jews from Spain—and continued for several pages up through 1997 and the establishment of Brazil's national antidiscrimination law. The cover of this calendar, with its blending of Brazilian and Jewish symbols into a hybrid Jewish version of the national flag (blue and white, with Stars of David on the dome of the universe), anticipated the upcoming quincentenary with the motto, "Brazil, 500 years of Jewish participation," extending Jewish presence to a more active cultural influence.

Examples of officially sponsored historical revisionism include Ministry of Culture publications, such as *Entre Moisés e Macunaíma* (Between Moses and Macunaíma), by two of Brazil's most prominent fiction writers, Moacyr Scliar and Márcio Souza, both of whom are Jewish.[3] In the book, each author separately explores the interlacing of his dual Brazilian-Jewish identity through his personal background, Ashkenazi and Sephardi, respectively. Another Ministry of Culture production, the musicological recording *Teatro do Descobrimento* (Theater of Discovery), traces the contours of colonial Brazil through its music, delineating the country's formative cultural influences. This heavily researched compilation includes several songs in Hebrew and the first Hebrew poem written in the Americas, by Rabbi Isaac Aboab da Fonseca.

These endeavors were further fueled by the rediscovery and renovation of the oldest synagogue in the Americas, built in the northeastern city of Recife in 1637 during the phase that Brazilians refer to as "the Dutch Invasion" (1630–54). The recognition of the historical presence and participation of this small population of Jews is corrective, but it is also strategic; the widespread publicity about the synagogue in Brazil and abroad is an example of the larger project to recast contemporary Brazil as a multicultural, modern nation. There is further evidence of this shift in orientation at many levels of Brazilian society, from national to local, and from official to popular. When considered together, the simultaneous acknowledgment and celebration of the Jewish presence in Brazil on multiple levels of Brazilian society constitute a statement about national values made explicit at this historical juncture.

Commemorative Stamps

Brazil's 500th anniversary celebrations coincided with another heralded commemoration, that of the turn of the millennium. The idea of a new era provided additional fodder for Brazilian repositioning, and on January 1, 2001, the Brazilian Postal Service released a set of commemorative stamps entitled *Novos Tempos: 2001, um novo milênio* (New times: 2001, a new millennium). The three stamps symbolized the calendars of the three major Abrahamic religions: Judaism, Islam, and Christianity. According to the Postal Service's description, they "allud[e] to the different forms used in distinct cultures to mark time." Each of the traditions was represented by religious symbols: Judaism was represented by a Torah, a menorah, the Ten Commandments, and Hebrew script; Islam was represented by a crescent moon, the Kaaba mosque in Mecca, the Prophet's mosque in Medina, and Arabic script; and Christianity was represented by a golden chalice with a sunlike host above it, a shooting star, the Three Wise Men on camels, and the dove of peace. On its Web site, the Postal Service explained each of the symbols on the stamps representing the Jewish and Islamic calendars, while for the Christian stamp the symbols were simply listed and summarized as "referring to the birth, life, and mission of Christ," this being presumed knowledge without need of further explanation. Each of the stamps could be purchased separately, and they were also available as a set of three, set against a backdrop of the heavens, with the month and year in each calendar corresponding to January 2001 printed outside the borders of the stamps. The stamps themselves offered no explanations; while the meaning of the Christian stamp was obvious, with its well-known symbols and self-explanatory "3° Milênio" [3rd millennium], the other two stamps provided no elucidation for those unfamiliar with Islamic or Jewish symbols or scripts.

Another revealing difference between the Christian stamp and the other two was in their assigned value. Whereas the Christian stamp cost R$0.40, equivalent to first-class domestic postage at the time, at R$1.30 the value of the other two stamps corresponded to the price for an international first-class letter. As the Jewish and Islamic stamps were clearly intended for use in international correspondence, it would appear that rather than a national educational effort, the stamps are an example of what is meant by the expression "*para inglês ver*" (literally, "for the English to see"), meaning a simulation to hide another reality, where the "English" stand in for "others" more generally.[4] In other words, it seems that the Jewish and Islamic stamps were intended to give those abroad an impression of Brazil as a place of religious tolerance.

A less cynical interpretation, and one that is in keeping with other gestures of inclusion within the country, would be that the stamps represent how Brazil would like to see itself, as well as be seen. Since the Jewish and Islamic communities in Brazil do not represent powerful or numerically significant electoral constituencies, the goal is not to court the vote of these tiny elements of the population, but rather to reinforce an image of modern Brazil that reaffirms its ambitions and ideals as an inclusive nation. Here the Postal Service commemoration signifies official government policy and practice and is therefore an instance of national discourse.[5]

Putting Jews on the Map

Another more literal instance of Jews being incorporated into the Brazilian social and political landscape occurred in 2001. São Paulo's Rebouças metropolitan train station near the Hebraica club was renamed the Hebraica-Rebouças station. Every day, many thousands of commuters pass the signs outside the station and on the overpass of the major thoroughfare, making the Hebraica a familiar part of the landscape even for those who will never pass through its gates.

In contrast to the lack of information accompanying the stamps issued by the national Postal Service, the commemorative plaque inside the station explains the significance of the name, though the existence of the text is likely more meaningful for the Jewish community than for the busy commuters who rush past it on a daily basis and are probably less concerned with the meaning behind place names. Loosely translated, the plaque reads: "The Brazilian 'Hebraica' Association of São Paulo offers its thanks on the occasion of the inauguration of the Hebraica-Rebouças station for use by millions of citizens and honoring the Jewish community of São Paulo. We offer our congratulations to the following accomplished and eminent public figures [men] for their grand social vision." Clearly this was a political move, the sort of social adjusting of which monuments and place names are the currency.[6] Prior to the renaming, city maps showed the other large clubs in the city, including the Pinheiros club, but not the Hebraica. However, the Hebraica station gives prominence to this Jewish institution in the city's evolving urban scheme rather than to the much larger and better known Pinheiros club immediately across the street from the Hebraica. All city maps now feature the name of the Hebraica; since the club stands for the Jewish community, this name change registers the Jewish presence in São Paulo.

These two examples, stamp and train station, national and local, give evidence to the recent trend in Brazil of incorporating the Jewish presence. It is also the kind of recognition and visibility that the Jewish community seeks. Every place that is named for an event or person tied to the community is a small victory of recognition that is celebrated and catalogued. Egon and Frieda Wolff, chroniclers of Jewish Brazilian life, point out that "it is very common in Brazil to name streets and plazas after distinguished citizens as well as people with an international reputation" (1988:66).[7] Both their *Guia histórico da comunidade judaica de São Paulo* (1988) and Henrique Veltman's *A história dos judeus em São Paulo* (1996) dedicate short chapters to listing the streets and plazas named after community members and other people, places, and events associated with Jews. While some names have direct Jewish connections, such as Estado de Israel (State of Israel), others are less obvious, such as Combatentes do Gueto (Ghetto Fighters), a reference to the Warsaw resistance. That the lists include names such as Dalíla, Canãa (Canaan), Belém (Bethlehem), and Jordão (Jordan), which are also part of the Christian Old Testament and thereby not the specific legacy of Jews, does little to diminish the impressive list of individuals who have been so honored, including Maimonides, Theodore Herzl, Stefan Zweig, David Ben-Gurion, Golda Meir, Sarah Bernhardt, and Albert Einstein, to mention a few of the internationally known figures.

The inauguration of these spatial markers is celebrated by events in the community. For example, the naming of a highway overpass after one of the recently deceased members of the community was celebrated by an event at the Hebraica club in the Adolfo Bloch Hall and attended by luminaries from the community. At the generously catered reception friends and family gave speeches remembering the honoree and his many contributions to the community and the city through public works projects. Photos of the overpass with its new plaque were displayed, and its location was clearly explained. The honoring of this individual extended to the community as a whole.

In addition to Jewish names on public spaces, another way that the public landscape has been marked by the Jewish presence can be found in the instances of Jewish symbols in public art, mostly large sculptures, some of which are sponsored by local Jewish organizations. For instance, large menorahs can be found in centrally located plazas, including one in São Paulo (near the Tietê bus station, due to the efforts of the Chabad movement), and another in Rio (outside the Copacabana metro station). The fiftieth anniversary of the state of Israel in 1998 was marked by the placement of a large modern sculpture of the Star of David on a traffic island in Higienópolis.

The different levels of state and city bureaucracy represented by these examples indicate that these examples are part of a larger trend and not the initiative of a single agency. While these symbols may hold little meaning for the larger population, for the Jewish community these commemorative public displays of Jewish names and symbols confirm that this community is acknowledged for its contributions to society and solidify its place in the city and in Brazil. The Hebraica train station considerably intensified this process, shifting the scale from micro-local (i.e., neighborhood) to metropolitan.

It should be noted that in contrast to this celebrated recognition where *public* space is concerned, most Jewish institutions in São Paulo, such as schools and synagogues, do not publicly mark themselves with Jewish symbols, or even with names in many cases, preferring to remain anonymous behind high walls, a point I return to in the following chapter. Although the community finds affirmation in the public acknowledgment of a general Jewish presence, security demands that its specific presence be hidden. This tension between the acceptance and inclusion made possible by visibility and the protection afforded by invisibility is one of the many contradictions that the community navigates as ties to São Paulo and Brazil strengthen with each generation.

In the case of the stamp, the national project is at least partly directed toward an international audience, one that gains greater significance in the contemporary context as Brazil solidifies its global position. The marking of the cityscape with an indelible acknowledgment of Jewish participation in local culture and politics is a pact with the future even more than an accounting of the past. Each gesture of acceptance signals a deepening alliance between Jews and Brazil, and a further integration of the humanist values espoused by each. This is a desire expressed by both Brazil and Jews in Brazil, as it confirms and furthers what each would like to transmit about themselves. The Jewish community's desire to be recognized as part of Brazil is complemented by Brazil's desire to reinforce its image as a tolerant nation, a consolidation of its modernizing project.

The High Holy Days, 5760

Another example of the mutual identity construction of Jewish Brazilians and Brazil through Jews can be found in the relationship between Brazilian politicians and Jewish institutions, especially the Hebraica. This relationship is not one of mutual patronage in the usual sense, but rather it is an exchange of symbolic capital, and one that reaches its apex during the observance of the Jewish New Year. The annual appearance of politicians at the Hebraica during the High Holy Day observances deserves special attention for the way it makes explicit the role of the Hebraica as the representative of the Jewish community, and for how this place and this occasion represent the relationship between Jews and Brazil.

Visits by important personalities are legitimizing, and the Hebraica has received such legitimization from some of the most prominent public figures in Brazil and the Jewish world. These visits are logged in the club's publications, with nearly every issue of the club's magazine containing some reference to a well-known personality who has made a visit to the club, spoken to a gathering, or attended an event in the previous month. The last page of the glossy bilingual (Portuguese-English) book about the club displays photos of some of the most illustrious visitors, including Israeli prime ministers David Ben-Gurion and Yitzhak Rabin.[8] A quote from Ben-Gurion confirms the uniqueness of the Hebraica on the stage of world Jewry: "When someone tells me they are going to Brazil, I always tell them to be sure to visit the Hebraica in São Paulo. It is an impressive club! An example of communal work for Jews all over the world."

The Hebraica's importance in the Jewish world is strengthened by its importance in Brazil, a message reinforced by the inclusion of photos of major Brazilian politicians who have visited the club, beginning with then-president of the republic, Fernando Henrique Cardoso.[9] São Paulo's governor at the time, Mário Covas, is also pictured, as are the former mayor of the city of São Paulo, Paulo Maluf, and Rodolfo Konder, municipal secretary of culture. The accompanying text makes explicit that "[t]he Hebraica is one of the major reference points at every level, communal, political, cultural, and artistic." Including non-Jews in the "mosaic" of photos reinforces the legitimization.

In the same vein, the book documenting the club's first fifty years (Cytrynowicz 2003) verifies the visits of famous personalities all along the club's history, including Nobel Laureate Shimon Peres, the grand rabbi of Israel, and Olympic swimmer Mark Spitz, as well as innumerable top Brazilian performers. The last chapter is dedicated to then-president Luiz Inácio "Lula" da Silva's participation in the celebration of the Hebraica's fiftieth anniversary, accompanied by Governor Geraldo Alckmin and Mayor Marta Suplicy, an event that was covered in the São Paulo edition of *Veja* (Canecchio 2003).

The importance given to visits by powerful men is nowhere more evident than during the Jewish New Year. For the New Year of 5760 (in September 1999) the liturgical choir accompanied the cantor Moshe Stern who had come from Israel to lead the most conservative of the four different services that were being held simultaneously inside the club that year. From my vantage point on the stage of the Arthur Rubenstein Theater, I could easily observe the steady flow of politicians. The first to arrive was the embattled mayor of São Paulo, Celso Pitta, the first black mayor of the city, who took the stage during the services and addressed the congregants. After a nod to the importance of Rosh Hashanah and Yom Kippur, Pitta launched into a brief discourse about the social and political problems affecting Brazil, which he concluded by stating: "Any effort by the government is insufficient if we do not have a community actively engaged in solidarity, a value [*preceito*] that is emphasized [*destacado*] in the Jewish tradition. That is why I am here, and I can assure you, in the name of the city of São Paulo, that we are proud of the Jewish community among us. With [the community] we have learned that now more than ever we must unite beyond races and cultures in defense of peace and life."[10]

Pitta's speech was quickly followed by a succession of disruptive appearances, including those of Governor Mário Covas and Health Minister José Serra.[11] They were accompanied by an entourage that included several congressmen,[12] some of whom remained at the service, joining others on the stage in the chairs reserved for important men of the community.[13] Governor Covas commented on the significance of the festivals for Jews and, by extension, all believers. Representing the federal government, Minister Serra also ascended to the stage and spoke to the assembled worshippers, reading a greeting from President Cardoso, solemnly intoning: "Today is a day that is especially significant for all of us when we ask God's pardon for our failures and inability to fulfill all that we have promised. The other meaning is that independent of race or belief, we are all equally humble before God."[14]

These reflections on Judaism by non-Jews visiting the Hebraica complement the reflections of Ben-Gurion and other prominent Jews: in the same way that the Hebraica is confirmed as an important institution within Jewish circles, by visiting the Hebraica and showing affinity for Judaism, Brazilian politicians reaffirm the importance of Jews in Brazil, thereby consolidating these two sources of the community's identity.

While the Hebraica is not the only point of contact, it is positioned as the major bridge between the Jewish community and *paulistano* and Brazilian society. Obviously, the presence of prominent politicians is significant for the Jewish community in São Paulo, as evidenced by the attention these guests enjoy while visiting communal institutions and subsequently in the community's publications. It is also worth considering what the visits from these politicians and their "affirmation of their ties to the community" say about Brazil as well.

Here I am making an argument parallel to that offered by anthropologist David Mandelbaum, whose lifelong work in India included studies of the Jews in Cochin. Although Mandelbaum began his research in the 1930s in a cultural context quite different from the hypermodern metropolis of São Paulo, several of his insights serve to illuminate the relationship between these two minority communities and their host nations.[15] Specifically, Mandelbaum examined the relationship between national-level politicians and the small Jewish population; in 1968, the four hundredth anniversary of the Paradesi synagogue in Cochin was the occasion for a major celebration attended by local, national, and international politicians, academics, and clerics. The event was supported by the Kerala state government and marked by the issue of a commemorative stamp and a volume about the proceedings that included the address given by the most notable of the guests, Indian prime minister Indira Gandhi.[16] "She took the occasion to remind her audience . . . that the ancient, harmonious, and honourable story of the Jews of Cochin demonstrated the historic tolerance of the Indian people and showed again how important it was for the modern Indian republic to be a secular state" (Mandelbaum 1975:202). She called this tolerance India's "great heritage."

Although the contexts and national goals of postindependence India and contemporary Brazil are different in significant ways, not the least of which is the secularism that Gandhi was attempting to secure, Mandelbaum's interpretation of the meaning of Gandhi's words and her presence at the event are pertinent to an understanding of the process of mutual appropriation occurring in the Brazilian context. As Mandelbaum explained: "The symbolic gesture of her attendance . . . was more than a purely political gesture since there is scarcely a smaller minority in India than the Jews. *It was rather a symbolic reaffirmation of a basic principle of national policy.* The Jews of Cochin offered a useful case on which . . . to focus and restate that principle. Other political leaders, in other places and at other times, have similarly taken *the example of Jews and Judaism to illustrate fundamental values they wanted to declare"* (1981: 228–29, emphasis added). In India in 1968, these values revolved around the assertion of secular nationalism.

In Brazil, another place and time, Jews and Judaism continue to serve as a useful prism through which to project fundamental national values. Similarly, Brazilians pride themselves on their reputation for being a tolerant and inclusive nation, though the idiom is multiculturalism rather than secularism. As in India, Jews in Brazil do not represent a significant voting bloc, nor do they wield the kind of political power at either the local or national level to warrant this kind of attention. These gestures of inclusiveness have less to do with Jews per se, and more to do with Brazil, with the way Brazilians would like to see themselves and be seen by others, and with the direction in which they would like to take their democratizing nation. The complementary gesture on the part of the Jewish community, that is, its solicitation of and contributions to these acts of inclusion, speaks strongly to the community's desire for belonging, recognition, and most importantly, participation in this national project of inclusiveness. It is hardly surprising that the most important Jewish holiday should be used for this dual purpose.

*　*　*

The Jewish New Year is really two holidays, Rosh Hashanah and Yom Kippur, at either end of a period totaling ten days. Together the two holidays are known as the High Holy Days (Grandes Festas in Portuguese). The two days of Rosh Hashanah (literally, the head of the year) begin the new year and are considered the anniversary of the creation of the world and the Day of Judgment. On Yom Kippur, the Day of Atonement (Dia do Perdão in Portuguese, the Day of Pardon), observant Jews fast for twenty-four hours and collectively pray.

Known as the Days of Awe, or the Days of Repentance, the seriousness of these holy days derives from the belief that on Yom Kippur God decides the fate of every individual for the coming year, and Jews extend to one another the desire that each be written into the book of the living for another year: "L'shanah tovah tikatevu" (May you be written down for a good year). The days between Rosh Hashanah and Yom Kippur are dedicated to repentance, to asking forgiveness from God and from other people. This is also the reason that individuals attempt to make amends, settle debts, and generally set things right before beginning this period of the year.

Another way to symbolically cleanse oneself of sins is through the ceremony of *tashlikh* ("you shall cast away"), which involves throwing pocket lint and breadcrumbs into flowing water, especially where there are fish.[17] Formerly performed primarily by Orthodox Jews, *tashlikh* has enjoyed a revival among other Jews in recent years. In São Paulo, the polluted rivers cannot serve this symbolic purpose, so the Hebraica installed a permanent fountain and pool with fish in the Carmel Plaza, easily accessed by the thousands of Jews who pass through the club during this period. The installation of the *tashlikh* fountain is just one of the ways that the club sees itself as fulfilling a mandate to be a Jewish club and not just a club of Jews.

A profound confirmation of this mandate can be found during those ten days from the beginning of Rosh Hashanah to the conclusion of Yom Kippur. During this time the Hebraica is transformed. Normal activities are all but suspended, and various spaces within the club are appropriated for religious services. Many of the synagogues in the city sell tickets in advance so worshippers are guaranteed a seat, and most fill to overflowing, accommodating regulars as well as those who do not otherwise participate. However, a considerable portion of the community prefers to attend services at the club for reasons ranging from social to political to economic to aesthetic to logistical, resulting in 4,000 to 5,000 people attending the multiple services there.

For years there had been three different services held at the club, each with a different orientation and set of participants.[18] The oldest of the services was held in the Arthur Rubinstein Theater, the stage of which was transformed into a golden temple with backdrop made to look like the Western Wall.[19] The Israeli *chazzan* Moshe Stern led these services every year starting in 1977. This was the service attended by the most "traditional" of the families in the club, and also the one that the politicians visited when they descended on the club during the Jewish holidays.

A second service was held in the multipurpose Marc Chagall Ballroom, accommodating a much larger crowd in a slightly less conservative atmosphere. This service was originally created for young people, but had since become popular with families and people of all ages. At this service *chazzan* Gerson Herszkowicz (who was also the principal of the Bialik Jewish school) was accompanied by the Zemer chorus.

The third service was the only one that pertained to a particular congregation; Comunidade Shalom in the nearby neighborhood of Itaim Bibi held its High Holy Day services in the Adolfo Bloch Hall, with children's services in the nearby Anne Frank Theater. All three of these services occurred simultaneously in the club during Rosh Hashanah and Yom Kippur.[20]

In 1999, a fourth set of services was introduced at the club. For the first time, the club's informal synagogue had sponsored the training of a professional singer, Cláudio Goldman, to become a *chazzan* and to lead a service to be held in the Ben-Gurion Room, a large multipurpose space on the second floor of the main building near the synagogue room (where the first services for young people were held nearly thirty years earlier).[21] As the little synagogue had grown both in the number of regular participants and in the services offered, a demand had also grown for it to provide High Holy Day services, a major undertaking involving not only the preparation of a new cantor, but also the provision of copies of the *machzor* (the prayer book for the High Holy Days) and the arrangement of space.

This tiny congregation was made up of people who, for a variety of reasons, felt uncomfortable or alienated in other synagogues.[22] Several people explained that the synagogue was the main reason they came to the club. Others described a return to both Judaism and the community through this very relaxed congregation. Without a rabbi, and with a part-time cantor during the rest of the year, the congregation is presided over by the ever-gregarious José Luiz Goldfarb, director of the Department of Jewish Culture.

Goldfarb's drive to be what he called "radically tolerant" and inclusive has helped incorporate this ragtag group of regulars at the club's synagogue into Jewish life in the city. Toward this, one of the innovations for the new Rosh Hashanah and Yom Kippur services in 1999 was that they were free of charge with no reservations required. They were open to all, and many of those who attended could not have afforded a seat at another service. This shift toward greater inclusiveness was yet another subtle but significant indication of the club's efforts to play a greater role as a center of community life. As Goldfarb explained in the club's magazine: "From Rosh Hashanah [until] Yom Kippur, . . . everyone will be able to fully enjoy being Jewish [*desfrutar da condição judaica em sua plenitude*]. In keeping with [*sintonizada*] the multiplicity of Judaisms there are in the world, the Hebraica reaffirms its democratic character and receives, with open arms, the various religious manifestations of its members for the arrival of the year 5760."[23]

Juggling the plural and sometimes contradictory ways of being Jewish, this "multiplicity of Judaisms" is more trying in practice than Goldfarb's enthusiasm suggests. While entirely in keeping with the Brazilian values of flexibility and acceptance, not all Jews are comfortable with stretching interpretations, nor do they necessarily share the goal of being "radically tolerant" or inclusive. Where these values clash, Brazilian Jews struggle to find common ground within their community. Emotions run particularly high around the High Holy Days.

* * *

This was not just any new year. The year about to begin, 5760 on the Jewish calendar, was expected to be an especially good year in numerological terms, since the component numbers (5+6+7+0) add up to eighteen. Among Jews, the number eighteen signifies good luck and long life. This is one of the more popular manifestations of mystic Judaism, as this association is rooted in Gematria, a kabalistic system for interpreting the religiosymbolic meaning in numeric equivalencies between words. Though this is a complex scholarly field unto itself, a brief explanation is in order.

The Hebrew alphabet, the *alef-bet*, is itself considered holy. It is said that the entire world was made with its twenty-two letters. Each of these letters is assigned a numeric value, and words with the same value are considered related, symbolic associations that are offered as proof of God's ordering of the world. Serious students of the Kabala dedicate themselves to minute readings of the Torah at the level of the letters, looking for hidden meaning that when properly interpreted could reveal important information about God's plans for the world, including the date of the coming of the Messiah.

In the case of the number eighteen, its significance derives from the word "*chai*," meaning "living."[24] This word is written with the Hebrew letters *het* (having a value of eight) and *yud* (with a value of ten), so that by adding the values of the component letters, the total for *chai* is eighteen. Therefore, eighteen is equivalent to "living." Because of this association, all things having the number eighteen or its multiples are considered auspicious. Good luck is also conferred through the number eighteen, such that monetary gifts, whether to charities or for a Bar Mitzvah, are often in multiples of eighteen. In São Paulo, many Jews took advantage of the new option of selecting their car license plates by including the number eighteen for protection and good luck. At the Hebraica club the phone prefix includes eighteen. Eighteen was also the number of members of the Shir Ha-Shirim chorus, which accompanied Moshe Stern through many hours of singing during the High Holy Days services in the Arthur Rubinstein Theater.[25]

The members of the *coral dos jovens* (young people's choir), as it was known, ranged in age from thirteen to thirty. Half of the members had been singing with this chorus for the five years of its existence. Those who were working or in college in 1999 had begun when they were in high school, selected through open auditions. Others dribbled in to replace those who had moved away or were overcommitted. The time commitment was a problem for everyone, and those who stayed remained out of a deep loyalty to the genial maestro. His personal appeal and professionalism elicited this kind of response from experienced musicians and singers as well, as we had seen during the production of *Porgy and Bess* the month before. In the months leading up to the celebrations several members of the chorus left due to the heavy time commitment. Others joined and had to keep pace with a chorus that was already well into the two books of music we had to learn for the many hours of singing.

The more experienced members already knew some of the material. However, while the prayers may have been familiar, often the melodies or their particular versions were not. Since we were to accompany the *chaz-zan*, we had to learn the melodies that he was used to singing, not the ones that might already be familiar. Stern had sent the sheet music as soon as it was determined that due to the downturn in the Brazilian economy in January 1999, the club could not afford the professional chorus of Russian men who had accompanied him in previous years. In addition to learning so much music there was also the added task of transposing both language and music, since some of the transliterated prayers had been in Yiddish and we were to sing in Hebrew, and since the harmonies for four men's "voices" did not always work with the young women singing alto and soprano. The excellent linguistic and musical abilities of several of the young chorus members were called on more than once to make the necessary adjustments. When Stern showed up a few days before Rosh Hashanah, it seemed we were impossibly far from attaining the desired level.[26] Nevertheless, when it finally came time to perform, we surprised not only ourselves, but the club's directors, who, it turned out, had had low expectations for the group of amateurs.

Given the many hours of rehearsal, it is remarkable that young people would dedicate themselves to such an arduous process. It was certainly not for the trip that was promised as compensation, which seemed to shrink in duration and distance with every decline suffered by the Brazilian currency on the world market. As Goldfarb termed it, the involvement of youth was fruit of seeds planted some five years before, when the club resolved to find ways to integrate young people into the religious services offered at the club. In addition to the creation of a liturgical choir, young men had also been taking courses to learn how to blow the *shofar*[27] and be *baal korei* ("master of the reading"),[28] responsible for reading from the Torah during religious services. The development of educational programs with Jewish content for very young children was also part of this drive to involve children and youths of all ages in communal and religious life, including the "Shabbatinho" (little Shabbat) services for preschoolers. All of this could be seen as another instance of the club's presenting its activities through the lens of youth participation, as the headline from the club's magazine reported the following month: "Juventude participa das Grandes Festas" (Young people participate in the High Holy Days).

*   *   *

The party that closed out the celebrations that year was also an example of youth involvement as well as an indication of the challenges to tolerance faced within the community. As the New Year approached an incongruous banner was hung at the entrance to the club: "Shaná Tová 99 'The Party'. . . . The last of the millennium!" The New Year was auspicious not for the numerological significance of 5760, but because it was the last Jewish New Year of the second Christian millennium. However, for some members of the community the incongruity lay elsewhere. Observant Jews bring the Day of Atonement to a close by breaking the fast with family and friends. The party was scheduled to begin at precisely 10:32 p.m., once the break-fast was complete. Restricted to those eighteen and over (because of the legal drinking age, not the numerological significance), the controversial annual party organized by the "Adventure" section of the club's Youth Department promised lots of drinking, music, and dancing to the band Ultraje a Rigor.[29] The idea that such a solemn occasion would be marked (or marred) by a rowdy party and heavy drinking, as happened every year, was offensive to many.

While the drinking was not the focus of the objections, this event did stand out as one of the few instances in which *paulistano* Jews would publicly drink alcohol in large quantity. In fact, alcohol is a notable exception to Jewish adoption of Brazilian consumption patterns; as a group, Jews in São Paulo do not drink much in public. Several people made a point of drawing my attention to the fact that I was seeing very little alcohol consumption among Jews, most significantly in places or under circumstances where other Brazilians generally consume large quantities. Having lived for years in the interior with ample time to observe drinking patterns at parties and *churrascos*, at bars and in clubs, this striking difference was first pointed out to me at a *churrasco* for the chorus, a situation in which other Brazilians would drink a lot of beer.[30] Instead, there was no beer at all and only one pitcher of *caipirinha* (a mixture of lime, sugar, and *pinga*, a strong spirit made from sugarcane) for the entire group of forty adults. I also noted very little beer drinking at the Hebraica club, whereas at non-Jewish clubs I had observed groups sitting for hours sharing tall bottles of cold beer. Clearly this distinction is not a question of prohibition, as among some Christian sects, since Jews regularly consume alcohol as part of religious observation. Indeed, the celebration of Simchat Torah, the holiday marking the beginning of the Torah reading cycle that follows immediately after Yom Kippur, is frequently celebrated with the consumption of large amounts of alcohol. For instance, I attended a local Chabad (Hasidic) synagogue during Simchat Torah, where the men on the other side of the room divider became increasingly boisterous in their vodka drinking and dancing (although the women did not). Aside from these particular circumstances, the difference between Jewish and non-Jewish Brazilians in the social consumption of alcohol was evident and empirically verified by the owner of a buffet house who had learned from years of experience to order less alcohol for Jewish events than those held by non-Jews.

The frequent statement that "Jews don't drink" was shorthand for the commonly held but unsupportable notion that Jews did not drink heavily. The phrase referred especially to group-level social practices and was only comparative, a statement about identity or ideology, rather than fact.[31] The unfortunate flip side of this widely disseminated discourse is that when Jews do drink, that is, when they do have problems related to alcohol abuse, they are often marginalized, their problems unacknowledged. In 2002, a Brazilian branch of the U.S.-based organization JACS (Jewish Alcoholics, Chemically Dependent Persons and Significant Others) was established; JACS-Brasil (Judeus em Recuperação de Álcool, Comprometimento com Drogas e Seus Parentes e Amigos) is responsible for the increased awareness of what had been an invisible problem in the community, especially among youths who engage more thoroughly in local practices than did previous generations.[32] The increase in drug and alcohol consumption that the founders of this organization have observed among youths is clearly tied to the deepening integration of Jews into the Brazilian social milieu.[33] That the Shaná Tová 99 party was publicized as offering *bebidas* (drinks) and that the annual party was known for heavy alcohol consumption made it stand out all the more.

More than simply controversial, this party was deeply offensive to Orthodox members of the community in particular. One chorus colleague reported witnessing a fight involving one of the young people selling tickets to the event who was confronted by an angry man who called those who were involved in the party planning "Nazis." Presumably, the slur was meant to accuse the party organizers of slaughtering Judaism and therefore the Jewish people.

While on the one hand, holding a boisterous party may not have seemed a fitting way to conclude days of atonement and repentance, on the other hand, the annual party is a way for nonobservant (or obligatorily observant) young people who might otherwise feel alienated from the community to participate at such an important time. It is a means by which those without religious affiliations can be connected to the community and a way for those with organizing abilities but no strong religious affiliation to exercise their leadership skills. There may also be parallels between this and the raucous *carnaval* celebrations that precede the austere period of Lent, giving this celebration a distinctively Brazilian flavor.

That the party is social and not religious nevertheless accomplishes part of the goals of the High Holy Days, that of communal affirmation. Furthermore, that the Hebraica club not only tolerates but even sponsors such an event suggests that the club's flexible spaces represent more than innovative architecture and creative multiple uses of space. Finally, that the club can be transformed from a place of worship to a place of festivity in a matter of hours is confirmation that the Hebraica is a club for Jews in the broadest sense. Confirming the oft-cited claim that the Hebraica is much more than a "club of Jews," Goldfarb asserted that the club did not subscribe to a particular interpretation of Judaism, a policy that often led to conflict where strong beliefs were at stake. The club's leadership actively seeks ways for the activities and events in the club to reflect deeply held Jewish values, "community" being one of them, even when these "Jewish values" clash. While they may be rooted in religion, these values find expression in other cultural manifestations, even those that may appear to be contradictory. It is in these contrasts and contradictions, the many junctures and juxtapositions of seemingly irreconcilable cultural influences, that Jewish culture is its most dynamic. The Hebraica provides a venue within which many relations to Judaism and Jewishness can be explored. Part of that exploration includes developing a relationship with Brazilian society and national culture, and enacting Brazilianness.

Jewish *Carnaval*

While the club is an obvious venue for the celebration of Jewish festivals, there used to be *carnaval* celebrations at the Hebraica club as well. Since *carnaval* is both Catholic in origin and emblematically Brazilian in its expression, Jewish commemoration of this festival sheds light on the intersection of Jewish and Brazilian identity and gets right to the heart of the tensions between being Jewish and being Brazilian.

Carnaval celebrations in Brazil reiterate the often-cited primary cultural distinction between house and street, *casa e rua*, the private and the public (DaMatta 1991a). Accordingly, there are two main categories of celebrations: *carnaval de rua* (street *carnaval*); and *bailes*, dance parties in clubs. Street *carnaval* has generally been interpreted by scholars as enacting a reversal of the social order, one which ends up reinforcing the status quo by "letting off steam," allowing the disempowered a taste of power (by dressing up and taking center stage), the high cost of which leaves them exhausted and impoverished, but happy.[34] In contrast, the safe and relatively controlled *bailes* within private clubs usually involve minimal inversion or mixing of classes.

The four days of *carnaval* culminate on the Tuesday before Ash Wednesday, the beginning of Lent. In spite of its evident Catholic origins and referents, and the pious period of penitence that follows, Brazilian *carnaval* is famous for ribald and luxurious celebrations. The date of *carnaval* each year varies according to the lunar cycle relative to the equinox, but it usually falls in February, toward the end of summer in the Southern Hemisphere. In Brazil, it marks the end of vacation, the beginning of the academic year, and a return to productivity, more meaningful for many Brazilians than the Lenten period itself.

The *carnaval* season is ushered in at the beginning of summer, in December just before Christmas, with the introduction of the new music and dances (especially *axé* from Bahia) that happily thump from every radio. Immediately following New Year's, the samba schools begin to leak their themes for the *carnaval* parades, and the television networks compete with station breaks featuring gorgeous women sambaing in nothing more than sequins and stiletto heels. It seems that all of summer is a buildup to the *carnaval* celebrations that include the music and dances that have become popular throughout the summer.

As at so many clubs across the city and throughout the country, *carnaval* parties were held at the Hebraica up through the 1970s. Many club members fondly recalled the popular parties of the past. However, it is unclear exactly when and why they were discontinued. One person speculated that influential directors might have thought it antithetical for a Jewish club to sponsor celebrations of a holiday with indisputably Catholic roots; if so, that logic has not been extended to the celebration of the Christian New Year, since the club sponsors an annual New Year's Eve party on December 31. Neither is it clear what would have stimulated a shift in policy, since that contradiction had not prevented *carnaval* celebrations earlier. Others speculated that the prohibition might have come from the state's Jewish Federation, FISESP (Federação Israelita do Estado de São Paulo), but that organization's director assured me that FISESP does not have the authority to impose prohibitions. (He did acknowledge "*poder moral*," the moral force of the organization, without making any explicit links to a *carnaval* prohibition.) Still another person was certain that the celebrations were canceled at the time of the Yom Kippur War in 1974 as part of an expression of solidarity with Israel in the form of a coalescing of Jewish values and identity. While compelling, this explanation was not borne out by fact; a search through back issues of the Hebraica's magazine turned up regular *carnaval* propaganda and post-*carnaval* reporting up through 1980 (including a February 1977 article on the history of *carnaval* in Brazil), so whatever consolidation of Jewish identity may have occurred in response to the Yom Kippur War did not extend to eliminating Jewish *carnaval* celebrations.

As of 1982 there were no longer references to the club's celebrations in the magazine.[35] My search for information on the end of *carnaval* at the Hebraica also turned up the fact that earlier *carnaval* celebrations were held jointly by the Hebraica and the other Jewish club, the Círculo-Macabi. A failure of the collaboration between the clubs must also be considered as a possible factor in the demise of Jewish celebrations of *carnaval*. Not surprisingly, these institutions still sponsor celebrations of the Jewish festival of Purim. Often compared to *carnaval,* because the two holidays fall within a month of each other and because celebrants in both wear costumes, Purim does not offer a focal point for a combined Jewish Brazilian identity.

A third possible explanation for the end of *carnaval* celebrations at the Hebraica may be financial. With their strengthening economic position, middle- and upper-class Jews preferred to retreat to the beaches for a calmer *carnaval* and a last chance for a beach vacation before the end of summer. This preference would have resulted in reduced attendance at the club's events and a consequent reduction in cost-effectiveness. In other words, rather than ideological, cancellation of *carnaval* could have been purely a business decision. Without further investigation, I can only speculate that financial inviability gave weight to the arguments of those who objected on religious or cultural grounds and resulted in the end of *carnaval* celebrations at the Hebraica in the early 1980s.

Regardless of the reasons, the implications of this change shed light on the continued integration of Jews into the social landscape of São Paulo. The fact that the Jewish collectivity has enjoyed *carnaval* the same way other Brazilians do is evidence of its absorption of Brazilian culture and society. That these celebrations occurred in a Jewish club suggests that there was more than a superficial participation in national events, but rather, an embracing of the practices that are emblematic of Brazilianness. While at first glance, cancellation of *carnaval* celebration at the club might appear to indicate a retreat from wholesale absorption of elements of Brazilian cultural identity, the continued integration and increased acceptance of Jews suggest quite the opposite. Those members of the community who are inclined to celebrate *carnaval* continue to do so. In contrast to earlier exclusionary times, the Pinheiros club across the street maintains an open invitation to Hebraica members to take part in their *carnaval* celebrations. Instead of celebrating in an ethnic enclave, community members celebrate in ways that are consistent with their class position, on the beach, at clubs, and in the streets. As such, whatever the rationale of the club and community leadership was at the time, rather than a rejection of a key element of Brazilian culture and, by extension, a distancing from that aspect of their identity, the cancellation of *carnaval* at the Hebraica represents a strengthening of Brazilianness within the community.

Carnaval is the ultimate symbol of Brazilian culture and nation, especially as it is celebrated in Rio de Janeiro. In recent years, the nationally televised Rio parades have provided a stage for working out Brazilian identity and incorporating Jewish themes that make them particularly rich for the discussion at hand, building on the other examples of inclusion of Jews in the nation discussed above. Whereas the Postal Service represents the Brazilian nation in an official capacity, the example of the transformed São Paulo landscape is a local concretization of the relationship between Jewish and Brazilian identity. The presence and pronouncements of prominent politicians during Jewish celebrations at the central community institution make explicit the shared benefits of this collaboration. Brazilian acknowledgment of Jewish festivals and Jewish celebrations of Brazilian festivals expose the terrain on which the contradictions of Jewish Brazilian identity get worked out. The incorporation of Jewish themes and symbols into the Rio *carnaval* parades is yet another instantiation of the current climate in which Jews are being actively integrated into national culture, in this case, at the level of popular culture.

These parades are a celebratory exercise in national identity. While the pageant has international reverberations, the discourse is internal, presenting ecstatic expressions of national pride and exorcising and transforming key issues at the popular level. Albeit a highly institutionalized form of popular culture, Rio's *carnaval* parades edify and unify the nation behind certain symbols and their interpretation. Their educational and national objectives must be kept in mind when considering endeavors on the part of several of Rio's samba schools to incorporate Jewish themes into their presentations.

The first attempts were timid, almost oblique. During the *carnaval* parades of 2001, two samba schools nodded toward Jewish contributions to Brazilian culture. A major samba school, Tradição (Tradition), paid homage to television mogul Silvio Santos, owner of SBT (Sistema Brasileiro de Televisão), the second-largest television network in Brazil, and host of a popular program on Sunday afternoons. Though Santos (born Senor Abravanel) has made public statements about his Jewishness and has extended gestures toward the community, the school did not mention his Jewish background, representing only his Greek origins.

That same year, a minor samba school, Tuiuti, addressed Jewish contributions more directly, albeit through a utopic narrative. The school's theme was Zumbi, the leader of escaped slaves in Brazil who was killed in 1695 and who has been resurrected as a symbol for the Movimento Negro and popular culture forms that celebrate African and Afro-Brazilian contributions to Brazilian society.[36] As reporter Shirley Nigri explained, "[i]n the samba school's version of the story, Zumbi was influenced in North Africa by Jews and Arabs who had fled the Spanish Inquisition. Dancers dressed as Jews and Arabs did the samba side by side, in what some interpreted not only as a historical depiction but as a contemporary message of coexistence. Other Jewish symbols also figured in the parade. A car in the shape of a Star of David, representing Jewish immigration to Brazil, carried a lion as a symbol of Judaism, a tall golden menorah and a model of the Western Wall" (Nigri 2001). The elaborate costumes and headdresses worn by the celebrants included Stars of David, menorahs, and pseudo-Hebrew letters. One float made to look like a ship's prow also featured these symbols, while a man wearing a *tallit* (prayer shawl) and *tefillin* danced with an exuberance that was decidedly lacking in piety.[37] This celebratory circulation of Jewish symbols and the coupling of Jews with the story of a national black leader is yet another example of the historical reinterpretation under way through which Jews are being reinscribed into Brazilian history.[38]

Jewish themes were addressed again in the 2003 parade, but much more explicitly and this time with organized Jewish participation. The resulting parade presentation was ostentatious: with the beat of nearly one thousand drums pounding in the chests of tens of thousands of cheering onlookers, and the eyes of 100 million accompanying the event on television sets across the land, Moses raised his arms and the shimmering aqua blue parted. "In an enchanted gesture," sang 4,500 participants, "the sea turned into a *passarela* (walkway)." Moses then walked through the passage in the ocean of gyrating, happy people with fish on their heads and was followed by ecstatic dancers portraying Hebrew slaves freed from ancient Egypt. While the Japanese technology employed to make Moses "levitate" at the front of the parade may have appeared miraculous, like so many extraordinary events of the contemporary world, this was the result of careful planning and political maneuvering and had engendered quite a bit of controversy.

Early in the planning stages for the 2003 parade, in search of financing for their presentation of the story of the Ten Commandments, members of the Mangueira samba school in Rio approached the Casa de Cultura de Israel (the Israel House of Culture), a Jewish cultural organization located not in Rio but in São Paulo.[39] Word of the plans that Mangueira, Rio's premier *escola de samba*, was going to present a "Jewish" theme began to circulate nearly a year before the 2003 celebrations. Mangueira is one of the oldest and best loved of the samba schools in Rio,[40] repeatedly winning the championship since the early 1920s. As a colleague from Rio commented, even though people from Rio may have other favorite schools, at heart everyone is a Mangueira fan, and everyone feels a certain satisfaction when Mangueira wins.

For the significance of this collaboration between Mangueira and the São Paulo Jewish community to make sense, a brief explanation of the structure of *carnaval* parades is in order. The themes to be presented by each *escola de samba* are arranged far in advance,[41] and planning begins in earnest as soon as the previous year's parades are complete. Details are kept secret for as long as possible to keep competing schools from finding out about innovations ahead of time, such as the Japanese levitation technology. Though often referred to in typical Brazilian hyperbole as "the greatest show on earth," the *carnaval* parades in Rio are a fierce competition.

In the summer months preceding *carnaval*, the samba schools each release their new *samba do enredo*, their original theme song, which narrates the story line each school will present in the parades that year. In addition to building up excitement, the radio play gives fans a chance to learn their school's song before the festivities so they can sing along. The quality of the song and its performance are just two of dozens of categories that are scored to the first decimal place and tallied on live national television on Ash Wednesday, after the parades are over, selecting the participants for the champions' parade and determining which schools will lose their ranking and which will rise.

Not only are the costumes and floats evaluated; there are also required components, including the twirling *porta-bandeira*, who carries the flag and colors of her school. Another obligatory component is the traditional wing of the *bahianas*—hundreds of swirling, big-skirted women whose costumes are loosely modeled on the dress of women in the northeastern state of Bahia—which can be difficult to work into many of today's samba school themes. Schools are also scored on the energy of their presentation as a whole. Each school can number up to 5,000 participants, but the upper number is limited by how many can make it through the entire parade route in an hour and ten minutes, from first note sung to the last flash of dancing feet at the end. A brilliant collective performance can be penalized for not meeting the time requirement, and there are always unforeseen calamities, such as small fires or mechanical breakdowns on the floats. Most of Brazil watches on television, and tens of thousands pack the modernist *sambódromo* (samba stadium) that lines the "Avenue."[42]

Anyone with the will and the money, including tourists, can buy a costume and parade in one of a school's *alas* (wings) representing elements of the story being told. Selling costumes is one of the ways that the schools raise funds for the following year and finance their other community programs. In the previous year, 2002, with a theme about the Northeast of Brazil, Mangueira once again claimed the championship, this time by a mere one-tenth of a point.

The Jewish community in São Paulo was abuzz with news about the 2003 *carnaval*, not only because Mangueira had decided to present a supposedly Jewish theme, but also because the Jewish community was collaborating in the effort. No one seemed troubled by the fact that the theme that was being presented, the story of the handing down of the Ten Commandments, is not the exclusive domain of Jews. This was being promoted as an opportunity for the community to stand out and to get noticed in a positive light, an opportunity to participate in one of Brazil's most important cultural institutions and to confirm the place of Jews in Brazil. In the words of José Luiz Goldfarb, one of the activists behind the collaboration:

> It will be an unequivocal demonstration that in Brazilian lands our community has succeeded in preserving its traditions at the same time that it remains open and involved in the social milieu in which it lives. Could our ancestors—who escaped terrible persecutions in European and Oriental lands in search of refuge in Brazil— have imagined that one day an organization of the importance of . . . Mangueira would be joined [*irmanada*] on the Avenue with our community, enacting the story of Moshe Rabeinu [Moses] and the receiving of the Ten Commandments? (Goldfarb, unpublished manuscript, 2003)

The Jewish community was by no means united behind this collaboration, and not just because part of the community saw even the highly transformed Brazilian *carnaval* as a Christian celebration. The greater resistance came from segments of the community concerned with what they saw as redirecting monies from charity organizations toward frivolous celebrations; in light of the growing impoverishment of the community, they saw this collaboration as a waste of resources that were needed elsewhere.

In response to this critique, supporters of the collaboration argued that not only was it important to take every opportunity to show that the Jewish community was part of Brazilian society and participated in its most significant cultural institutions, but also that Mangueira was itself a charitable organization. In communal publications they detailed the thirty different social projects that the samba school provided to the Mangueira community, serving 8,000 people and creating 400 jobs. Mangueira has been successful putting the proceeds from each year's *carnaval* to use in the community, creating schools and day-care centers, classes in information technology and other vocational training, sports and health programs, and programs for the disabled and the elderly. Indeed, as Goldfarb extolled, Mangueira is a "champion" during the rest of the year as well. Its efforts are recognized as among the best in the country, he said, having been "cited as an example for the world by the United Nations, having been presented with an award from UNESCO for the best social program in Latin America. It's not surprising that when President . . . Bill Clinton visited Rio, he insisted on visiting . . . Mangueira to kick around a soccer ball with Pelé. Mangueira is a champion samba school, but it is also one of the few communities . . . that knows how to take the fruits of success on the Avenue and carry out exemplary social work" (Goldfarb, unpublished manuscript, 2003). This emphasis on *tzedakah* (charity) was submitted as the link between the Jewish community and the community of Mangueira and cited by several other community commentators as being what made the collaboration *coerente* (logical).

The collaboration occasioned other fund-raising opportunities, the most significant of which was the celebrations for the fiftieth anniversary of the Hebraica club, just three weeks before *carnaval*. On this occasion, members of Mangueira, including segments of the percussion section and others wearing parade costumes, came to São Paulo to perform in the Yitzhak Rabin gymnasium at the Hebraica. All proceeds from the event went directly to the two most prominent Jewish charities in São Paulo, Ten Yad and UNIBES.

In an interview with the *Globo* newspaper, Flávio Bittelman, director of the Torah-shaped Casa de Israel, interpreted the meaning of the collaboration between these two disparate institutions: "We will be parading, celebrating harmony between religions, symbol of Rio's *carnaval*."[43] This time it was Jews commenting on Christian celebrations and employing the same message of equality and coexistence that the politicians had offered during the Jewish holidays, reinforcing these most central elements of Brazilian ethnic ideology.

The collaboration proceeded, and Mangueira's presentation in the parade was a grand spectacle that included a sphinx and a pyramid, Ramses' palace, and giant, monstrous plagues. José Luiz and his wife, Ana, ecstatically paraded; later, he sheepishly admitted they were in the wing of the plagues, dressed as locusts. The costumes were beautiful, he said, but quite heavy. As they say, it is one thing to samba; it is quite another thing to samba in high heels all the way down the Avenue, or in his case, to bounce enthusiastically while dressed as a locust.

As always, famous people participated in the parade. One wing of Mangueira included Luciano Huck, guru of hip youth TV, who had recently come out as Jewish in a major ad campaign to publicize Jewish charitable contributions to Brazilian society; Luciano paraded wearing a *kippah* (also known as a yarmulke or skullcap). Also wearing a *kippah* in the parade were the *chanteuse* of *carnaval* music, Beth Carvalho, and former soccer star Raí, neither of whom is Jewish. The *kippah* was part of their costume. During one televised moment, Gilberto Gil showed up in the midst of this crowd of famous people wearing *kippot* (pl.) and embraced each of them.[44] More than a circulation of Jewish symbols, in a context in which Jewish men struggle over whether to wear *kippot* in public, this could be even be seen as a political act of solidarity.

While all of the festivities were in good spirits, slaves and plagues notwithstanding, the message was clear. The school titled its presentation "The Ten Commandments: The Samba of Peace Sings the Saga of Liberty." With haiku-like minimalism, the song lyrics told the story of the slaves in Egypt (without mentioning Jews or Hebrews) and told the life story of Moses from birth to the receiving of the Ten Commandments. The Ten Commandments were recast as the textual basis for peace and love. The illuminated word "*PAZ*" (peace) inscribed on the tablets held aloft by Moses eliminated any doubt about the message, emphasized by the song's refrain: "Quem plantar a paz, vai colher o amor" (Those who plant peace reap love). In the midst of extreme violence in Brazil's urban centers, and the conflicts in the Middle East and Gulf regions, the call for peace was heartfelt. It was literal instantiation of what Robin Sheriff calls the "prescriptive commandments" of the ideology of racial democracy (2001:224), in which Moses himself called for an end to violence.

This is a far cry from the assertion that reversals reinstate the status quo that has been the standard for interpreting the inversions that characterize Carnival celebrations on many points on the globe. These collaborations—the harnessing of cultural and financial resources, the endorsement by famous people—are all about deploying power. The mutual appropriation of symbols—of major Brazilian institutions like Mangueira taking up Jewish themes, and of Jewish institutions taking on Brazilian themes—serves the needs of both communities. While Brazilian society seizes opportunities to tell a different story about Brazil, one that is not about impoverishment and degradation, but rather of release and liberty and creativity, the Jewish community seeks to find a place for itself within this narrative. As Sheriff insists, rather than dismiss the ideology of racial democracy and its corollaries as mere "myth" or political obfuscation or false consciousness, it is possible to see the transformative powers of an ideological "dream" of what Brazil "ought to be" (2001:221). That Jewish Brazilians share in that dream and participate in discourses about it can have potentially powerful transformative effects.

Though the enthusiastic members of the Jewish community who paraded with the school were convinced it was a winning combination, Mangueira took second place. First place was secured by the popular Beija-Flor school with its hopeful celebration of the life of the newly inaugurated president, Luiz Inácio "Lula" da Silva. Of course, that was also political. Nevertheless, the outcome of the competition did not detract from the significance of the collaboration. A colleague in São Paulo commented on the parade, which she said "left some Jews in a bad mood." Usually far more jaded, she enthused: "I thought it was fantastic! It was all really confused, as the stories told in *carnaval* usually are. But they didn't demonize us, or say that we're bad and all-powerful!" In other words, the effects of the presentation reached far beyond reestablishing the status quo. The presentation of a "Jewish" theme in Rio's nationally televised *carnaval* parade, and the participation of the Jewish community in this event, represented a discursive shift to a more explicit Jewish participation on the national stage.

When harnessed together, these institutionalized forms of cultural expression can turn out to be powerful vehicles for social transformation. A projection of a desired future, they are the current form of what Brazilian anthropologist Renato Ortiz called a "cosmology which precedes its own reality" (1985:38). In Sheriff's terms, they are "prescriptive" rather than "descriptive" (2001:220). They are about imagining new pasts and about creating new futures.

With its floats and costumes and fantasies, *carnaval* lends itself to this sort of hopeful projection. The day after *carnaval* is somber, everyone perhaps a little exhausted. Some of the pall of Ash Wednesday is cast by the grim reality of waking to face things as they are rather than as one might wish them to be. So it is with Jews in their everyday existence: no matter the rationale that they might use to explain their broad acceptance in Brazil, the country of the future, where all differences are tolerated if not celebrated, their condition as transnationals sets them outside this celebratory drama as they continue to draw on sources of identity from beyond the borders of Brazil.

6

Doubly Insecure

What is unique about Jewish Brazilians is their Brazilianness. The ideologies that are central to Brazilian national identity have created a space for Jews to be able to become fully incorporated, participating citizens. More significantly, these same ideologies are reproduced within the *paulistano* Jewish community, buttressing a set of hybrid beliefs and practices such that they enact their Jewishness in Brazilian ways. What set *paulistano* Jews apart from other Brazilians, including other Brazilian transnational groups, are the external and very contemporary qualities of the hostility directed against them. Without a strong history of organized anti-Semitism in the country, there is little room within the Brazilian framework for apprehending these active forms of intolerance, but its existence and the clear threat of transnational enactments of this sort of violence force the Jewish community to engage directly with their transborder identities. It is a particular irony that in this tolerant nation, where Jews have attained such social acceptance and economic success, it is their transnational condition that places limits on their belonging, not necessarily because of their own external ties but because of the external sources of violence directed against them. Within the context of generalized crime and violence, *paulistano* Jews respond in ways that are consistent with that of other middle- and upper-class *paulistanos*, blending the local and transnational in their practices.

Living in the City

The city of São Paulo is more than a backdrop, more than merely a setting in which Jews live their lives. It is practically a character in their daily dramas. Much of what it means to be Jewish and Brazilian in São Paulo has to do with the city itself, its sheer size and complexity, its ethnic and class tensions, and the incessant noise, filth, congestion, and crime, all of which conspire to make life in the city both exciting and precarious. Living in São Paulo means living with insecurity, and this urban danger is also part of the identity of *paulistano* Jews. It couples with the insecurity that Jews feel almost everywhere as part of their condition as Jews. The insecurity of *paulistano* Jews is a dialectic in which they simultaneously share in the risks of the population around them while managing the risks that are peculiar to them as Jews. It is this difference in risk, and their collective response to it, that distinguishes Jewish Brazilians from their compatriots and limits their belonging in this otherwise accepting nation.

The street, *a rua*, is a powerful concept in Brazil (DaMatta 1987 and 1991a:63–69), synonymous with public, often informal, space. *Na rua*, on the street, is where errands are run, random encounters occur, and unstructured learning takes place. It is where *meninos de rua*, street children, make their existence uncomfortably known.[1] It is also where class boundaries are negotiated. Street vendors dodge police as they attempt to make a living selling cheap goods imported from China via Paraguay and dangerously unregulated foodstuffs. At the other extreme, the privatization of public thoroughfares is hotly contested as the residents of wealthy areas attempt to close themselves off to incursions from outsiders by the creation of walled and guarded "fortified enclaves" (Caldeira 1999, 2000). In popular parlance, *a rua* is a place of problems.

Certainly, the streets in São Paulo are a source of difficulties, with daily traffic jams measured in kilometers.[2] When not immobilized by gridlock, vehicles of all sorts and sizes move much too quickly along well-rehearsed paths. Confronting street traffic impinges on quality of life, but it is also central to the experience of the city for its residents, "traveler-inhabitants" who move through the city and do not merely reside in it (García Canclini 2009:57). Those who depend on public transportation are subject to robbery on the buses, deepening the miserable conditions of mass transit. Waiting for a bus can be an anxiety-provoking experience, as one maintains one's senses alert to the presence of possible sources of danger while hoping that the bus is not overly delayed by too many vehicles, accidents, floods, and street repairs. One day, as we made our way through the traffic, my friend Raquel suggested that I call my book *São Paulo: The Chaos*. Though she knew my work was about the Jewish community, her comment underscored the extent to which the city streets figure prominently in their day-to-day lives.

The streets are also a source of danger. More than just rumored danger, robbery and assault are common occurrences, touching everyone's life. Rosa, who had been held up several times at intersections, quickly cranked her windows up each time the car stopped, as if this could protect her against the occasional armed bandit mixed in among the beggars and vendors and windshield washers working at major intersections. At night, drivers frequently go through red lights, slowing at intersections only enough to look for oncoming traffic. What might appear to be reckless disobedience of the law is in fact a defensive move by people not wanting to sit at intersections vulnerable and unprotected. On the day the Jerusalém choir sang at the new Sala São Paulo music hall, while we were in final rehearsal the car belonging to one of the choir members was stolen from the heavily guarded street outside the Hebraica. A few hours later, our piano player arrived late at the music hall, having been held up at gunpoint in the backseat of a taxi; his assailant simply opened the rear door of the cab and got in. This sort of occurrence is normalized such that responses range from nods of recognition to humorous swapping of similar stories. People adapt as best they can.

Most people can recount stories of being held up, and this discourse about crime contributes to public perceptions of danger.[3] Caldeira terms these frequent narratives "the talk of crime," which is both a coping strategy and a vehicle for disseminating stereotypes and contributing to a "culture of fear and suspicion" (Caldeira 2000). Although Caldeira's analysis stems from her research in São Paulo, she finds continuities in other metropolises, including Mike Davis' apocalyptic view of Los Angeles (1990). Similarly, anthropologist Setha Low (1997) finds the "fortress city" in many global settings. In order to avoid repeating the phenomenon of reifying the discourse, it is important to reiterate Scheper-Hughes' "caveat" (1997:475–76) that a focus on dramatic violence in Brazil is neither an attempt to characterize that society in terms of violence nor to ignore the everyday violence experienced by many people in other countries, including the United States. Part of what Scheper-Hughes draws attention to through the concepts of "everyday violence" and "peace-time crimes" is the normalization of violence, not only in Arendt's sense of making it "banal" (1977), but also in the sense of the less obvious but nonetheless injurious forms of routinized and coercive control (see Bourdieu 1977, Foucault 1979).

So prevalent was this sort of crime that the radio station Joven Pan carried out a campaign against holdups on the street.[4] The station's bright yellow logo on car and bus windows proclaimed: "Já fui assaltado" (I've already been robbed). An acknowledgment of this widespread phenomenon, the campaign sought to shake off the complacency that accompanies normalization. The campaign sparked a disagreement between Raquel and another woman who claimed that because it was "negative," displaying the sticker violated the Jewish religion. Raquel dismissed this as ridiculous, since there is certainly no prohibition against negativity in Judaism, and proudly displayed her car sticker in what she considered "passive protest" against rampant crime. It is doubtful that this resistance to the normalization of crime had any impact beyond stirring up a few agitated conversations and wan grins of recognition.

This criminality is part of a larger pattern of violence in São Paulo that is perceived to be greater there than in other parts of this country characterized by endemic violence (Scheper-Hughes 1992, 1997; Linger 1992; Caldeira and Holston 1999). There is a double irony in the popular belief that the major events in the country's history have been "bloodless," most notably the end of slavery, the end of the monarchy, the beginning of the republic, and the end of the military regime. Part of the irony is in the belief that the groundwork for today's violence was laid during colonial times, making this view of Brazilian "nonviolent revolutions" contradictory. More importantly, social change in Brazil has been anything but bloodless, as evidenced by the government's quashing of major uprisings, such as the "rebellion" in Canudos, the Revolution of '32, the political repression during the military regime of the 1960s and 1970s, and the numerous *chacinas* (mass killings) in *favelas*, on indigenous reserves, and on street corners in major cities that continue today in which the state is often directly or indirectly implicated. The continuation of death squads after the military regime in Brazil and other "peace-time crimes" (Scheper-Hughes 1992, 1996, 1997) have posed serious challenges to the emergent democracy. Similarly, increased violent crimes and police violence undermine confidence in the process of democratization (Caldeira and Holston 1999, Caldeira 2000).

In an attempt to address some of the widespread violence, Brazilian cities considered legislating the hours of operation and the amount of money that could be retrieved at one time from bank automatic teller machines, effectively eliminating the convenience of twenty-four-hour access, and with it the rationale for the machines. This was intended to protect the citizenry from *sequestros relâmpagos*, "lightning kidnappings," the name given to the rapid abductions from which the victims ransom themselves with cash from automatic teller machines.[5] Brazilians have a remarkable ability to make light of all sorts of difficulties and calamities, as evidenced by this sort of linguistic play, as well as other forms of folklore, popular culture, and jokes (D. Goldstein 2003). I noted another example in Higienópolis, where a car parked at an elite tennis club behind the Buenos Aires Plaza had an "arm" sticking out of the trunk dressed in a long white sleeve with a "gold" watch on the wrist, a three-dimensional joke on kidnapping.

However, wealthy people are not the only target of *sequestros relâmpagos*; in fact, the wealthiest have the protective advantage of guards, gates, armored cars, and bullet-proof glass. These heavily advertised, burgeoning businesses promise protection with their slick storefront window displays along the streets of Jardins and other upper-class neighborhoods, offering security systems for homes, businesses, and automobiles, private solutions to social problems. In October 1999, the São Paulo edition of the national weekly newsmagazine *Veja* reported that the city had 105,000 private security guards, three times more than the number of military and civil police in the city.

Somewhat more collective responses to the urban violence are found in the high-rise buildings throughout the city. Businesses and medical offices share security services, ranging from solitary doormen to high-tech systems. Depending on the region of the city and the nature of the businesses in the building, an individual arriving for a doctor's appointment, for instance, might need to present identification and have a photo taken before receiving a magnetized card permitting her to pass a turnstile or enter the elevator. In apartment buildings, doormen sit behind tinted bulletproof glass and talk to visitors through intercom systems. After phoning the apartment residence to announce a visitor, they buzz the guest through a double set of gates, one of which must close before the second one will open, protecting the visitor from the dangers of the street and making it more difficult for someone to rush the entrance. A similar double-gated system for cars entering and exiting underground garages is gaining currency.

Many neighborhoods pay private security guards to maintain vigil outside the walls and gates of homes and apartment buildings, keeping an eye out for suspicious persons or activities. There have also been some problems with underpaid or otherwise unsatisfied security guards who, armed with the knowledge of security systems and the comings and goings of residents, have actually helped if not orchestrated robberies. The resulting climate of distrust only aggravates these already strained class relations. The well-off are entirely dependent on the labor of those from whom they wish to be separate in order to run their households, raise their children, and protect them from incursions from the unruly street. This is just one example of the many ways in which attempts to segregate along class lines have backfired.

Security and standards of living are such central concerns for the *paulistano* middle classes that in September 1999, the *Folha* published the first of its bimonthly reports on the quality of life, which was evaluated as "unsatisfactory" by the residents polled by the newspaper's researchers.[6] In spite of relative economic stability with regard to inflation, the gap between the richest and the poorest had grown, as had high unemployment, facts related to the role that the city plays in the internationalization of the national economy that polarizes the population at the social extremes. With three million people living below the poverty line (34 percent of the municipality's population), the socioeconomic inequalities in São Paulo, home to 10 percent of the country's population, were consistent with the social calamity that existed throughout the country,[7] where half of the wealth was in the hands of 10 percent of the population.[8] Several programs during the subsequent administration of Luiz Inácio "Lula" da Silva sought to redress these inequalities and lifted over thirty million

Brazilians out of poverty. Although poverty and inequality are certainly part of the equation of crime, especially insofar as the poor are more frequently the victims of violent crime, they are insufficient as explanations.[9]

Caldeira's analysis of the crime statistics also shows that while overall crime rates increased between 1973 and 1995, the rate of increase was greater in the outlying areas of the city, where the poorer populations are concentrated. Another indication of how increased crime is felt differentially by different social strata, "the rates of crime against property are highest in the upper- and middle-class neighborhoods, whereas the rates of homicide are highest in the poorest districts of the city" (Caldeira 2000:118).

More than the perception of a hypersensitized population, São Paulo saw violent crime increase so that it made up a greater percentage of overall crime. Murder rates in São Paulo, while not the highest in the world or in the Americas, nevertheless translated into disturbing absolute numbers: the rate of 30–50 murders per 100,000 people meant roughly 7,000 murders per year in the metropolis. Where some of the city's violence statistics may be comparable to those in other global metropolises, police violence makes São Paulo unique. With an average of 1,000 people killed per year by the Military Police in the early 1990s (as compared to 25 and 24 in Los Angeles and New York, respectively, in 1992; Caldeira 1999:118), police violence considerably raises the overall tenor of fear and insecurity, even if the middle classes are rarely targeted. The end of 1999 saw a 63 percent increase (from 67 to 109) in the number of people killed by the Military Police in São Paulo, and a 200 percent increase (from 2 to 6) in the number of officers' deaths over the same period in the previous year. Police violence is one of the aspects of contemporary Brazil that is most difficult to reconcile with the return to political democracy that began in the late 1980s (Caldeira and Holston 1999). "The police, far from guaranteeing rights and preventing violence, are in fact contributing to the erosion of people's rights and the increase of violence" (Caldeira 2000:137). Clearly, this lack of confidence in the agents of the state translates into a lack of confidence in the state. Given the difference in perspective that socioeconomic class affords, it is not surprising, but is nevertheless disturbing that for some, including members of the Jewish community, the exhaustion of these daily tribulations evoked a nostalgia for the military regimes of the past and their associated social order (at least for those who were not part of the opposition).

Stemming from and aggravating the infamous socioeconomic inequalities in Brazil, social barriers increasingly take physical forms, including the many kinds of walls described by Caldeira in her ethnography of this city. The walls and surveillance systems and other "aesthetics of security" available to the more privileged classes appropriate public space, transform it into private space, and perpetuate exclusion and social inequality. In her discussions of the class-segregated communities that have emerged in the United States and in other locales, Low points out that these walls and gates represent material expressions of the anxieties of the populace (1997). Similar to the self-perpetuating loop that Caldeira describes in her discussion of the "talk of crime," the resulting "landscape of fear" also reproduces social exclusion. The acceptance of the structures and rhetoric of security, with its corollary willingness to forgo certain kinds of privacy and civil rights, aggravates the different experiences of alienation all along the class continuum, reinforcing the perceived need for increased security that is the constant theme of life in São Paulo.

As part of this fraught landscape, Jewish institutions are neither the special targets of this kind of violence, nor are they immune from it. Indeed, they might be targeted for class reasons, rather than ethnic ones. For example, in the mid-1990s, a bank branch located just inside the main entrance of the Hebraica was held up and the manager was killed. Following that incident, security was stepped up and banking services were moved to more remote locations within the club. Within the larger context of frequent bank robberies, this particular bank robbery cannot be read as an act of anti-Semitism merely because it occurred in a Jewish institution. Even if stereotypes about wealthy Jews influenced the choice of site, the bank was the target, not the Jews in it.

While Jews are not any more subject to violence of this kind than any other group, the Jewish community obviously lives in and responds to this general climate. Since the community is generally better off economically than the population at large, as a group Jews tend to experience the problems of crime and violence through the lens of the privileged classes. This means that the community focuses on individual and institutional security and takes measures to protect itself and its institutions that are consistent with the cultural milieu. As such, Jewish institutions in São Paulo have adopted a whole range of security measures, most of which are typical of those installed in similar institutions.

The Imaginary Jew

Where protection of Jewish institutions also involves protection against attacks directed at them *as* Jewish institutions, the extent and nature of anti-Semitism in Brazil must be considered along two different axes. The first is the difference between abstract prejudice and codified or operationalized prejudice, and the second has to do with the place of Jews in Brazilian society and the way they disrupt a color-based racial model.

On the first axis, there is abundant evidence of prejudice in Brazil against an *imaginary* Jew, a medieval holdover maintained by official Catholic doctrine taught in the schools until the 1970s (in some cases until much more recently) (Lesser 1995, Elkin 1998). Brazilian folklore is replete with references to biblical Jews, including plant names (for example, a vine called *sapatinho de judeu*, Jew's slipper, has little shoelike flowers) and festivals (i.e., Holy Week [Semana Santa] reenactments of the events leading up to Christ's crucifixion). In addition to the familiar European anti-Semitic repertoire, Nachman Falbel further suggests that the association of Jews with criminality and trafficking in South America in the early twentieth century added a layer of stigmatization to the word *"judeu"* (Jew) (1998:249), supplementing the cycle of negative stereotyping and reinforcing the imaginary Jew against which the community constructed itself. Historian Jeffrey Lesser also identifies this imaginary Jew as having a more contemporary referent, "framed in an unsophisticated reading of European anti-Semitism" and derived from "an inaccurate image of Jewish life outside of Brazil" in the first half of the twentieth century (2001:70). In other words, there are some more recent formulations of anti-Semitism in Brazil, but these are neither well developed nor widespread.

Jewish Brazilians were well aware of the difference between abstract and active prejudice, especially in a country where a small, concentrated Jewish population means that most of the citizenry has little or no contact with Jews, and where a general lack of knowledge about Jews (both mythicohistorical and contemporary) means that for most Brazilians, Jews exist in the *imaginary* plane. When I asked one man in his sixties what it was like to grow up as one of the few Jews in a small city in the interior, especially during the 1930s, a period of overt political anti-Semitism, he responded that it was irrelevant, that most people were so ignorant that even if they made anti-Jewish statements they did not connect these to the

Jew standing before them. This imaginary Jew was so abstract as to have no direct referent in lived experience.

Nevertheless, it is against the *imaginary* Jew that Jews in Brazil (and likely elsewhere) construct their identities and practices. For Brazilian Jews, the ever-present fear or perceived threat of anti-Jewish hostility is not imaginary, even if it does not often find explicit expression in Brazil. As transnationals, Jews are intensely aware that the hostility toward them can also be transnational. Ongoing conflicts involving Jews, as well as hostility and violence against Jews in locales near and far, serve to remind Jews of the fragility of their status even in a country as tolerant as Brazil.

Contradictions are central to Jewish-Brazilian identity—contradictions between Jewish and Brazilian cultural elements, between visibility and invisibility, and between desires for inclusion and experiences of exclusion. Jews are simultaneously part of Brazilian society and outsiders. Nowhere was this tension more evident than in Felipe's critique of the community's understanding of the low incidence of organized or violent anti-Semitism in Brazil. Speaking from his place at the community's margins, Felipe was something of a jester, prodding and critical. Like so many of his overstated assertions, Felipe's own position was contradictory, both celebrating Brazilian tolerance and questioning its solidity: "Since we have never had a crisis of anti-Semitism, a racial crisis, the community considers itself assimilated in national society. This is a lie. We are tolerated. We are not wanted [*queridos*]."

Indeed, without a history of organized or violent anti-Semitism, most Jewish Brazilians have comfortably accepted the national ideology of racial tolerance. In 2003, Brazil recognized anti-Semitism as a form of racism punishable under the antidiscrimination statute of the 1988 Constitution; an active public-private collaboration oversees successful and well-publicized prosecutions under the statute. Most of the likely sources of disruption of this ideology are external to Brazil and find difficult resolution in a context where ethnic and racial harmony is sought as part of the national identity.

However, these external threats and their associated sources of identity are also what place limits on the Brazilianness of Jewish Brazilians. Ironically, the social integration that has allowed Jews to feel accepted in Brazil has also transformed Jewish practices in Brazil in relation to Israel. The relative economic security of many in the community has permitted the development, active maintenance, and promotion of positive relations with Israel on the part of individuals, the community as a whole, and the Brazilian nation. Not surprisingly, as elsewhere there is considerable disagreement about Israel among Jews in São Paulo. Some members of the community engage in educational efforts to raise awareness of Israel, such as publication series, while others work closely with the consulate to secure the diplomatic and cultural relationships between the two countries. Celebrations are organized whenever Israel attains significant milestones (such at the sixtieth anniversary), and when the conflict in Israel/Palestine escalates and occupies the headlines, members of the São Paulo Jewish community organize manifestations of support for Israel. Furthermore, with the situation in Israel at a sustained crisis point that has polarized Jews around the world, there are certain to be transformations in the Brazilian Jewish community.[10]

The existence of the state of Israel stands as an attractive counterpoint to the comfort and familiarity of living in diaspora and for many Jewish Brazilians casts doubt on an otherwise strong sense of belonging in Brazil. There is a long-standing Zionist movement in Brazil, though many people who emigrated to Israel ("made *aliyah*") for ideological reasons have subsequently returned to Brazil.[11] It is a widely held view in the community that those who make *aliyah* are "quem não deu certo aqui" (those who didn't work out here), that is, those who did not adapt socially and especially financially in Brazil. These impressions are supported by long-term data from demographer Sergio DellaPergola, who has found that increases in migration from Latin America to Israel follow crises in the countries of origin rather than being stimulated by the draw of Israel (1999).[12] In fact, during periods of crisis in Israel, the rate of *aliyah* has decreased, a refutation of the ideological claim.

In light of his criticism of the São Paulo Jewish community, Felipe expressed regret that he was never able to emigrate to Israel, explaining the place and purpose that he felt Israel holds for Jewish people everywhere: "Israel means everything. It is our home (*casa*). The day Israel ends you won't be able to walk free in the United States as a 'Yid,' as an Israelite. If we are free to say 'I'm a Jew' in this world it's because Israel is there. It's the heart. It's the brain. It's the pillar . . . It holds up everything [*segura tudo*]." Extrapolating from his own experience of loss and instability, Felipe added, "When you have a house, you have more security to be able to do the other things, to work, to study, to love [*namorar*]. That's the case of Israel, our house. The door is open." In effect, Felipe was saying that he could live comfortably in Brazil because of the existence of Israel. Having a "home" in Israel meant being able to be at home in Brazil.

Bernardo, the doctor, took a more utilitarian view of Israel, calling it "an insurance policy" for Jews. As someone with options, he could afford to express a pragmatic ambivalence: "It's a *country*, it has its contrasts . . . It's not the Promised Land." Beyond concerns over the geopolitical problems that plague Israel, Brazilians are especially distressed by the infamous antipathy of the Israelis. While Felipe joked, "I love those arrogant people," Bernardo explained the consequences of an affective dissonance for many Brazilians' relationship with Israel: "I've been to Israel. I love Israel. I think it's everyone's second *pátria* [homeland]. It's a point of balance for security, but . . . people are distancing themselves . . . When you arrive in Israel, you are not treated well. If I go to Disney [World], Mickey [Mouse] treats me very well. So, I've been to Disney [World] twelve times, and only went once to Israel." Bernardo's consumer comparison of Israel and Disney World makes it clear that at least for some Brazilian Jews, there is an element of choice rather than obligation in their relationship to Israel.[13] Israel might be a safe house, but that does not mean they need to take refuge there, especially if they perceive it as unpleasant, and especially when they already have a home.

There are numerous youth movements in São Paulo that encourage young people to take an interest in Israel. The popular Israeli dance groups at the schools and clubs are among the activities that encourage exchange programs. In spite of these and other Israel-oriented activities and organizations, Jews in Brazil are generally speaking less able to and less interested in financially supporting Israel. Their perspective is from within a "developing" country, one that has suffered economic instability. Some believe that it is they who should be receiving support from Israel, not the other way around. Bernardo explained that "with the impoverishment of the community and . . . internal problems and needs, people look inward more and more." This internal gaze reinforces the ties and investment that Jewish *paulistanos* have with their local communities. The *abrasileiração* (Brazilification) of the Jewish community means a greater orientation within Brazil, not only toward Jewish Brazilians, but toward other Brazilians as well.

Transnationalism on the Ground

Just as living in São Paulo means living with insecurity, being Jewish also means living with insecurity. Though the urban violence that has become so common in Brazilian cities does not specifically target Jews, Jews experience it just like other Brazilians. Additionally, Jews are more vulnerable to another sort of violence from a different source and with another rationale. For Jews in São Paulo, security concerns are redoubled, since in addition to the generalized urban violence that city residents know so well, the Jewish community must concern itself with international anti-Jewish and anti-Israeli violence. The coexistence of the two security problems means that most of the measures taken against specifically anti-Jewish violence are absorbed into the general environment of high security in São Paulo, though others are more specific.

Many of these specific measures are discreet. In contrast to the public spaces that are disassociated from specifically Jewish locales, many Jewish institutions opt to disappear behind the high walls that are common throughout the city, undistinguished by any identifying signs so that it is possible to pass a place day after day without ever imagining that a Jewish school or synagogue is just on the other side of the unmarked wall. I lived just doors away from a synagogue that I had heard about but could never find, and only learned of its exact location once I was invited to attend Shabbat services there. The protection wrought by invisibility is but one precautionary approach that extends the standard practices in this security-conscious city to address the particular concerns of Jewish institutions.

Some institutions have more extensive, often high-tech, security systems attended by uniformed guards. This kind of added defense brings with it the disadvantage of higher visibility. In some cases, this visibility not only identifies a Jewish institution as such, but may also actually aggravate latent stereotypes about Jews wishing to exclude themselves from the social milieu. Deliberate ethnic segregation contradicts the Brazilian ideology of racial equality, and where it overlaps with normalized class segregation, as in the case of Jewish communal institutions, this can provoke anti-Jewish sentiments that may have lain dormant or been previously nonexistent. In other words, by protecting themselves against the sort of attacks that are familiar to Jews around the globe, Jews unintentionally provoke feelings of mistrust in a country with little history of anti-Semitism.

Jews throughout the world maintain a heightened awareness of their vulnerability to sudden changes in fortune, subject to the effects of geopolitical shifts, objects of displaced hostility during swells of nationalist sentiment. Their long experience in diaspora means that Jews live in anticipation of these shifts, even through long periods of stability. The creation of the state of Israel has not ameliorated that sense of vulnerability, and increases in the Israel/Palestine conflict have in fact contributed to the targeting of Jews in distant places on the globe. Territorial conflicts have been globalized and are no longer played out exclusively on the ground in question. More than a distant or abstract concern for Brazilian Jews, several incidents in the 1990s in other countries in the Americas were brutal reminders of the transnational nature of contemporary anti-Jewish violence, leading to intensified security efforts in Brazil.

The most deadly and destructive of these incidents, and the one that has generated the greatest response in the community in São Paulo, was the bombing of the AMIA in Buenos Aires. In July of 1994, a bomb went off in the Asociación Mutual Israelita Argentina (AMIA), the Argentinean Jewish Mutual Aid Association,[14] collapsing half of the multistory building, reducing it to rubble. It was the worst mass killing in Argentinean history: 86 people died along with the bomber, and another 300 were wounded. The building housed both the AMIA, the main cultural organization of the majority Ashkenazi population,[15] and the DAIA (Delegación de Asociaciones Israelitas Argentinas), the Delegation of Argentine Jewish Associations, the political umbrella organization. The bomb also destroyed 100 years of community archives. Nearly two decades later, this incident continues to reverberate in Argentina and Jewish communities throughout the region.

The AMIA bombing was the most lethal, but it was not the first of its kind in Buenos Aires. In 1992, a car bomb at the Israeli embassy killed 29 and injured over 100. The attack on the Israeli embassy is not cited nearly as frequently as the AMIA bombing, nor does it have the same resonance for Jews in São Paulo. The difference may lie not only in the extent of the destruction and number of casualties, but also in the nature of the institutions attacked, a distinction that is decoded by Jews in Brazil and suggests their own greater vulnerability.

It is not entirely surprising that these events occurred in Argentina, which has Latin America's largest Jewish population and a long history of anti-Semitism. Neither is it insignificant that the first attack in 1992 was on an institution representing Israel. The Argentinean events were an extension of regional conflicts in another part of the globe. In the literature on interethnic violence, the focus is almost always on clashes between groups with a stake in the territory in which the violence occurs, whether in Bosnia, Rwanda, Ireland, or East Timor. International terrorism, violence with a message, calls the world's attention to a regional conflict. Airplane highjackings and bombings have been another platform for drawing eyes to a particular conflict; the supranational nature of air travel, even where a national airline is the target, puts the "location" of these attacks in the international arena, making all potential air travelers take note. Another example of an international arena was the murder of eleven Israeli athletes and coaches during the 1972 Olympics in Munich, which gained significance as an especially heinous act in the context of an event with the explicit goal of overcoming international conflicts.[16]

The simultaneous attacks on U.S. embassies in Kenya and Tanzania in 1998, which left 224 people dead, should also be considered in light of this discussion. Clearly, the 2001 attacks on the World Trade Center in New York and the Pentagon targeted locations that would draw the greatest attention because of their symbolic and real prominence on the international stage.[17] Certain institutions, including airlines, embassies, and Olympic teams, represent nations, making them potential targets in national conflicts and offering opportunities to focus the world's attention on local conflicts. Ironically, international cooperation, institutionalized with the establishment of the United Nations, has helped create this international stage. The rapid economic and technological changes that fall under the rubric of globalization have also contributed to making international terrorist events possible. The same flows of people and information that facilitate international commerce similarly foster fluid relations between transnational people who are scattered over the globe; they also facilitate the transnationalization of political organizations, resistance movements, and terrorist groups.

The bombing of the AMIA was different from these other examples of targets with a more international profile, including the attack on the Israeli embassy. The "audience" for this Argentinean performance was the international Jewish community and other supporters of Israel. It was not an event calling on the "international community" to take note and take action. Its target was too specific to call the attention of anyone other than those who already had ties to Argentina, Israel, or other Jewish communities. The conflation of Israel with Jewish people links these two events, confounding the conflict in the Middle East with historical anti-Semitism.

The AMIA bombing was a transformative moment for many people in the São Paulo Jewish community and has remained a continual point of reference. When one of the national Jewish papers reported on the September 1999 desecration of graves in a Jewish cemetery in Buenos Aires, the story was accompanied by an archival photo of the destroyed AMIA building from six years before, along with the caption: "um trágico atentado que continua sem solução," as-yet-unsolved tragic attack.[18] "Yet another episode of anti-Semitism in Latin America," the article began. "Once again in Argentina. This time the stage used was La Tablada cemetery in the province of Buenos Aires." Here, the "stage" was one of many on which the drama of anti-Semitism is played out internationally, this time carefully scripted. The grave desecration took place during the early hours of September 18, in the week between Rosh Hashanah and Yom Kippur. Two of the major Jewish organizations in Argentina pushed for the case to be handled by Federal Police rather than by the police in Buenos Aires, since the latter had been implicated in the attack on the AMIA. In order for it to be considered a federal case, it has to fall within the purview of the antidiscrimination laws, something which was made more difficult by the absence of swastikas or other recognized anti-Semitic graffiti. The fact that the incident occurred in a Jewish cemetery during the Jewish High Holy Days was not sufficient to define it as a hate crime.

The Brazilian article cited the lack of Nazi symbols as proof that the perpetrators were informed and organized, as if they knew not to employ the symbols that would categorize their attack as a hate crime and set certain procedures in motion. Further evidence of their organization was read into the number of graves desecrated, sixty-three, nearly corresponding to the number of months, sixty-two, that had transpired since the attack on the AMIA. This numerical significance was not lost on a people with a long tradition of seeking numerological meaning in words and dates, following kabalistic logic. This is a peculiar type of violence the effectiveness of which is intensified by symbolic communication, an exchange of coded messages between the perpetrators and their targets. Each new incident reopens the wound of the AMIA attack and reinvigorates the fear that has gripped Jewish communities in the region ever since. Other Jewish community centers in the Americas have also been attacked, such as the one in Los Angeles invaded by a machine gun–wielding white supremacist, or the Sacramento synagogue that was burned.[19] Every time an attack of this sort occurs, Jewish leaders and security specialists strain to come up with new, more effective ways to protect their scattered communities from future violence. Certainly, the motives and planning that go into an event like the bombing of the AMIA are considerably different from the smaller-scale and comparatively disorganized attacks of the sort that occurred in Los Angeles and require different sorts of responses. Jewish community leaders must simultaneously consider all of these levels.

The need for developed security systems is perceived not only because of the community's strong sympathies with Jews in other locales. Jewish institutions in São Paulo regularly receive direct threats, whether or not they have explicit ties to Israel. It is precisely this possibility and the knowledge that the location of the AMIA attack in Argentina was a strategic choice, and not an accident or coincidence, that forces Jewish community leaders around the world to respond with new standards of security for Jewish institutions. Clearly, this is a strategy of deferral, one which may leave less visible or poorer institutions vulnerable as a second or third choice for determined attackers, as in the Los Angeles incident.

The investigations into the 1994 bombing in Argentina continue, but it appears to have been carried out with the help of some Argentinean police with neo-Nazi ties. The trail has been followed to the notoriously porous triple-border area where Brazil, Argentina, and Paraguay meet, a region with significant Arab and Muslim communities and rumored to have Hamas and Hezbollah training camps. Without any precedent for similar problems in Brazil, government officials caution against unfairly targeting these communities in the post–September 11 agitation. The Israeli ambassador to Argentina has repeatedly accused Iran of "ideological" responsibility for the attacks, which he says were carried out by members of Hezbollah.[20]

Although the AMIA bombing and the subsequent developments in the case have been reported in the Brazilian press, these events have gone largely unnoticed by the general Brazilian population, the majority of which is too concerned with the immediacy of problems at home to pay attention to events in other countries, even neighboring countries, that do not directly affect them. However, for Jewish Brazilians this event was close to home and demanded an immediate rethinking of the already high security that surrounded most Jewish institutions in urban areas. Following the attack in Argentina, FISESP, the umbrella organization for the majority of not-for-profit Jewish institutions in the state of São Paulo, made a series of recommendations that resulted in stepped-up security for Jewish institutions, in some cases with oversight from specially trained consultants.

Many of the security measures to protect against anti-Jewish violence are discreet, especially when layered onto the security systems that are normalized throughout the city. The simultaneity of the two security problems means that most of the measures taken against anti-Jewish violence can be absorbed into the general environment of high security. As in many parts of the contemporary world, most people move through these highly monitored spaces unaware of the extent to which they have been planned with these questions in mind and ignorant of the degree of vigilance to which they are subjected.

Only rarely is it obvious that a particular measure is taken specifically to protect against terrorist attacks. For the most part, community members have absorbed these measures, and they recover quickly from the frequent reminders that they are potential targets of violence. With its separate social spaces protected by tight security, the Hebraica club can be seen as an example of the segregation and reinvented public spaces that Caldeira critiques. From the perspective of those who frequent the club, it is a sanctuary from the stresses of the streets of São Paulo. For the club's members, safety is found not only in the guarded gates and walls, but also in the relief from the Christian hegemony of the rest of the city.

Ironically, the very size of the club and the fact that thousands of Jews congregate there make it a potential target for anti-Jewish violence. A reminder of this came at the start of the Jewish High Holy Days in 1999, when just before the beginning of the Rosh Hashanah services the liturgical choir was asked to wrap up rehearsals in the Arthur Rubinstein Theater an hour ahead of time to give the security personnel an opportunity to search the theater for bombs. The young people in the choir were unperturbed. When I asked about their nonchalant attitudes to this reminder of the threat of violence, several responded: "We're used to it." In another incident, when a threat was phoned in to the Department of

Jewish Culture, the two young women who worked there, Sílvia and Kátia, were visibly disturbed, but they also commented that it was the kind of thing that happened all the time. In much the same way that *paulistanos* of all classes normalize the violence that permeates their daily lives, members of the Jewish community learn to take in stride the reminders of their vulnerability as Jews.

In spite of these stoic dismissals, the combination of fear of immanent attack with the high level of tension from living in such an aggressive urban environment often leaves people on edge, quick to imagine the worst. For instance, the Hebraica club's council elections in 1999 occurred the week following Brazil's first "American-style" public shooting.[21] The tension in the group became evident when one of the chorus members burst in on a rehearsal and the first startled reaction in the group was the assumption that something terrible had happened; instead she wanted to announce that she had won a seat on the club's council.

This state of alert heightened at the beginning of the Second Intifada in September 2000. The São Paulo Jewish community maintains a good relationship with local police, who work with the community's security services and provide added support outside Jewish institutions during major events, like the High Holy Days. Given the brewing anger toward Israel that easily extends to Jews as a whole, in October 2000, the *Folha de São Paulo* reported that four divisions of the Civil Police were monitoring the Israeli consulate and over thirty synagogues around the city. The police chief reiterated a version of the national ideology when he assured that "this sort of thing does not happen in São Paulo." Nevertheless, the police force swung into action when an abandoned bag was found in the building housing the FISESP; they evacuated the building, blocked off a major street in the Pinheiros neighborhood, and were preparing to blow up the bag when it was found to contain nothing more than forgotten tools.[22]

With the conflict in the Middle East reaching an explosive peak in April 2002, the FISESP renewed its security recommendations (drawing on those of the Anti-Defamation League) in light of the "exportation of the Middle East conflict" and the threats directed at Jewish institutions. Together with the national Jewish federation CONIB, the FISESP organized a march "for peace, against terror, and against anti-Semitism" in São Paulo, which brought together an unprecedented 10,000 people.[23]

The AMIA bombing serves as a constant reminder that the threats could manifest in an attack in the São Paulo community.

On an individual level, the attack in Argentina was meaningful for many in São Paulo. For some, it strengthened an already growing desire to "become more Jewish," to publicly demonstrate an ethnic identity, a sentiment that these individuals had felt was more internal and private up to that point. One friend described a dream he had shortly before the incident in Argentina in which he wore a *kippah* on the street for the first time.[24] After the AMIA bombing members of the São Paulo Jewish community organized a protest on the Avenida Paulista, gathering under the suspended modernist structure of the Museu de Arte de São Paulo (MASP art museum).[25] Fulfilling the premonition of his dream, my friend wore a *kippah* on the street for the first time that day and has worn one ever since.

In this electrified context, the *kippah* is transformed from a religious garment into a symbol of ethnic assertion and even political protest.[26] Anthropologist Manuela Carneiro da Cunha argues that as a native category of group definition, ethnicity itself "is an important form of eminently political protest" (1986:108). However, when politically energized Jews assert their ethnicity through public displays of difference they do so at the risk of jeopardizing the security of their national identity as Brazilians by deliberately casting aside their ability to pass as undifferentiated Brazilians.

Almost exclusively an issue for men, the question of whether to wear a *kippah* "on the street," that is, in the public sphere of danger, operates at the intersection of religious and ethnic practice where the social context plays a central role in the meaning of such a choice. One aspect of the question has to do with sacred space; men are expected to wear a *kippah* whenever they enter a synagogue, covering their head out of respect.[27] Another has to do with sacred time; men are supposed to cover their heads during prayer or ritual. Whether or not to wear a *kippah* was constantly an issue for the men in the Jerusalém chorus whenever these two aspects diverged. Some of the men contended that whenever we rehearsed in the club's makeshift synagogue *kippot* should be worn, because in spite of the multiple uses of the synagogue, it was nevertheless a sacred space.[28] Others contended that *kippot* should be worn whenever we sang liturgical material, since we were singing prayers and the name of God was being spoken.[29] Those men who were not observant were just as likely to forget to take off their *kippot* to sing Gershwin as they were to forget to put them on to sing "Oseh Shalom." Since these discussions provided guidelines but not firm rules, at any given moment in the chorus there were men wearing a *kippah* alongside bare-headed men.

Discussion about the circumstances under which the *kippah* should be worn also arose in contexts that had less to do with respecting sacred space or time than with reconciling religious observance with the secular and potentially hostile world. For men who were "ultra-Orthodox,"[30] whether to wear a *kippah* was not an issue, since this was a core practice. However, men in less rigorous denominations, including the Modern Orthodox movement, varied in their public use of religious garments and sometimes explained their decision not to wear a *kippah* in terms of the responses of others. One man who drove all over the city as part of his work would have preferred to wear a *kippah*, but wore a baseball cap as a head covering instead in order to avoid the conflicts that his religious garment had previously provoked. Lesser describes his father-in-law's insistence that he remove his *kippah* as they stepped onto the street following Friday night services so as not to "take any chances," though there had never been any known incidents of aggression (Lesser 2001:66).[31] One young man who was completing his studies at the University of Campinas and in the process of becoming more deeply observant did not feel comfortable or entirely safe wearing a *kippah* in Campinas, where there is only a very tiny and dispersed Jewish community. He had resolved to begin wearing a *kippah* on the street upon completing his studies and returning to São Paulo. Not only did the larger community afford a degree of safety allowing him to more fully observe his religion, but this possibility also reinforced his deepening sense of ethnic identity, moving it from the private to the public realm.

In large part, what is at stake for *paulistano* Jewish men in their decision to wear a *kippah* in public has little to do with risk taking or provoking anti-Semitic hostility, since they have generally suffered little harassment or violence as Jews in São Paulo. Instead, by wearing a *kippah* or otherwise marking themselves as different they forfeit their ability to "pass" as nonethnic, to be taken for *just* Brazilian. While those groups defined by color or "race" cannot opt whether to reveal their ethnicity, Jews have the privilege of being able to choose under what circumstances to "come out" as ethnic. Invisibility, whether of institutions or individuals, is a tactic for survival and success that is available to those who are not "marked" as different.[32] The choice to intentionally differentiate themselves can be interpreted by some as a rejection of Brazilian national identity and its projected desire for a racially and ethnically blended future. When Jews choose to distinguish themselves from other Brazilians they not only invigorate latent anti-Semitism but they also raise doubts about their exclusionary practices among Brazilians for whom cultural miscegenation is the idealized goal.

Wearing a *kippah* in public, whether in the context of a political protest or everyday life, extends far beyond an expression of religious piety and into the realm of identity. Another example of a religious obligation transformed into an ethnic symbol is in the way that some people put *mezuzah* casings on their doors without the parchment, since it is the parchment and not the casing which fulfills the *mitzvah*; the casing becomes a literally empty but nevertheless meaning-laden symbol. Where the *mezuzah* serves as an ethnic symbol, the relationship is the reverse; the scroll is invisible and therefore not as significant as the external display, one that is indicative not of compliance but rather of *belonging*. As such, these religious objects undergo what DaMatta calls the "process of symbolization," by which objects become imbued with symbolic meaning, or, in this case, move from "one domain to another" (1991a:70). Where these symbols have different valences for Jews and non-Jews, the task for Jews is to navigate between what the intended meanings of these symbols are and the way they are interpreted by others.

In some cases, what is intended as largely functional may be transformed into a symbol, as in the case of the blocks of concrete in front of some Jewish institutions, which acquire added significance in the Brazilian context. These concrete blocks are a potent example of the protective measures that draw uncomfortable attention to the limits of Jewish belonging in the Brazilian nation. They do so because the response to the security problems posed by both national-level urban violence and international terrorism highlight some of the ways that local, national, and global contexts intersect in the practice of ethnic community identity. The need to create safe spaces often translates into the creation of separate spaces that reinforce a distinct ethnic identity and suggest a desire for separation and exclusion, even if that is not their intention.

Antiterrorist Flowerpots

The most obvious and the most problematic of the security measures recommended by the FISESP following the attack on the AMIA are the concrete barriers placed on the sidewalks in front of the entrances to several
edifices housing Jewish organizations in the city, including synagogues
and schools. Placed on the street, that is, in public space, these concrete
barricades are key elements of the security systems of these institutions.
Poorly disguised as ungainly *floreiras*, flower pots, their purpose is to de-
ter car or truck bombs. Without a history of this kind of violence in Brazil, and given the general population's minimal knowledge of Jews and
international events, the fortifications appear to the non-Jewish neighbors
of these institutions as little more than inhospitable invasions of public
space. For the general population without ties to the Jewish community
and without the memory or an appreciation of the local significance of
the events in Argentina, the concrete barriers appear preemptive. They
are seen as hostile rather than defensive, and as an indication of the Jewish community's unwillingness to integrate into Brazil, evidence of the
Jewish community's presumed desire to close itself off from the broader
society. Anecdotal evidence of exclusive Jewish clubs and business practices and endogamous marriage practices are offered by non-Jews with
minimal contact with the community. Rarely are these security measures
seen within the context of globalized anti-Jewish or anti-Israeli violence.

It is just this kind of violence directed at Jews scattered throughout the
world, and the clear demonstration that international borders are per-
meable, that forces the Jewish population in Brazil to recognize its own
transnational status. It imposes a kind of invisible limit on the extent to
which even fully "assimilated" Jews can be *just* Brazilian.[33] Frequent reminders of Jews in Germany or Egypt who thought they had successfully
integrated into their respective societies only to find that they were the
first to be rounded up or expelled in times of conflict remind Jews that
they will always be seen as Jews.

While the concrete barriers are unique to Jewish institutions, they are
an extension of the heightened concern with security and the elaborate
security systems deployed in edifices throughout São Paulo. Like the "talk
of crime" discussed by Caldeira, these security systems are also part of a
feedback loop, as their existence reinforces the perception of a security

problem, encouraging further investment in and elaboration of security systems.

Although the problems of violence are common to urban centers throughout Brazil, the *paulistano* response is particularly intense, and the response of the Jewish community and its institutions is consistent with this local cultural milieu. The situation in Jewish institutions in Rio de Janeiro provides an illuminating contrast. Though I did not carry out formal or structured research in Rio, home to Brazil's second-largest Jewish community, I did visit some key institutions and conducted a few interviews with members of the community and community leaders. While Rio de Janeiro suffers from arguably worse endemic violence, significant cultural differences between the two cities offer a distinct repertoire from which the respective Jewish communities draw their responses to violence. Among the many differences between the Jewish communities in Rio and São Paulo is the lack of concrete barriers in front of Jewish institutions in Rio. Significantly, the general level of security at Jewish institutions is considerably lower than at their São Paulo counterparts. This difference is not because of a reduced risk of international anti-Jewish violence, but because Rio operates under a different set of norms for responding to the dangers of urban life and navigating ethnic and racial differences.

There are four Jewish clubs in Rio, none of which bear much resemblance to the Hebraica in São Paulo. When I asked people in Rio about this, they responded that because they had the beach they did not need a club. The exaggeratedly urban setting certainly conditions how the São Paulo community is organized. How these institutions respond to the question of security reveals key cultural differences between these two cities, each of which is emblematic of Brazil in distinct ways.

On one occasion, a friend's father took me to one of the four Jewish clubs in Rio where he used to be a member. Though he did not explain to me where we were headed or why, he clearly had something in mind. We got off the bus, walked off the street, and right through the front entrance of the club without so much as showing identification, let alone a membership card. He then led me up the stairs and right into the president's office, where he sat me down and told the president that I needed to talk to him. The contrast with the norm in São Paulo, where I had grown accustomed to the obsession with security, left me stunned, and at first all

I could think to ask the club president about was the lax security at his club. He responded: "You and I, we don't have security. Nobody can *give* you security—they can only *transmit* [a feeling of] it." When I pushed the question further, raising the FISESP recommendations and commenting on the low security I had come across in Rio institutions in general, he admitted, "They are right, and we are wrong." However, he added that the social consequences of raising walls and barriers and enforcing institutional segregation would be far more damaging to the community relative to the gains made through what he considered a false sense of security. The security equation has vulnerability on one side and discrimination on the other. The ideology about Rio having greater racial and ethnic openness poses another layer of problems for the *carioca* Jewish community in deciding what measures to take to protect itself from the possibility of attack.[34]

Without wishing to oversimplify the many distinctions between Rio and São Paulo, it appears that the Jewish communities in these two cities differ in ways that are consistent with their broader cultural and social contexts. Jews in São Paulo are *paulistanos*, and it is as *paulistanos* that they respond to the risk of attack and to events in Jewish communities in other locales. In other words, they respond within the cultural repertoire of São Paulo. The question of security is where these registers of experience, the local and the global, overlap, exposing contradictions between general *paulistano* norms and Jewish *paulistano* needs. The redoubled security efforts in the face of both local and transnational sources of potential danger are situated within the local response to the broader condition of violence.

Back in São Paulo, when I asked official permission to take pictures of the concrete barricades lined up on the sidewalk in front of one of the major Jewish institutions, I knew that I would very likely be denied. The director balked, of course, when I asked if he would in effect allow me to take photographs of an important part of the institution's security system, and a controversial part of it at that. I explained that I wanted to be able to illustrate the double problem of security faced by the Jewish community in São Paulo, that I understood that the concrete barriers represented a double bind, as both protection from violent attacks in the form of car bombs and as a measure that had drawn negative attention to the community by suggesting that Jews wished to close themselves off from the rest of Brazil. In presenting my research, I explained, I would need to talk about the barriers, and preferred to be able to show them.

If I had tried to take pictures without authorization I would have risked having the security guards come after me and even confiscate my camera and call the police, as had happened to a colleague while he was taking photos of the barriers in front of another Jewish institution.[35] I also could have driven quickly past in a taxi and taken the pictures, as the reporter from the national newsweekly *Veja* had apparently done for an article criticizing the barricades. Acknowledging these alternatives, I explained to the director that my purpose was not simply to take the photos, and was certainly not to make him uneasy. I sought his collaboration, wanting him to understand what the photos were for and why I felt they were necessary. He called in another director, and I explained the whole story again, showing them the gold-sealed letters of introduction from the University of California that explained my research. It turned out that what carried the most weight in establishing my legitimacy and sincerity was the letter from one of the directors at the Hebraica giving me blanket permission to photograph on the club's grounds. This letter had become necessary after an earlier incident when the club's security guards prevented me from photographing a banner hung near one of the club entrances on which a politician congratulated the community for the Jewish New Year. Though I never needed these documents again at the Hebraica, I carried them with me at all times and had many occasions to present them. The permission and confidence that I was granted at the Hebraica carried more currency within the local idiom of security than my passport and university affiliation.

By the end of our conversation, we were clearly in agreement that the barriers posed a dilemma and caused misunderstanding. I was given permission to take as many photos as I needed with the understanding that I would not mention the name of the institution or take any pictures that showed the front entrance, thereby protecting the rest of the security system from scrutiny should my photos fall into the wrong hands. Toward that end, I was accompanied by one of the uniformed security guards, who kept a rather watchful eye on the angle of my camera and corrected my position more than once. In truth, I was grateful for his company and protection so I could concentrate on taking the photos and not have to worry about my two cameras being swiped as I shifted my attention from street vigilance to photographic composition.

I ended up taking many fewer photos while doing fieldwork than I had expected, partially as a consequence of the usual state of alert necessary while out in the city. Like millions of others I felt vulnerable on the streets of São Paulo. I followed the advice of those with a lifetime of experience in making their way through the city and avoided carrying valuables, chose my routes carefully, and did not stop along the way to look around and marvel at modernity reaching skyward. I saw photo opportunities everywhere, but knowing full well that static images cannot describe the complexity of the city, I heeded the warnings and preferred not to risk drawing attention to myself or being caught unawares. Having the guard by my side allowed me to drop that defensive stance, if only for a few moments.

Upon taking the last photo, a close-up of one of the flowers planted in the strips of dirt on top of the barriers, I realized that there was something more than utilitarian defensiveness being communicated by these clunky concrete blocks. As with the grave desecrations in the Buenos Aires cemetery, these blocks also contained a coded message, perhaps intended for potential perpetrators of violence, perhaps for the surrounding community. It was with a certain sadness that it dawned on me that the flowers planted in these homely antiterrorist flowerpots were *Spathiphyllum*, popularly known as *lírio-da-paz* (peace lily). The offering of peace was there for whoever wished to look for meaning.

For Jews in São Paulo, security measures express the overarching tensions in their lives, those between visibility and invisibility, between wanting recognition and wanting anonymity, and between distinction and belonging. While living comfortably with contradictions is a familiar condition of life in Brazil, some of the ambivalence among Jews is due to the distant but ever-present reminders of their vulnerability. The redoubled security efforts, or better, their double *insecurity*, is one facet of the tensions inherent in being both Jewish and Brazilian. Global and local levels of experience are intertwined such that Jews in São Paulo respond to dangers in local ways, even while their responses threaten to destabilize precisely that desired national identification. As Jews, they cannot afford to ignore what happens beyond the borders of Brazil. Yet it is precisely this orientation that marks them as different, as something other than simply

Brazilian. It is not so much their diasporic identity per se but rather their transnational status and practices that set them apart, in some ways that appear quite literal. Where they feel the tension the most is in their embrace of Brazilian openness even while having to construct their own barriers against it, effectively blockading the unqualified inclusion that is the hope that Brazil offers.

7

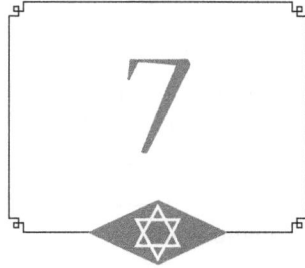

Cosmopolitans at Home

The theme of contradictions permeates anthropological studies of Brazil. Scholars seek to account for a democratic nation that so clearly excludes a majority of its citizens from the full rights of citizenship (i.e., Holston 2008). Some wonder at the continual clash of traditional and modern institutional forms (Hess and DaMatta 1995). Others try to make sense of the continued embrace of the ideal of racial democracy in a nation with such obvious and extreme racial inequality (i.e., Sheriff 2001). Still others seek to explain how humor and unbridled joy can coexist along-side brutal violence (Goldstein 2003). Brazilians themselves simply shrug and say, "This is Brazil," elevating the fact of contradiction as if it were a national characteristic. Perhaps this is simply the modern condition, one in which the process of becoming is exposed. It is certainly a process for Jewish Brazilians, who, according to some views, seem to contradict some core notion of what it means to be Brazilian. If accepting contradictions is another element of national culture, alongside racial ideologies, then perhaps being Brazilian gives Jews an edge; rather than expecting the contradictions to resolve, they become integrated into core beliefs and practices, part of being and becoming Brazilian, even as their condition as Jews and transnationals places limits on their belonging.

Porgy and Bess

Although ethnographies typically begin with an "arrival scene" (Pratt 1986), I began this exploration with a departure scene, since departures so often crystallize what months of fieldwork have not made clear. Similarly, reflections at the end of a project make sense out of seemingly opaque occurrences at the outset, so here I return to the opening scenes of my introduction to the people who would become my community for those dense months of fieldwork.

The beginning of my fieldwork and integration into the Jewish community in São Paulo and "the city called Hebraica" corresponded to the intensification of the rehearsals for a production of George Gershwin's *Porgy and Bess*. The Jerusalém chorus had performed a few songs from the opera in the past, but this time it was joining with the theater and dance sections of the club's Youth Department to put on a full production, a formidable project.

The chorus was already familiar with the maestro's ambitious undertakings. He had sealed his reputation for being able to squeeze blood from stones (the stones being an amateur chorus and the blood being beautiful music) with a prize won at a choral competition in Israel. Even more impressive was the gala event the previous year celebrating Israel's fiftieth anniversary when the chorus performed Beethoven's Ninth Symphony with a full orchestra. The selection had been the maestro's choice, since the symphony is associated with peace. When several chorus members protested that they were unwilling to celebrate Israel's anniversary by singing in German, a compromise solution was found: a group of chorus members translated the entire choral arrangement into Yiddish, which they believed was unprecedented. After these experiences, the chorus members trusted the maestro's ability to pull off an opera in English, even one as musically complex as Gershwin's opus.

The maestro had simplified and reduced the score so that it could be played by six musicians, and only the key pieces were to be performed by the chorus and a group of six professional singers, five of whom were black, something that especially pleased the maestro. In order for the audience to follow the sung English, the maestro pulled strings and arranged for the use of the municipal opera company's overhead translation board. The remainder of the storyline was condensed and told in Portuguese through a combination of theatrical presentation and narration.

At the point when I began to participate in the chorus, the maestro and the theater director (an established actor whom everyone delighted in seeing in humorous television commercials for household products) were considering having the chorus put on blackface, or at least dark makeup in order to represent the black people whose lives are represented in the opera. Since we would be performing an abridged version of the piece, we would not be violating Gershwin's stipulation that the complete three-hour opera be performed by an all-black cast. Nevertheless, performing in blackface certainly seemed to be a violation of the spirit of Gershwin's intent. Somehow I got involved in the conversation, perhaps because I had already been enlisted to help with the English pronunciation, but I soon registered my concerns. For my concerns to make sense, I needed to explain a little about the racist significance of blackface caricatures in the U.S. historical context. That the opera had opened the doors for hundreds of black artists in the United States was later echoed by the black Brazilian professional opera singers who played the lead roles in our production.[1] Eliseth Gomes and Edna de Oliveira, who played Serena and Bess, respectively, commented that even in Brazil these many years later they owed their careers to Gershwin.[2] Wearing blackface seemed to also contradict the maestro's intended message in selecting this piece for presentation, which he explained as an exploration of common experiences shared by blacks and Jews. In the end, an alternative was found, and the solution contributed greatly toward advancing the maestro's humanist project and tying it explicitly to Jewishness.

Following Gershwin's overture, the production opened with a narrator setting the context, addressing the audience in the Arthur Rubenstein Theater:

I ask your permission to tell this story. I appeal to the imagination of this distinguished audience. We are in the 1930s in a city in the United States. This stage is now the patio of an old, abandoned mansion . . . a *cortiço*,[3] to be more specific! Here on the margins live good people . . . and some, not so good. It is this world, marginal, oppressed, hopeful, black, that Gershwin decided to sing . . . Gershwin, a Jew. As you will see, not all the singers, actors, dancers, and musicians who will tell this story are black. (Laughs.) This is, so to speak, in honor of Gershwin, black people, and liberty! It is with the permission of our esteemed composer and your attention that we now begin.[4]

This appeal to the imagination was reinforced by the minimalist stage set and understated costuming, which presented a simplicity that belied the tremendous amount of work involved. The months of preparation culminated in a single, sold-out, evening performance, one that exceeded even our most hopeful expectations.

On the night of the performance, following the final preparations, the fifty or so members of the chorus gathered on the stage to warm up our voices. During rehearsals we had always completed warm-ups with one of the songs from the production. That night, however, someone spontaneously suggested we sing "Oseh Shalom."

Oseh shalom bimeromav,
hu yaaseh shalom aleinu
veal kol Yisraeil,
veimeru: amen.

He, who maketh peace in high places,
May he make peace for us,
And for all Israel,
And say ye, Amen.

These brief words have been sung to many melodies and the chorus regularly sang three versions. In addition to the simple melody sung in many communities, and the lovely and difficult version set to music by Felix Mendelssohn that the liturgical choir was especially fond of, there was a lyrical version in three voices sung by both choirs. It was the last that we all knew by heart, and we sang it while standing in a semicircle in the halo of light on stage in the final moments before the doors were opened to the crowd waiting outside. The resonance of our voices filled the darkened theater as we sang for ourselves, leaving many with a sensation of floating that some reported carrying with them throughout what turned out to be an emotionally powerful performance.

As in the full version of the opera, the performance ended with Porgy and the entire cast singing the finale, "I'm on My Way . . ."

I'm on my way
. . . to a Heav'nly Lan'
oh Lawd, It's a long, long way,
but you'll be there to take my han' . . .

When the curtain closed on the final chords the entire cast let out a loud whoop of elation (for which the maestro later chided us) and set about embracing each other. One woman from the chorus turned to me and said, "Well, you'll certainly have a lot to write about, won't you?" I was startled and pleased that she understood that this collective experience had everything to do with what I sought to understand about being Jewish in Brazil. Porgy's search for Bess against all odds was simultaneously spiritual and material, just as the Jewish search for home is an incomplete process, one that never finds complete resolution.

At Home in the World

The going "home" of return migrants is different from making someplace home for those without a place to return to, and it requires the deployment of different sorts of symbols.[5] Both require imagining community. Both draw on certain memories and reconstructions of the past. The former justifies itself in relation to physical place, whereas the latter occurs in spite of geographic continuity.

The concept of home or homeland is integrally connected to the concept of diaspora. For some dispersed peoples, home is a nation-state, a specific place from which they have been exiled and to which they hope, one day, to return. For other dispersed peoples no place is home, meaning that there is no physical, knowable, geographically delineated space for which they long. Their origins are embedded in irretrievable layers of movement, prior to the existence of nation-states. Their deterritorialized existence is integral to their identity as a people. Both kinds of dispersed peoples employ symbolic representations of home in the maintenance of their group identity, and the more heterogeneous the group the more obvious the constructed nature of this symbolic capital.

Insofar as national identity is constructed out of a shared sense of the past, ethnic differentiation within a nation threatens the cultural resemblances that are the mainstay of national unity. It is to this "imagined" unity, an identity in the literal sense, to which Anderson refers with his concept of "imagined community" (1991[1983]). It is the will to overlook internal variation for the sake of creating a unified whole (Herzfeld 1997). Nationalizing projects depend on this appeal to shared past, insist on shared language, and, wherever possible, erase cultural difference. Under certain circumstances, heterogeneous ethnic groups engage in similar processes of construction through imagination, bridging, and erasure. The ongoing and active nature of transnational relations poses direct challenges to both of these endeavors, the assimilating processes of national identity and the unifying processes of ethnic identity, as transnational peoples seek to create home in their nations of origin while simultaneously reaching across national and cultural boundaries in search of a sense of extranational belonging.

Throughout this book I have considered examples of the diasporic and transnational qualities of Jewish Brazilians. Their condition of diaspora is most evident at the moments of immigration, when Jews came to Brazil from so many points on the globe, bringing with them significant cultural differences. Their common identity as Jews, based on a belief in a shared origin, has been central to the creation of a community in Brazil through mostly secular organizations. Drawing on national ideologies of inclusion, these communal organizations have facilitated the Brazilification of the Jewish community through the use of Portuguese and the incorporation of Brazilian practices, including holidays, into the Jewish repertoire. The deepening of their Brazilian identity is reflected most significantly in the ways they have embraced Brazil's reigning racial and ethnic ideologies to explain the way the community has been accepted in Brazil with minimal experiences of anti-Semitism and the way the community has blended its many cultural differences, but also in their reproduction of certain exclusionary practices that are typical of the national social class hierarchy. It is their transnational condition, indicated by their external ties as well as by the possibility of violence directed against them, which places limits on their national identity, thereby reinforcing this transnational identity.

In Brazil, ethnic differentiation poses a particular sort of problem, especially when it concerns a group that has been welcomed, has done well, and after generations can *pass* as Brazilian. Overt and intentional markers of difference, whether a *kippah* or a concrete barrier, are taken as an affront, a rejection of the ideology of inclusion and equality among races that is espoused by the nation. For a group that is both diasporic and transnational, differentiation acknowledges another past, but also another present, and these markers are about honoring their distinct past(s) and dealing with their insistent present.

For Jews, it might appear that the problem of homeland was resolved with the creation of the state of Israel, and Israel capitalizes on its purposeful existence as the homeland for world Jewry. However, regardless of earlier historical ties to the land and the present significance that Israel holds for Jews throughout the world, modern Israel is not the nation of origin of most of the world's Jews. As I have said, it is a *product* of the Diaspora, not its solution. For Jews who are at home in Brazil, their relationship to Israel is a constant reminder of the overlapping valences of their diasporic and transnational status.

The dueling relationship between diaspora and transnationalism was made clear to me following a presentation I made at the Jewish bookstore Livraria Sêfer toward the end of my fieldwork. During the discussion, one man's comment about the continued interest in *aliyah* confused those present. Though the earlier ideologically driven interest among Brazilians to make *aliyah* had diminished considerably, this man insisted that the drive was still there. I knew the man speaking, and knew that he and his wife had made *aliyah* in their youth, and that like many others they had returned to Brazil with their two small children in the mid-1980s. As he sought to explain his point it became clear that he was extending "*aliyah*" from its usual meaning of taking citizenship and permanently settling in Israel to include *visiting* Israel. In other words, Jews can enact their diasporic identity by traveling to Israel, to maintain ties with family and friends living there, and to engage in the kind of "heritage tourism" that is practiced by other diaspora groups as well.

The fact that Jews today can take advantage of modern technologies of transport and communication to maintain active contacts in Israel and in other locales is an expression of their transnationalism. That Brazilian Jews can employ these same technologies to visit Israel and call it "*aliyah*" is an expression of their diasporic imagination. Decol sets Zionism and *aliyah* within the larger "circular movement between Brazilian and other big Jewish population settlements, mainly Israel, Argentina and [the] United States" (2009:106). This economically motivated "circular movement" is typical of the "transnational *habitus*" to which Guarnizo (1997) refers and provides a practical framework for diasporic imaginings. In other words, however much Israel may hold a special place in the hearts and minds of Jews scattered about the globe, in the contemporary world practical considerations make Israel one of many points in a constellation of homelands.

Perhaps these are not such new phenomena, but are simply familiar experiences dressed up in new academic terms. Joining the fray of imprecise terms, "cosmopolitanism" has returned with chameleonic versatility. By reminding us of some of its past negative meanings, David Harvey underscores the recent transformation of the term: "Shaking off the negative connotations of its past (when Jews, communists, and cosmopolitans were so frequently cast as traitors to national solidarities), [cosmopolitanism] is now portrayed by many . . . as a unifying vision for democracy and governance"(2000:529).

Nevertheless, as Pollock et al. (2000) note, it is possible to talk about cosmopolitanism without reciting its genealogy from the Stoics through Kant. Paul Rabinow's explanation offers useful clarification: "Let us define cosmopolitanism as an ethos of macro-interdependencies, with an acute consciousness (often forced upon people) of the inescapabilities and particularities of place, characters, historical trajectories, and fates" (1996:56). In its current usage to indicate a mode of being, then, cosmopolitanism encompasses an awareness of the role of history in making the present, and the contingencies of place, such that identity cannot be tied to territory alone.

Historically, charges of cosmopolitanism have been levied against Jews during times of rising nationalism. In the Brazilian context it seems possible to reorient the relationship between national and cosmopolitan through the framework of *antropofagia*, the modernists' call to cultural cannibalism that seeks to break down rigid categories in favor of blended identities and practices. By enacting a grounded sense of belonging (*cidadania*) with the righteousness of *tzedakah*, perhaps Jewish (and other transnational) Brazilians can find their equilibrium within their nation of origin. Changes since the 1990s have found Brazil in seventh place in the world economy, while social programs have lifted thirty million out of poverty. It will be interesting to observe the changes in the meaning of transnationalism and cosmopolitanism as Brazil's footing in the world economic power structure grows more secure.

Perhaps this view of a "balancing act" can help to make sense of the contradictions that are evident in the lives of Jewish Brazilians. Recalling

Caldeira and Holston's analysis (1999) of the tension between political and civil democracy in Brazil as being reflective of the *process* of democratization, I would like to suggest two sources of tension for Jewish Brazilians that are reflective of the processes of both Brazilianization and ethnic-identity consolidation. These processes occur simultaneously, such that we see within the community contradictory trends toward greater religiosity and greater secularization. Pollock et al. also stress the need "to learn to live tenaciously in terrains of historic and cultural *transition*" (2000:580). Being cosmopolitan means having an acute awareness of not having arrived, of being continually in flux, of learning to live with instability (and insecurity) as part of the condition of being.

These processes are continuous, fed by the tensions and contradictions that are also their product. In this way, the question of identity that is at the heart of cosmopolitanism is not so very different from the accepted understanding of ethnicity as constructed at its borders rather than as consistent in its content (Barth 1969). When Pollock et al. refer to instances of cosmopolitanism as evidence of "ways of living at home abroad or abroad at home—ways of inhabiting multiple places at once, of being different beings simultaneously, of seeing the larger picture stereoscopically with the smaller" (2000:587), they are echoing the concepts of situated and multiple identities developed during earlier studies of ethnicity.

Where all of this comes to bear on being Jewish and Brazilian is in the tension between the desire for recognition and the desire for invisibility, the former being an expression of integration and participation in national society and culture, and the latter being a defensive posture taken by those accustomed to living in fear.[6] Other contradictions stem from the desires for group continuity and belonging, but belonging can have many objects, differently defined, including local group, nation, and the imagined, extended Diaspora. Perhaps the biggest contradiction is a reflection of just how much local, class-based values and practices have been incorporated into the community and become consolidated as "Jewish" in that context.

Jews in São Paulo have embraced the ideals of inclusion while engaging in the practices of exclusion. In this, they are expressing both their Brazilianness and their Jewishness. The club, the expensive *kit*, the increasing poverty of the community as a symptom of its Brazilification, and the ways in which the community explains its internal integration in terms of the nation are all ramifications of these tensions. The irony that the community protects itself from transnational threats in ways that are both local and translocal reveals the highly dynamic articulation between these levels of experience.

This is the essence of diasporic experience: no ideal, no ideology, no amount of integration can erase the past. The present is imbued with it, and the future is limited by it. Those who forget lose a part of themselves (and run the risk of losing all). Those who remember are always outsiders.

Living Comfortably with Contradictions

There are similarities among the identities, experiences, and aspirations of diasporic and transnational peoples across the globe, and yet there is something particular about the Brazilian context that shifts the meaning of these parallel experiences of being in the world. Part of this difference can be explained by the national ideologies of Brazil, and part by the tolerance for contradiction that imbues Brazilian culture. Clearly, a facile understanding of national belonging as being based on legal citizenship does not begin to explain the symbolic and emotional aspects of *cultural* belonging that are at the core of what it means to be Brazilian. Scholars have introduced the concept of "cultural citizenship" as a way of illuminating the extralegal sense of pertaining to a place and a culture, in the broadest sense.

First introduced by Renato Rosaldo as part of a multisited group research project on Latino identity in the United States, for Rosaldo "cultural citizenship" emphasizes the tension between a concept that is technical and legal and the nuance and flexibility of culture (1994a, 1994b). According to Rosaldo, the concept of cultural citizenship "refers to the right to be different" (1994a:402). For Chicanos, these differences range across linguistic, religious, racial, and ethnosocial distinctions from majority society, as well as across differences among Latinos.

The idea of cultural citizenship is an explicit rejection of assimilationist ideology that would have immigrants and ethnics abandon their differences at the door of national belonging. It rejects homogenizing forces and implies a construction of nationhood that does not merely tolerate difference, but instead depends upon it. Like many ideologies, it is a goal to be attained rather than a reality to be explained, a hope, an objective, a guiding principle.[7]

Rosaldo intended the term "cultural citizenship" to be a "deliberate oxymoron" (1994a:402). However, it strikes me as a familiar paradox for transnational peoples for whom their identity is rooted elsewhere and whose position in the here-and-now is always conditional and suspect. Further, in thinking about what she called the "flexible citizenship" of transnationals, Aihwa Ong (1999) introduced another view of cultural citizenship, one that takes into account state power. Whereas Rosaldo discusses the agency of ethnic minorities to assert their cultural difference, Ong highlights the power of the state to "establish the criteria of belonging" (1996:738). Drawing on Foucault, Ong points out that citizens undergo a dialectical "cultural process of 'subject-ification'" (1996:737) such that they are both made by and make themselves within prevailing power relations. Ong asks us to consider the place of "minorities of color," specifically, of "immigrants of color" in the First World, in order to understand the elements of power associated with cultural citizenship.

However, it is important to examine these processes not only in the First World, but in the Third World as well. In the Third World context of places like Brazil, where "color" is differently constituted, it is worth considering what Ong calls the "processes of normalization: an ideological whitening or blackening that reflects dominant racial oppositions" (1996:737) in the context of Brazil's racial spectrum. What is meant by "minorities of color" is not self-evident outside of the United States, and it takes on an entirely new meaning within other regimes of racial/color and cultural hierarchies. With regard to Jewish Brazilians, I am considering the place of a First World minority in the context of a Third World nation, and their acceptance into the dominant social and racial ideology.

In examining the experiences of Jewish Brazilians in São Paulo I am considering a different set of intersecting power relations that shed light from a different angle on the idea of cultural citizenship. The majority of Jews in Brazil, though certainly not all, descend from European nations. Most of their family members left as emigrants, refugees, and exiles at a time when Jews were defined by an inferior racial status. In the First World, they became marginalized minorities, racially and culturally inferior, and stripped of their status and rights as citizens of the nations in which they were born and had lived for generations, if not centuries.[8] Many arrived in this developing nation as impoverished peasants and peddlers, and they rapidly moved up the economic ladder from itinerant salesmen to industrialists and "liberal" professionals. The potential for acceptance was readily evident to racially marginalized refugees from war-torn Europe. They were eventually able to blend into the Southern European framing of whiteness in Brazil such that most Jews hold a place at the "white" end of the socioracial spectrum.

As such, it is not racial differences that mark or separate them. Nor is their religious difference an issue, except for the most Orthodox among them. Rather, it is their condition as transnationals that introduces an element of doubt to an otherwise felicitous relationship between Jews and Brazil.

Toward the end of my field research, I had occasion to talk about the interplay of legal and cultural citizenship with Samuel Malamud, a distinguished representative of the Brazilian Jewish community in Rio de Janeiro. Among Jewish Brazilians, Samuel Malamud was iconic, a quintessential Brazilian Jew, if there is such a thing. It was not that his self-presentation was particularly Jewish.[9] He did not wear a *kippah* or *peyot* (sidelocks). In contrast to the heavy black suits worn by Orthodox Jews, he wore white linen suits that were more appropriate to the tropical and social climate of Rio de Janeiro. In fact, he abandoned religion just after his eighteenth birthday, except for observing the rituals of *kaddish* and *yizkor*, the mourners' prayers of remembrance for his diseased parents— out of filial respect rather than religious piety. Born in the Ukraine in 1908, Malamud recalled watching the Russian civil war from the window of his home before he and his family fled in 1920. On the opposite side of the world, in the final months of the twentieth century, Samuel Malamud gave lucid testimony to his role in the changing place of Jews since his arrival in Rio in 1923 at the age of fifteen.

I spoke with Malamud in November of 1999, just four months before he passed away at the age of ninety-one. A colleague in Rio thought I should talk with him, so we arranged to meet after the second annual national Judaic studies conference, where Doutor Samuel was given yet another in a long line of awards for his lifetime of work on behalf of the Brazilian Jewish community.[10] I accompanied him to his apartment overlooking the famed Copacabana Beach and the sparkling Bay of Guanabara, to his living room filled with books and art, where our conversation was occasionally punctuated by his maid offering *cafezinho*, the strong Brazilian coffee that is a mark of Brazilian cordiality.

Doutor Samuel illustrated numerous points in our conversation with experiences from his own remarkable life. He did not merely witness the welcome and absorption of Jewish immigrants into Brazilian society; he played an active role in their acceptance as *Jews* over the course of the better part of a century. He did so by carving out a space for himself, deliberately, as both Jewish and Brazilian, simultaneously operating from both of these sources of his identity, unwilling to favor one over the other, insistent that these two identities could be reconciled in an overt way. Malamud operated within a particular concept of citizenship such that his life offers a way to think about, extend, and perhaps discover some of the limits of the concept of "cultural citizenship."

The tension introduced by the perceived foreignness of Jews and the contours of Jewish Brazilian citizenship in the twentieth century were clearly illustrated in Doutor Samuel's life. Like the portentous beginning of some great historical saga, Malamud arrived in Brazil on November 15, the anniversary of the Proclamation of the Republic—the equivalent of the 4th of July in the United States. Having fled Russia, and then Romania, Malamud and his family found refuge in Rio de Janeiro, then the capital of Brazil, where, as he explained, there was "no need to say who you are or where you come from . . . No one denies you Brazilian nationality because you are a Jew." His family soon moved to the immigrant neighborhood of Praça Onze, what Malamud described in his own writings as the "nerve center" of the Ashkenazi community (Malamud 1988:13), where he attended high school and got involved in community activities. With a gift for languages, he picked up Portuguese without a detectable foreign accent, acquiring the soft shushing of the *carioca* accent of Rio. A polyglot, Doutor Samuel spoke eight languages: Portuguese, Hebrew, Russian, Yiddish, English, French, German, and Spanish. The only language he ever forgot was Romanian, having lost his ability to speak it almost as soon as the boat pulled away as his family headed to Brazil. Like so many European Jews, especially Polish Jews who no longer spoke the languages of their home countries, Doutor Samuel explained that the language had become tainted for him "because of anti-Semitism." Interestingly, this association was personal and psychological rather than ideological, or he would not have retained some of the other languages in his repertoire.

Like so many Jewish Brazilians, Malamud felt a strong dual identity: "I feel Brazilian, but I also feel Jewish," he explained. Throughout his long life, he was accepted as both. Malamud felt this dual loyalty and a dual purpose when he was still a young man. He became a Brazilian citizen in 1929, at the age of twenty-one. Although he had already been in the country for six years, he encountered difficulty obtaining his citizenship when an official of the Ministry of Justice noted on his application that he was Russian and would need to be recommended by an established person known to the minister, not unlike the "recommendation" necessary to gain entry to an exclusive club. Malamud later speculated that even though he had left Russia at the age of twelve, the official must have thought he "carried the communist revolutionary virus" and that he "represented a threat to the nation" (Malamud 1992:346–47). Having lived in what he characterized as a Jewish ghetto, Malamud had no connections to the politically powerful, but a member of the community was able to put him in touch with a lawyer who personally knew the minister and who formally took responsibility for Malamud's conduct, so that he was able to acquire his citizenship.

Upon being naturalized, the first thing he did was to sign up for "*tiro de guerra*," the military service that is required of all Brazil-born men. However, the service was not required of naturalized Brazilians, and most immigrants never questioned the distinction. Malamud went to the Ministry of War where he learned that without military service he would be a "third-class" citizen and would not be able to occupy public office. This limit on the practice of citizenship for immigrants was not revealed up front. "I would not have been a full citizen of Brazil. I did military service with the intention of becoming a citizen with equal rights." Without military service he would have been legally equal for most purposes, but still marked as different, foreign, presumably unprepared to defend the nation, and therefore unqualified to represent it.

He graduated with his law degree in 1932 from the Faculdade de Direito (Law School) of what is now the Federal University of Rio de Janeiro just as the nationalist integralist movement was gaining strength in Brazil, especially in the nation's capital. The Brazilian movement's fascist tendencies were tempered by antiracist sentiments, although there were strongly anti-Semitic leaders in the movement. In contrast to his experiences in Europe, where anti-Semitism was rife, Malamud acknowledged the existence of anti-Semitism in Brazil, but added that it did not lead to anything. Brazilians "are not anti-Semites *de berço*," from the cradle, he explained.

Malamud eventually became a judge, a position he could never have held had he not done military service. This drew some attention, and Malamud caught wind of a story that was circulating about a "Jewish judge" right there in the nation's capital—where the significance of "Jewish" as foreign was all the more meaningful in the context of growing nationalism.

Historian Maria Luiza Tucci Carneiro notes that Malamud was among the most active in Rio in helping Jews find refuge in Brazil during the war, even as there were secret efforts within the Ministry of Foreign Relations to exclude Jews from immigrating to Brazil (1997:20).[11] Malamud also played an important role in creating organizations to help other Jews integrate into Brazilian society.[12] As the Second World War began, he wrote a weekly column in the *Iidiche Presse* (Yiddish Press), in Yiddish, about the international political scene.[13] As the nativists gained control during the Vargas regime, all publications in a foreign language were suspended, and Malamud's commentaries on the war shifted to radio transmissions which he continued up through postwar evaluations in 1945.

He became an early and adamant supporter of the creation of the state of Israel. His activities turned international when in the immediate postwar period he represented Brazil at the World Zionist Congress. He served as secretary general of the Organização Sionista Unificada do Brasil (Unified Zionist Organization of Brazil) and president of the organization's Political Committee, 1945–48. He also served on the editorial board of the periodical *A Voz Sionista* (The Zionist Voice), founded in 1947. When the vice president of Brazil traveled to the new state of Israel, Malamud was there to interpret his meeting with Israeli prime minister Ben-Gurion. Malamud was selected to serve as Israel's honorary consul in Brazil for three years until diplomatic relations were established in large part through his negotiations with the Brazilian government.

His multiple activities in support of the establishment and recognition of the state of Israel in no way diminished the importance of his Brazilian identity, and specifically his *carioca* identity, as it was from his place within the community in Rio that he developed into a community representative.[14] He consistently made personal and professional choices that allowed him not only to be both Jewish and Brazilian, in equal measure, and with equal pride, but to *act* from that position, as a Jewish Brazilian. For his many contributions to the community and to bridging Jewish and Brazilian societies he was recognized with multiple honors, including the prestigious Order of Rio Branco (in 1966) from the Ministry of Foreign Relations for distinguished service to the Brazilian nation, and Honorary Citizen of the state of Rio de Janeiro (in 1973), an especially meaningful title given the choices he had made in his life.[15] Importantly, his efforts on behalf of Israel were not taken to mean that he was less committed to Brazil.

Clearly, these are not the accomplishments of an ordinary man. Malamud was able to simultaneously represent Jewish Brazilians and stand out as unique among them. Because of the deliberate way he went about acquiring and deploying an active form of legal citizenship he was able to extend the limits of cultural citizenship for other Brazilian Jews. Where he was able to push the limits and make unique contributions actually highlights the very place where the citizenship of Jews within the Brazilian nation is limited—their foreignness. It is their condition as transnationals, with active ties and commitments to people in other nations, that continues to pose a problem for the full, stable, and comfortable membership of Jews in the Brazilian nation. Whether they are involved in supporting Israel economically or politically, or visiting and marrying across other international boundaries, these active relationships shed doubt on their commitment to the nation.

For Jews in Brazil the concept of nation is centrally part of their identity, even as it poses limits to their belonging in any modern nation. Their cultural citizenship, their "right to be different," is always literally in relation to other nations. It is their condition as transnationals that continually throws doubt on their commitment to their national home. Yet, as a diaspora people, they cannot be anything other than transnational. When they set themselves apart from other white ethnics, when they mark themselves by dress or alliance with difference, they signal a distance that some interpret as rejection and others as threat, an alliance with something foreign, as if Jewishness were a form of exclusive nationality.[16]

In spite of these imposed limitations, Malamud was able to assert his citizenship, both cultural and legal, the latter specifically in relation to state power. He had access to and the ability to move in relation to state power, to overcome his status as immigrant while making use of his status as Jew. He used his Jewishness to make space for other Jews and to establish relations with the Jewish state. He drew on state power to affect state power.

In Malamud's case, as an immigrant, and a young man in the nation's capital during the height of nationalist ferment, the need for him to prove his loyalty to his new nation was even greater. Instead, he explicitly, publicly, and formally deployed both sources of his identity. Not only did he always operate from a base as both Brazilian and Jewish; he asserted a unified Jewish-Brazilian identity in relations with the state, as well. He spoke as a Brazilian Jew in favor of the creation of a Jewish state, and as a Brazilian Jew he represented the Jewish state in relations with the Brazilian state. Perhaps Doutor Samuel understood the centrality of state power in the dual processes of making oneself and being made. His sensibility was not one that can be explained in terms of being a minority or immigrant "of color," since these are not constructs that make sense in the Brazilian context. Nor did his understanding derive from an analysis of First World–Third World relations. Instead, his status as a member of a diaspora group, a group that has frequently been stripped of rights and citizenship, helped him understand the centrality of power in securing a place for Jews. This was his understanding at the international level. At the personal level, his sensibilities remained with Brazil, and his home in Rio, where he was "*ambientado*"—accommodated to the familiar environment, at *home*—and it was from this solid sense of home that he exercised his dual transnational identity.

Throughout his life, whenever prominent Jews came to Brazil, Malamud was involved, such as when Albert Einstein visited Brazil in 1925. As a young man, Malamud befriended and legally represented the cosmopolitan writer Stefan Zweig when he took refuge from the European atrocities. Malamud was also central to the establishment of key Jewish institutions in Rio, including the Jewish Federation of Rio and the Jewish Confederation of Brazil. He was cofounder (and eventually honorary president) of ORT (Organização, Reconstrução e Trabalho; Organization, Reconstruction, and Work) in Brazil, a school providing secondary education and professionalization courses originally for Jewish refugees to develop the necessary skills for survival, which he described as a Jewish school with mostly non-Jews. He was also vice president of World ORT (1980–90) and honorary vice president from 1990 to 2000, and remained active until his death. At the centenary celebration of Malamud's birth in August 2008, ORT Brazil director Hugo Malajovich said that "[h]e died . . . with his passport in his pocket in preparation for his journey to Jerusalem for the

World ORT General Assembly" (World ORT 2008). At the centenary cel-ebration, historian Paulo Geiger emphasized the "symbiotic relationship between his Brazilian and Jewish identities . . . [he was] a Brazilian, a Jew, and a Zionist Brazilian" (World ORT 2008). Of course, it was a Brazilian passport that he was carrying to that international meeting.

Malamud's example is interesting because he pushed the limits of xe-nophobia and showed that it was possible to be both Jewish and Brazilian. In exercising his citizenship, he insisted on full legal citizenship, which gave him a platform from which to speak as a Brazilian Jew. In so doing, he was part of opening a space for other Jews in Brazil to be Jewish in Brazil—that is, not to just assimilate, but to be transnational subjects with external ties and still strongly feel and exercise their Brazilianness.

Havdalah

Shabbat is time outside of time, and its end on Saturday evening is marked by the ceremony of Havdalah, separation. It signifies the return to secular time. Because the blessing makes reference to plural "lights,"[17] the candles are different from those used in other Jewish rituals. They are braided, and the multiple wicks make for a bigger flame and a brighter light. It seems fitting to leave this here, with the image of a braided candle made of strands representing multiple pasts and multiple presents.

Notes

Chapter 1. Departures

1. This is the Portuguese spelling, *carnaval*, in contrast to the norm in English-language publications which have favored the translation "Carnival." The Brazilian forms of this festival are culturally distinct and deserve to be linguistically marked as such. See also Hintzen (2001).

2. All names given here are fictitious, unless the individual was so well known and distinctive that it would be impossible or impractical to hide his or her identity, such as in cases where the person occupied a prominent or significant position vis-à-vis the community and spoke from that position.

3. B'nai B'rith translates as "Sons of the Covenant," and the international organization of this name is the best known Jewish humanitarian and community service organization in the world.

4. *Ashkenazi* refers to Jews from Central and Eastern Europe, originally from France and the Rhineland; Ashkenazim is the plural form.

5. The literature on religion in Brazil is enormous and encompasses studies of Catholicism and new Christianity (Burdick 1993, 1998), African-based religions such as Candomblé and Umbanda (see, e.g., Bastide 1978[1960], Johnson 2002, Landes 2006[1947], Ortiz 1991[1978]); Japanese-based religions old and new, including Buddhism, Seicho-no-ie, and the Church of World Messianity (Matsuoka 2007); various forms of Protestantism; and new syncretic religions such as Santo Daime.

6. In addition to Jews, other non-Christian groups include the many nonmissionized indigenous peoples throughout the country, as well as Muslims, who make up a small portion of the largely Christian Middle Eastern/Arab population (Karam 2007).

7. Myerhoff's film of the same name was awarded the best short documentary by the Academy of Motion Picture Arts and Sciences in 1976, the only ethnographic film that has received this distinction to date.

8. Barbara Kirshenblatt-Gimblett suggests that this may have also been the unintended consequence of Boas' approach to combating anti-Semitism through the repudiation of the concept of race; "if Jews did not exist as such, how could ethnographers describe their culture?" (1995:x).

9. According to Frank, Mandelbaum's article "The Jewish Way of Life in Cochin" is "probably the first ethnographic account to appear in print about a Jewish community by an American anthropologist" (1997:736). A student of Herskovits, Mandelbaum had already established himself as a scholar of India, and his research on Cochin's Jews is not among his best-known work. While anthropologists have subsequently studied other Jewish communities around the world, Mandelbaum's work is still remarkable for its focus on one of the lesser-known communities, which by definition and by his interpretation, continues to challenge our understandings of Jews and Jewishness.

10. This research does not address the many Brazilians who are descended from the *cristãos-novos*, *marranos*, or other forced converts, or "crypto-Jews," many of whom are not aware of their Jewish ancestry. See Ramagem (1994) for a discussion of the descendants of *cristãos-novos*, some of whom are now converting to Judaism in Brazil.

11. On the concept of double consciousness, see Du Bois 1990[1903]; see also Chandler 2000, Gilroy 1993.

12. The original dispersal refers to the *galut*, Hebrew for "exile," beginning in the sixth century B.C.E., at the time of the destruction of the first temple in Jerusalem.

13. In this, I depart from a precept of some forms of Zionism which posit that contemporary Israel does negate the original dispersal by bringing Jews from all corners of the world back to their homeland.

14. This concept is defined by Rosaldo as "the right to be different and to belong in a participatory democratic sense" (1994a:402). See also Ong 1996.

15. For a discussion of scientific racism in the significant period of 1870–1930, which saw the transition from slavery to immigrant labor, see Schwarcz 1993.

16. It is worth noting that Sorj is originally from Uruguay, part of the significant presence of Latin American Jewish scholars and professionals who immigrated to Brazil and became part of the transnational Jewish community.

17. An earlier generation of Brazilian scholars sought to understand contemporary Brazil through its past, most significantly in the seminal works of Gilberto Freyre (*Casa grande e senzala*, 1933, translated as *The Masters and the Slaves*, 1986a), Sérgio Buarque de Holanda, 1936 (*Raízes do Brasil*, 1995), and Caio Prado Jr. (*Formação do Brasil contemporâneo, colônia*, 1942, translated as *The Colonial Background of Modern Brazil*, 1967). For a discussion of these and other works that are central to social thought in Brazil, see Veloso and Madeira 1999.

One of the most celebratory and widely circulated examples of this construct is Zweig's *Brazil: Land of the Future* (1942, written in his native German and subsequently translated into numerous languages, including English and Portuguese). See also Hernane Tavares de Sá 1947. A more recent example is historian Marshall Eakin 1998. According to Bernardo Sorj, this ideology was consolidated in the 1950s with the establishment of the middle classes (1997:17). In addition to reiterations of the *"país do futuro"* (country of the future) construct, nowhere is this more evident than on the national flag, bearing the country's positivist motto: "Ordem e Progresso" (order and progress, which Freyre took as the title for his second volume on Brazilian civilization, 1986b). The rationale behind the invention of a new capital (abandoning the old colonial capital in Rio) and its high-modernist design also gives *concrete* evidence of the future orientation of the Brazilian nation (Holston 1989).

18. For a historical discussion of immigration policy and ethnicity in Brazil, see Lesser 1999. For reviews of the concept of a Jewish race, see Patai and Patai 1989, and Novinsky 1996.

19. Historians and literary scholars began to examine the experiences of groups outside of the three races in Brazil before anthropologists. In particular, Jeff Lesser's work has addressed Jewish, as well as Arab, Japanese, and Chinese, immigrants in Brazil.

20. Sephardi Jews are those whose ancestors lived in Sepharad, as the Iberian Peninsula was known during medieval times. Sephardim is the plural.

21. Some descendants of New Christians have organized the Abradjin, Associação Brasileira dos Descendentes de Judeus da Inquisição (Brazilian Association of the Descendants of Jews of the Inquisition), though this is an explicitly Christian organization.

22. The adjusted figures derived from the Brazilian census accounted for 86,000 Jews in Brazil in 1994 and 2000 (down from a peak of 90,000 in 1980) (Decol 1999, 2009). The larger estimates usually cited are derived from community sources and from calculations based on these numbers following a formula developed by demographer of world Jewry Sergio DellaPergola and used to estimate the size of the "extended" (as opposed to the "core") population of Jewish communities (DellaPergola 1993, 1999).

23. The other program, *Shalom Brasil*, suffered some setbacks while I was conducting research due to the sale of its cable transmitter to an evangelical Christian organization, which promptly removed the program from the air. Since then, *Shalom Brasil* has moved to another cable station, but one without the same level of national distribution.

24. In her study of "liberal" Jewish identity, Hemsi found that this ability to "agglutinate" (*aglutinar*) elements of the community that synagogues "pulverize" was part of what drew community members to the club (1997:106).

25. According to Jewish law, a Jew is the child of a Jewish mother; therefore neither my mother nor I would be considered Jewish.

26. Club officials estimated that non-Jews represented around 1 percent of the membership, including the staff of the U.S. consulate, which recommends the club to its employees. A 2003 article in the São Paulo edition of *Veja* commemorating the club's fiftieth anniversary made an unattributed claim that 95 percent of the membership was Jewish (Canecchio 2003). Federal antidiscrimination laws prohibit the exclusion of potential members on the basis of race or ethnicity, but very few non-Jews other than those married to Jews are likely to be interested in joining a Jewish club.

27. *Paulista* refers to people from the state of São Paulo, while *paulistano* refers to people from the state's capital city.

28. The club garnered attention for its innovative design from the time of its 1957 inauguration, when its gymnasium, by modernist architect Gregory Warchavchik, was featured (for the first but not the only time) on the cover of a prominent national architecture magazine (Cytrynowicz 2003:45). In 1960, a special issue of the international

architecture magazine *L'Architecture d'Aujourd'hui* focused on Brazilian architecture to commemorate the inauguration of the capital city of Brasília and included a section on the Hebraica club, which had continued to expand with the involvement of some of Brazil's most renowned architects (Cytrynowicz 2003:60). The club's landscaping was designed by none other than Roberto Burle Marx, responsible for the distinctive designs around government buildings in Brasília, the famous promenade along Copacabana beach in Rio, and Ibirapuera Park in São Paulo. The main building of the Hebraica club was designed by architect and urbanist Jorge Wilheim, who was also responsible for the Albert Einstein Hospital, among other structures in São Paulo, and numerous urban plans for major Brazilian cities. In 2001, he became the planning secretary for the city of São Paulo.

29. Fortuna is a Brazilian of Syrian Jewish descent who researches and records Sephardi music. Some of her recordings have gained international distribution.

30. Now called "Feliz Idade" (Happy Age), in the past these programs have been alternately called "Universidade Idade de Ouro (University for the Golden Age) and "University for the Third Age," drawing on other metaphors to frame these popular events for the elderly. See Debert (1997) for an analysis of the use and meaning of the concept of the Third Age in Brazil and public discourse about aging and the elderly.

31. I discuss the practice of naming public places in Chapter 5.

32. Ladino, also known as Judeo-Spanish, is a blend of old Spanish and Hebrew historically spoken among Sephardi Jews. I do not recall Hebrew being among the languages spoken by this group of women, which might be attributable to their age and gender, as it was not common for women of their generation (they would have grown up in the 1930s) to have received formal religious education. Furthermore, this particular group of women was not religious, so they were less likely to have acquired Hebrew at a later stage.

Chapter 2. Braided Lives

1. A *cavaquinho* is a ukulele-like instrument that is standard in samba and its variations.

2. Moreira da Silva cowrote the song with Jorge Faraj and recorded it in 1964.

3. The Demônios da Garoa have been playing for over six decades (since 1942) and claim the Guinness record for the oldest vocal group in Brazil. Their name, Demons of the Drizzle, refers to the faint mist that has earned São Paulo the nickname Cidade da Garoa, City of Mist. They got their start in the neighborhood of Mooca, where many immigrant groups were concentrated, including Italians and Mizrahi Jews.

4. The Demônios recorded the song written by Américo de Campos in 1964 on their album *Trem das Onze*.

5. Chain migration contrasts sharply with mass immigration, especially where those masses are either forced immigrants or refugees. In chain migration, members of the community arrive in the new country and establish themselves before sending for relatives, who in turn establish themselves in order to send for others. In this way, new immigrants have a safe place to land and the benefit of *patrícios* (people from the same

country) who speak the same language and can interpret the new culture and who have the experience to help guide the transition.

6. Scliar's 1997 historical novel, *A majestade do Xingu*, includes one of these salesmen. Street peddling is still an important means of economic survival for migrants from other regions of the country, selling door-to-door everything from fruit and garlic to cleaning products. Whether carrying their load directly on their shoulders or in beat-up cars, hawking with only the power of their own voices, or blasting staticky announcements from loudspeakers, this informal economy still sustains many families throughout the country. Street sellers (*ambulantes* or *camelôs*) who set up tables at informally agreed upon points in the city of São Paulo have repeatedly clashed with city government over their extralegal occupation of sidewalks.

7. This practice of purchase in installments is distinguished from the layaway plans that are more familiar in the United States in that the customer gets the product with the first payment.

8. For a discussion of Armenians in Brazil, see Grün 1992.

9. See Truzzi 1992, 1997; Lesser 1999; and Karam 2007 for historical and ethnographic analyses of Syrians and Lebanese in Brazil and the creation of this ethnic group.

10. See Lesser 1995 for discussions of these policies with regard to Jews, and 1999 regarding Asians and Middle Easterners. See also Schwarcz 1993 on popular conceptions of race in Brazil, and Seyferth 1996 and Ramos 1996 on their implications for immigration.

11. See Lesser 1991 for a history of these settlements. See Brumer 1994 for a profile of the contemporary Jewish community in the state of Rio Grande do Sul, the descendants of these settlers. Most Jews left the rural settlements, migrating to the city. Porto Alegre, the state capital, is home to approximately 10,000 Jews, the third-largest community in Brazil.

12. See Tucci Carneiro 1988 for a discussion of anti-Semitism during this period in Brazil. See Lesser 1995 for a discussion of Brazilian policies and practices regarding Jewish immigration to Brazil in the first half of the twentieth century.

13. See Cytrynowicz and Zuquim 1997 for the school's seventy-five-year history.

14. In Portuguese, "*dona*" is the term of respect for women, a title that precedes the first name.

15. Margolis (1994) notes that this expression is now used by Brazilians to refer to immigration to the United States.

16. See, for example, Malamud 1988, Wolff and Wolff 1988, Worcman 1991, Reibscheid 1995, Mizrahi 1996, Morris 1996, Veltman 1996, Blay 1997, Egler 1997, Fausto 1997, Igel 1997, Pfeffer 1997, Kleinsinger 2000, and Scliar and Souza 2000.

17. Reibscheid identified another corner, Rua da Graça, with Rua Correia de Melo (1995:51).

18. See Mizrahi 2003 for a history of Middle Eastern Jewish (Mizrahi) families in Mooca.

19. On a return visit in 2006, I found that Jairo Freidlin, the owner of the Livraria Sêfer Jewish bookstore (and press) had updated his "Jewish Guide to Higienópolis" (with an additional synagogue, two schools, and many more services, stores, and restaurants),

and had dispensed with hiding locations, since information is so easily available on the Internet. The expansion of Jewish businesses and services gave further justification to the motto of the "new Jewish center of South America" maintained on Freidlin's map.

20. Anthropologists Roberto Cardoso de Oliveira (1976) and Manuela Carneiro da Cunha (1979) explain ethnicity as ideological. Where there are subethnic differences, these group identities are also ideologically based.

21. *Revista da Associação Brasileira "A Hebraica,"* January 1967, 1977, and 1987.

22. I am grateful to Cristina Franco de Mattos of the Centro Pró-Memória Hans Nobiling of the Esporte Clube Pinheiros for confirming and supplementing this information (personal communication).

23. Falbel notes that the Macabi club was founded in 1927 following an incident in which a Jew was expelled from the presumably non-Jewish "Sport Club" for wearing "a large Star of David on his chest"(2008:537). The "discontented" quotation is from *Revista "A Hebraica,"* January 1967:22.

24. *Revista "A Hebraica,"* January 1987:4. Feffer's prominence in the community was in part due to the fact that he furnished the paper for many Jewish publications. In fact, paper moguls figure prominently in both the history of the Hebraica club and the rapid rise of the community in *paulistano* society.

25. *Revista "A Hebraica,"* January 1967:22.

26. Jewish continuity is also the driving question of much social scientific research on Jews. The continued existence of Jews, in spite of and probably because of remarkable mutability, has been a challenge to philosophers and scientists, as any review of the literature will reveal. This is the central question of Henrique Rattner's important sociological essay on the Jewish community in São Paulo: *Tradição e mudança* (Tradition and change), 1977.

27. *Revista "A Hebraica,"* January 1967:23; January 1977:3.

28. *Revista "A Hebraica,"* January 1967:23.

29. The titles were sold at 30,000 old cruzeiros apiece, or 30 new cruzeiros, as reported in the December 1968 issue of the club's magazine (30 contos was reported in the January 1977 issue), indicating that hyperinflation had begun, with monetary adjustment reflected in the new currency created by lopping off the last three zeroes. Brazil underwent many of these adjustments and subsequent currencies, with increasing frequency, in the early 1990s, until 1994 and the introduction of the relatively stable Plano Real by the then–finance minister Fernando Henrique Cardoso, which formed the basis of his successful bid for the presidency.

30. *Revista "A Hebraica,"* December 1968:5.

31. *Revista "A Hebraica,"* January 1967:23.

32. *Revista "A Hebraica,"* December 1968:5.

33. I discuss the security issues in São Paulo and those of the community in detail in Chapter 6.

Chapter 3. Kosher Feijoada

1. The use of titles is ubiquitous in Brazil, where the language allows the simultaneous registry of formality/respect and affection and may be used in combination with a first

name, such as in the use of "Dona" (Mrs. or Miss) to address women, or when university students address a professor by title and first name rather than last.

2. *Tefillin* are used by Jewish men for prayer. Small leather boxes containing scripture are tied onto the forehead and wrapped around the left arm (against the heart) with leather straps forming a pattern that is said to spell out one of the names of God. See Frankel and Teutsch 1992, and Unterman 1991.

3. This mandate is shared by the organizations of other ethnic groups, including the Seinen Bunkyo, the Youth Department of the Brazilian Society of Japanese Culture, for instance.

4. Bila Sorj (1997) discusses exogamy among Jews in relation to conversion to Judaism, problematizing the concept of "*casamentos 'mistos.*" Elkin found this use of the concept of "intermarriage" to refer to marriages between Sephardim and Ashkenazim in other communities in Latin America (1998:190).

5. Dowry practices came up occasionally in casual conversation, but it is not consistently practiced. It appears to have been inconsistently employed in past generations as well. One couple told me they were teasing their son, considered a "good catch," about his apparent "value" because interested families had been approaching them with increasing offers, though they did not take this form of negotiation seriously. One woman who married about forty years prior to our interview recalled that the lack of dowry had been a source of contention between her father and husband. Those who brought up dowries in discussions generally thought they were "absurd," or an antiquated form which treated women like chattel. A far more common practice among middle- to upper-class Brazilians, including Jewish Brazilians, is for the families on both sides to help the young couple set up their new home; depending on financial means, wedding gifts can include apartments and major appliances, as well as sets of dishes, cutlery, linens, and so on.

6. Comunidade Shalom in São Paulo may be the only Reform synagogue in Brazil. In Rio de Janeiro, the Associação Religiosa Israelita (ARI, Jewish Religious Association) is a Liberal congregation, and the Congregação Judaica do Brasil (CJB, Jewish Congregation of Brazil) blends Conservative and Renewal approaches. The CJB is the congregation of the well-published Rabbi Nilton Bonder, known as the "*rabino surfista,*" the surfer rabbi, for his youthful appeal and laid-back *carioca* style. (*Carioca* refers to the qualities associated with people in the city of Rio.) These congregations have been shifting toward deeper religious practice while maintaining the gender equality that is one of the hallmarks of progressive movements in Judaism. Both men and women lead the services, read from the Torah, and wear religious garments ranging in style from the most traditional to the most colorful, artisanal interpretations of *tallit* and *kippot* (pl.). Some of the most significant changes are the inclusion of more Hebrew in the services, the greater use of religious garments such as *tallit* and *kippot* (by women as well as men, an important difference), and use of the *mikvah*. See Avigdor 2004 for a history and analysis of Comunidade Shalom in São Paulo. Many Reform congregations in the United States have also begun to make these changes, engendering considerable controversy. While some see it as a deeper engagement with Judaism, others see it as a move toward conservative practices or even orthodoxy.

7. The Second Temple in Jerusalem was said to have been glorious and luxurious. Its destruction by the Romans in 70 C.E. began the dispersal of the Jews, creating the Diaspora. It is believed that the Third Temple will appear from heaven in the messianic era. See entry for "temple" in Frankel and Teutsch 1992 and Unterman 1991.

8. Several people who had visited the synagogue mentioned that they were disappointed by the elegant but institutional style of the new synagogue; rather than a romantic Orientalist reproduction, they thought it looked like the Knesset, the Israeli house of parliament.

9. Lesser (2001) and others have suggested that the CIP, with about 8,000 members, may be Latin America's largest synagogue.

10. In contrast, the Jewish community in Mexico City, for example, is divided along Ashkenazi/Sephardi lines, and these enclaves are segregated from the larger Mexican community.

11. Bernardo was especially fond of sprinkling his speech with English phrases.

12. His son was eight years old at the time of the interview.

13. Although all three of these are amulets thought to offer some degree of protective power, the blue eyeball, popular throughout the Middle East, is most explicitly worn as protection against the "evil eye." The overlap in Jewish and Brazilian evil eye beliefs deserves more attention than I can give it here. See Dundes 1980 and 1981 for analyses of the evil eye, and Rebhun 1995 for a discussion of Northeast Brazilian evil-eye beliefs.

14. Beatriz Kushnir and Sara Gruman reported on a study of these Messianic Christian churches at the national Jewish studies conference in Rio de Janeiro in 1999. See Kushnir 1999.

15. See Parker 1991 on eating as a sexual metaphor.

16. See, for instance, Freyre's discussion of the influence of "Negro culture" on Brazilian cuisine (1986a:459–70).

17. See Kalcik 1984 on the relationship between food and ethnic and national identity.

18. I have used the Brazilian spelling of these snacks. *Sfiha* are open-faced meat pies and *kibbeh* are fried oblongs made of minced meat and bulgur. Karam (2007) notes that this increased visibility and consumption of Arab food came about at the end of the twentieth century.

19. The synagogue's name combines the singular masculine Portuguese article "*o*" (the) with the Yiddish word for synagogue, "*shil*" (a variant of "*shul*").

20. Chabad is one of the sects of Hassidic Judaism that has grown in popularity in Jewish communities in many countries. Binyan Olam is also an ultra-Orthodox sect, but is less well known and has smaller outreach. In São Paulo, both organizations emphasize teaching Judaism to youths and encouraging them to deepen their religious practice. See Topel 2008 for a discussion of this "new Orthodoxy" in Brazil.

21. Here he made a separation between a national identity, Portuguese, and a Jewish one.

22. He was referring to Deodoro da Fonseca, 1889–91.

23. He was referring to famed Brazilian model and male-to-female transsexual Roberta Close.

24. Although there is no evidence that the Portuguese explorer credited with "discovering" Brazil, Pedro Álvarez Cabral, was a New Christian, his wife was from a well-known New Christian family, and many among his crew were New Christians. Felipe understood these connections as coloring the entire enterprise.

25. Ephraim employed a common phrase applied to Brazil, "um país maravilhoso," a marvelous country.

26. In the Southeast there remains tremendous prejudice against the largely impoverished labor force that migrated en masse to the industrial cities during the twentieth century. *Paulistas* discriminate against the populations of the Northern and Northeastern regions for being poor, underdeveloped, and, according to some, "black," in direct contradiction to the ideology of racial democracy. See O'Dougherty 2002 about regional prejudice against *nordestinos* (people from the Northeast).

27. Recent editions of the estimable Aurélio dictionary note that this use of the word is derogatory. Also see the entry for "*judeu*" in Câmara Cascudo 1972. Derogatory uses of "Jew" exist in English as well.

28. The term is also used by Jews elsewhere in Latin America, and Finkielkraut (1994) chronicles the divergence in the use of "Israelite" and "Jew" in France.

29. There are variations in the spelling of *iídiche* in Portuguese, including the simpler form, *ídiche*.

30. This use of the language to refer to the people is the inverse of the use of "Jewish" in the United States to refer to the Yiddish language (Boyarin 1996:95).

31. Topel (2008) notes that such mixed-sex gatherings are one of several techniques used by "proselytist rabbis" to reach less religious or secular youths. Part discussion session, part lecture, part social club, in these sessions, these youths explore Jewish identity, and some may begin a process of greater religious participation that may result in a "return" (or conversion) to Orthodoxy.

32. Igel cites an example of another blended construction from semiautobiographical novelist Adão Voloch, whose characters seek "conciliatory" identities, blending Jewish and indigenous into "judeu-guarani" and "caboclo judeu" (1997:117).

33. Rebhun discusses the range and meaning of nicknames in Brazil (1999:78–81).

34. See Finkielkraut 1994 for a discussion of what could be considered a contemporary instantiation of "hidden" Jews in post-Enlightenment Europe. By contrast, see Kaye/Kantrowitz 2007 for a discussion of "Jews of color."

35. For a thorough examination of this form of social Darwinism in Brazilian immigration policy, see Lesser 1995. Interest in the social construction of race has also extended to a growing body of literature on the construction of "white" as a category (where this pertains to Jews, see Brodkin 1998, and Grün 1998). See Gilman 1991 for an analysis of Jewish bodies and phenotypic stereotypes underlying the development of modern scientific racism. There is a tendency for much of this literature to reproduce some of the same essentialism that it seeks to deconstruct through reiterating a singular "Jew." Furthermore, this Jew tends to be unabashedly male; a significant portion of the literature analyzes "the" racialized (and sometimes feminized) "Jew's body" through the concept of the circumcised penis, confusing the bodily (that is, the cultural) with the

biological). In her critique of these twin phenomena, Pellegrini (1997a, 1997b) points out the irony that Jewish women are displaced in the recent innovative work on race, gender, and Jewishness and asks in what way these analyses would be transformed if we were to take seriously the "interarticulations" of these categories. For Gilman, Jonathan Boyarin, Daniel Boyarin, and Said before them, it is apparently self-evidently negative for a people to be "feminized," whereas a deeper analysis of what this means and how it is put into practice would reveal much more about relations of power not only between nation-states and dominant and subordinate groups in society, but also in the gendered relationships from which the metaphor is drawn.

Chapter 4. The High Cost of Jewish Living

1. O'Dougherty notes that for the Brazilian middle class, Disney World vacations, or what she calls "the accomplishment of Disney" (2002:97), have the added value of "being associated with modernity and a transnational social circuit" by "position[ing] Brazilian travelers symbolically among the citizens of the First World" (2002:101).

2. "*Pau*" means "stick" or "wood," so a literal translation of *cara-de-pau* is "wooden face," not unlike the idea of a poker face in English. In describing how he found ways to get free services (including dental work and hair implants), Felipe (whose story I tell later in this chapter) played with the literal meaning of the expression and joked while pointing to his face: "I shave with furniture polish because this is a *cara-de-pau*." In this expression, brazenness, or chutzpah, is clearly a point of pride.

3. When considering expenses in Brazil, in addition to looking at the exchange rate, it is essential to look at prices in relation to the federally determined monthly minimum wage (*salário mínimo*), the unit of reference for salaried employees. Salaries are calculated as multiples of the *salário mínimo*, such that when the rate increased, from R$120 to R$130, for example, someone making three minimum wages (three units) saw a jump in income from R$360 to R$390. Something that might not seem expensive by U.S. standards on the basis of a simple currency exchange is often entirely out of reach for the majority of the Brazilian population. This difference was considerably aggravated by the loss in value of the Brazilian real in January 1999. For the purposes of comparison, if the U.S. minimum wage were monthly, at the 2002 federal hourly minimum of $5.15, at eight hours/day, the monthly minimum wage was roughly $950 (or R$2,328 at the exchange rate of 2.45). While extremely low, and just below the "poverty line" for two people as determined by the U.S. federal government, it is nevertheless well over ten times the concurrent Brazilian minimum of R$200 (or U.S.$81.63).

4. In his capacity of director of Jewish culture, José Luiz Goldfarb is also responsible for the club's synagogue and is often the first point of contact for these families.

5. Lesser notes that a similar structure was used negatively during debates about Jewish immigration in 1947 when the neighborhood of Copacabana in Rio was called "Copacabanovitch" in reference to the concentration of Jews living in that region of the city (2005:318).

6. Article 20 of Federal Law 7,716/89 classifies as a crime "practicing, inducing, or inciting discrimination or prejudice against race, color, ethnicity, religion, or national origin."

7. The protagonist's unusual name is a feminized reference to the Maccabees, Jewish warriors of the second century B.C.E. Apparently the only time in Lispector's significant oeuvre that she offered any indication of her Jewish background was in this single short novel completed not long before her death (Vieira 1995). It is because of this scarcity of Jewish themes in her writing that Igel (1997) does not discuss Lispector's work in detail in her volume on Jewish writing in Brazil.

8. Donna Goldstein (2003) discusses the mutually dependent and strained relationship between maids and their employers from the maids' point of view, as well as her own awkward relationship to both employers and employees in this intimate system of interdependence and miscommunication.

9. This was the topic of periodic articles in the club's magazine, charting the changes in rules and attitudes.

10. Also "shiksa" and "shikseh," this Yiddish word is derived from the Hebrew word "*sheques/sheketz*," meaning "blemish," and is used in the Torah to refer to the flesh of a taboo animal; the extension of the term to non-Jews is because of the marriage prohibition against them (Eisenberg and Scolnic 2001:146). According to Unterman's entry for "gentile," in which he explains with considerable understatement that "negative attitudes towards Gentiles are expressed in the names used for them," "shikse" literally means "abominable woman" (1991:84).

11. In her master's thesis at the University of São Paulo, Hemsi (1997) found that "liberal" Jewish parents delegated the responsibilities of transmitting knowledge of Jewish culture and traditions to the schools, while they left the socialization of their children in a Jewish atmosphere to the clubs.

12. In April 2011, the president of the Hebraica announced the club's decision to open a new Jewish elementary and middle school; the details have yet to be elaborated (José Luiz Goldfarb, personal communication).

13. A "thirteenth" month's salary is paid at the end of the year to all regularly employed workers and is built into the tuition in this school as well.

14. At the exchange rate at the time, he was paying the equivalent of roughly U.S.$700/month, though prior to the drop in the value of the real, it had been closer to U.S.$1,300. Because it was the end of the year, the adjustment in the exchange rate was not yet reflected in the school's fees. The following year's fees would reflect the drop by near half in the value of the real in relation to the dollar that occurred in January 1999.

15. See the Frankel and Teutsch (1992) and Unterman (1991) entries for discussion of the symbolic significance and protective qualities of the *mezuzah*.

16. For comparative purposes, proportionally, just the parchment for the *mezuzah* would cost over U.S.$400.

17. The Bat Mitzvah for girls is not considered a commandment according to Orthodox interpretations.

18. Collection plates are not passed during weekly services in synagogues, and synagogue attendance increases greatly during these celebrations. Therefore, seats at religious services during Rosh Hashanah and Yom Kippur can be expensive, since these prices offset the costs associated with these services in particular, and with maintaining the synagogue throughout the year.

19. *Kashrut* comes from *kasher*, meaning "fit" or "proper," as decreed by God in the Torah and interpreted by rabbis in the Talmud.

20. Margarine usually has a milk-derived product, and only margarine made exclusively from plant products and denoted as kosher can be eaten with meat.

21. In contrast, the *barya* (slaves) of the Beta Israel in Ethiopia underwent a truncated ritual conversion to Judaism in order to be able to work in Jewish homes (Salamon 1999:73–74).

22. A summary of the rabbinical interpretations of the lessons to be derived from the laws of *kashrut*, especially those related to slaughter and consumption—explanations that include curbing an instinct for violence and developing a sense of justice and teaching self-restraint—can be found in Frankel and Teutsch (1992).

23. While not in gross violation of the laws of *kashrut*, the sushi that is served at the club is not kosher (because of the means of slaughter and preparation). This was the reason a colleague and I could not have our sushi lunch appointment inside the *sukkah* (the palm frond–covered, hut-like structure built for the festival of Sukkot, the Festival of the Tabernacles, which follows immediately after the High Holy Days and celebrates nature and the harvest). People were encouraged to meet and eat in the *sukkah*, but only kosher food was allowed inside.

24. The club made unconfirmed claims to be the only private club in the world with a McDonald's operating within it.

25. Jewish funerary ritual is a religiously and symbolically rich topic that deserves far more attention than I can give it here. In addition to the associated high costs, there is also conflict within the community surrounding policies for the burial of non-Jewish spouses.

26. The word "*nobre*" (noble) is used to mean "elite," "select," "preferable." For example, prime time on television is called "*horário nobre*."

Chapter 5. Inscribing Jews into the Nation

1. Unlike in other countries in the Americas, the 1992 quincentenary of Columbus' arrival was not given much attention in Brazil, where the separate date of "discovery" is one of many distinctions that set Brazil apart from the rest of the region.

2. The Keren Kayemet LeIsrael (KKL, also known as the Jewish National Fund, JNF) is a Zionist organization founded in 1901 to raise funds to purchase land for Jewish settlement and the future state of Israel. It is known for ecological initiatives, including large-scale tree planting, developing water conservation systems, and now promoting awareness of global warming.

3. Souza is not known as a Jewish writer, as his Moroccan Jewish ancestry has only recently come to light. Macunaíma is an emblematic Brazilian character, from the novel of the same name by modernist Mário de Andrade (2000[1928]).

4. Peter Fry's book with this expression as its title (1982) explores what he calls "politically convenient" appropriations and the appearance of conformity, often within a rubric of unequal power relations.

5. This use of postage stamps as a medium for nationalist messages in Latin America is also discussed by Child (2005).

6. See Lesser (1999:55–59) for another example of this phenomenon, the creation and placement of the Amizade Sírio-Libanesa (Syrian-Lebanese Friendship) statue in São Paulo.

7. Obviously, this is a practice that is quite familiar elsewhere, but it is taken to greater heights in Brazil. Perhaps only the current trend of corporate sponsorship in the United States whereby buildings and stadiums and academic chairs are branded by their source of funding can rival the self-conscious memorialization as it is practiced in Latin America.

8. Ben-Gurion was Israel's first prime minister (1948–53 and 1955–63). Rabin (Israel's prime minister in 1974–77 and 1992–95) shared the 1994 Nobel Peace Prize with former Israeli prime minister Shimon Peres (in his role as foreign minister) and Palestinian Liberation Organization chair Yasser Arafat, prior to being assassinated by a radical Jew when leaving a peace rally in 1995. Both Ben-Gurion and Rabin have spaces in the club named after them: the Ben-Gurion Room, where the new services were held; and the Centro Cívico Yizhak Rabin, one of the largest multisport gymnasiums in the city (4,200 square meters), where sports competitions are held and where the main stage is built every year for the annual Israeli folk dance festival.

9. Politicking and community outreach aside, Cardoso has proven to be a Philosemite on various occasions, including an event in 2001 at which he declared that he had always wanted to be a rabbi. Brazil's crypto-Jewish history weaves together contemporary national politics with identity politics; Lesser cites a Jewish genealogical society newsletter that suggests that Cardoso is descended from Jews (2001:66 and n3). Cardoso's comment must be seen in light of an earlier, infamous, comment in which he said that he, like all Brazilians, "had a foot in the kitchen," an expression that indicates someone has black ancestry (see Chapter 3). Cardoso positioned himself as having affinities with a range of ethnic affiliations.

10. Pitta's speech was quoted in the Revista "A Hebraica," October 1999:33–34, which dedicated three pages to text and photos documenting the prominent political figures who made their presence known that day.

11. Covas was a neighbor of the Hebraica and had long-standing ties with the Jewish community. Serra was a founding member of the president's party, the PSDB (Partido Socialista Democrático Brasileiro, the Brazilian Social Democratic Party), and was favored to succeed Cardoso after his second term. When Luiz Inácio "Lula" da Silva of the PT (Partido dos Trabalhadores, the Workers' Party) won the presidency, Serra successfully ran for mayor of São Paulo and then governor of the state of São Paulo.

12. The list of visiting politicians on that day is long, including Marcos Arbaitman (state secretary for sports and tourism and three-time former president of the club), congressman Alberto Goldman (whose visit was especially significant, since his son Cláudio was making his debut as a cantor in the new services), former governor Miguel Colassuono, and congressmen Walter Feldman, Romeu Tuma, Arnaldo Madeira, and Cunha Bueno. Although less than half of these men were Jewish, according to the club's magazine all of them were "reaffirming their ties to the Jewish community by their presence at the services" (Revista "A Hebraica," October 1999:35). For the Jewish politicians,

the High Holy Days give them an opportunity to assert their dual identities and celebrate the solidity of Jewish integration into all levels of Brazilian society.

13. Roberto Grün's (1994) discussion of Jewish Brazilian political life in São Paulo provides one example of an ethnic practice that is rooted in opposition to widely held stereotypes. In contrast to the enormous success of Brazilian politicians of Armenian, Syrian, and Lebanese descent, such as former São Paulo mayor Paulo Maluf, and in contrast to the involvement of Jews in other political regimes, such as the United States or England, Brazilian Jews have generally eschewed major elected positions in favor of appointed ones. Grün attributes this to the money involved in financing electoral campaigns and the fear of reinvigorating stereotypes of Jewish avariciousness and other elements from an "anti-Semitic repertoire" (1994:132). The success of Jaime Lerner, former mayor of Curitiba and governor of the southern state of Paraná, provides one of the counter examples of political behavior. However, since he has been subject to considerable anti-Jewish invective from opponents, his example also reinforces the fears that keep *paulistano* Jews from risking further involvement in electoral politics. Not wishing to expose the community to revived stereotypes while simultaneously desiring the social ratification that comes from public participation is yet another instance of the contradictory desires between visibility and invisibility. In spite of these external pressures and an apparently coherent logic that supports keeping a low profile, there have been Jews who have successfully entered the realm of politics, most notably members of the extended Lafer-Klabin family, whose prominence on the national political scene dates from the 1930s and includes elected and appointed positions (Elkin 1998:92).

14. Quoted in *Revista "A Hebraica,"* October 1999:34.

15. The strong connections with the Portuguese in both contexts is little more than a coincidence. Of greater comparative significance is the fact that both India and Brazil are known for the cultural hegemony of major religions, Hinduism in the case of the former, and Catholicism in the latter.

16. Prime Minister Gandhi's remarks were broadcast nationally at the time of the celebrations, and the published version was widely circulated. See Mandelbaum (1975, 1977, and especially 1981) for details of the speech and ceremony.

17. As in other religions, in Judaism water and fish have considerable symbolic meaning. Flowing water is spiritually cleansing. Its importance in Judaism is evident in the use of the *mikvah*, or ritual bath, by women prior to marriage or following menstruation, by both sexes prior to the High Holy Days, and prior to Shabbat among Orthodox Jews. Fish symbolize God because they have eyes that do not close and are protected from the evil eye because they are covered with water. Fish also symbolize fertility (many eggs) and are an important part of ritual meals. Fish are important in the *tashlikh* ceremony because they are said to eat the breadcrumbs invested with past burdens and carry them away. For greater detail, see Dundes 1980, 1981 on the evil eye, and the entries for "fish" and "water" in Frankel and Teutsch 1992, and "fish" and "*tashlikh*" in Unterman 1991.

18. The Hebraica began celebrating Rosh Hashanah and Yom Kippur in 1966 (Cytrynowicz 2003:91).

19. The original design for the theater anticipated its use for religious services, which

were held at the club beginning in the mid-1960s (*Revista "A Hebraica,"* September 1999:24).

20. Additionally, Hebraikeinu, the department in charge of activities for small children, sponsored educational play activities for children in the Carmel Plaza, occupying the children and teaching them about the meaning and traditions of the celebrations.

21. To the amusement of many, less than a month before his debut as a religious leader, Cláudio Goldman played the conniving, drug-dealing character Sportin' Life in the club's production of Gershwin's *Porgy and Bess.* One of the enduring songs from the opera is "It Ain't Necessarily So," which playfully mocks a series of biblical stories, warning all to take them "with a grain of salt": "De t'ings dat yo' li'ble to read in de Bible, it ain't necessarily so." Two years later, Goldman took over responsibility for the services in the Arthur Rubinstein Theater.

22. As the congregation continued to grow, renovations to the main building included rearrangement of the space, resulting in significant upgrades for both the synagogue and the library. The synagogue now has a beautifully designed dedicated space and well-attended services throughout the year.

23. *Revista "A Hebraica,"* September 1999:x.

24. The *chai* is a very popular amulet among Jews in Brazil and is also related to protection from the evil eye. For further discussion, see the entries for "eighteen" and "kabbalah" in Frankel and Teutsch 1992, and "alphabet" and "gematria" in Unterman 1991.

25. Much of this information is included in an article I wrote for the magazine "*A Hebraica*" (October 1999:31–32), one of two articles I was asked to write for the club's magazine during the course of my fieldwork.

26. Several languages were in constant use in and around those rehearsals. In spite of twenty-two years of annual visits to Brazil, Stern spoke no Portuguese (though several suspected he understood more than he let on). The maestro suddenly showed himself to be conversant in Hebrew, the only language he and the *chazzan* had in common for discussing the details of arrangement and timing. Stern and I spoke in English.

27. The *shofar* is the ram's horn, one of the most important symbols of the Jewish New Year. It is blown during the services and at the end of Yom Kippur and is said to awaken the community into spiritual awareness. There are three distinct symbolic blasts, and the ram's horn itself recalls Abraham's near-sacrifice of his son Isaac, who was replaced by a ram at the last moment, told in the portion of the Torah that is read during Rosh Hashanah.

28. That year, the club's synagogue trained five young men—"enough for a *futebol de salão* (indoor soccer) team"—to be *baal korei* and take on this responsibility in the services held at the club. This "team" now offers classes to those preparing for the Bar Mitzvah and helps maintain the services at the synagogue.

29. The band's name is a play on words. "*Traje de rigor*" means "formal dress," and "*ultraje*" means "outrage" or "affront," so the resulting combination means something like "strictly outrageous" or "rigorously offensive."

30. This generalization excludes those Evangelical Protestants, known in Brazil as *crentes*, or believers, who abstain from all alcohol consumption.

31. The discourse about Jews not having problems with alcohol or alcoholism is common in the United States as well. Indeed, Jewish sobriety has been a scholarly topic for over 200 years (Heath 1976), an idea that has so thoroughly penetrated popular consciousness that it frames the research on Jews and alcohol. There is a body of research that accepts this assertion as a starting point for investigations into the possible genetic basis for this supposed fact. More critical researchers on alcohol use among Jews must counter the assumptions that the "solidarity" of the Jewish community or the religious or emotional sustenance provided by Jewish teachings gives Jews some kind of immunity against alcohol, and they bemoan the negative effects of these assumptions on the identification and treatment of Jewish alcoholics, as well as the way in which they make it difficult to gather accurate data (Vex and Blume 2001, Flasher and Maisto 1984).

32. The Jewish Telegraphic Agency reported (May 19, 2002) on the 2002 inauguration of a Brazilian branch of JACS at the Hebraica club, citing the stigma associated with substance abuse as one of the contributing factors to the problem and its invisibility (Moraes 2002).

33. This phenomenon of increased drinking among younger generations, who are more distant from immigration and who follow patterns that are similar to those of the larger society, has also been observed in the United States (Knupfer and Room 1967).

34. See Bakhtin 1968, Stam 1989, and DaMatta 1991a for discussions of the social inversion and release that occur through *carnaval.*

35. Memories conflicted and definitive evidence was not available, so I was unable to pinpoint the exact year when *carnaval* at the club was cancelled. Not surprisingly, the club's magazine is largely a propaganda vehicle that reports on events that have already occurred, with the apparent intention of reminding members of all the opportunities for leisure and recreation in the club while encouraging those who did not attend to frequent the club so as not to miss future events. Controversial or negative topics rarely appear on its pages. Even major crises with special significance for the Jewish community, such as the assassination of Yitzhak Rabin, the bombing of the AMIA Jewish community center in Buenos Aires, or trouble in Israel are only reported through the prism of events held at the club, such as commemorations or debates. Thus, where controversy has arisen, it has not been evidenced in the magazine. Given the laudatory nature of the magazine, rather than search for an announcement of the cancellation, I searched for the first absence of reporting. With the 1981 and 1983 volumes of the club's magazine missing from the library, I was only able to approximate the year and was left only with the speculative and faulty memories of community members to provide explanations.

36. See Lima and Toneto (1999) about the celebration of Zumbi by rappers in São Paulo. Zumbi's name has also been taken up by the popular music group Nação Zumbi (Zumbi Nation), and even by a bishop (see Toneto 1999).

37. This uncomfortable relationship between spirited celebrations and somber themes resulted in a controversy in 2008 when on the cusp of *carnaval* the samba school Viradouro was prohibited from including a float representing the Holocaust. The school's theme was "É de arrepiar!" (roughly, it gives you goosebumps, or it is frightening), and the float representing genocide was supposed to be an example of the extremes caused by intolerance. However, the Jewish Federation of Rio de Janeiro asked a judge to prevent

the school from including its display of piled, emaciated cadavers when it learned that the float would be topped by an actor dressed as Hitler. The public discussion of the controversy was detailed in a cover article in *Época* magazine (equivalent to *Time* magazine), which both cited Russian theorist Mikhail Bakhtin's analysis of the role of Carnival in the Middle Ages and quoted Brazilian anthropologist Roberto DaMatta's analysis of this particular episode (Gurovitz and Aquino 2008), evidence of the role of public intellectuals in Brazil, as well as providing a less harmonious example of the relationship between Jews and *carnaval*. The designer intended the float to be critical of the horror, but it was deemed disrespectful and was banned. This is hardly the first legal intervention in *carnaval* representations, as there have been numerous instances of banned Christian symbols when the representations have crossed the invisible line of decorum.

38. This association between peoples who have suffered is a frequent theme in Brazilian popular culture, from Gilberto Gil's reminder that both blacks and Jews were prohibited from practicing their religion in colonial Brazil (Stam 1997:39) to the refrain in the song "Luta de Classes" (Class struggle) by the band Cidade Negra, which links Jews and blacks in a single trajectory: "escravo da Babilônia, trabalhador do Brasil" (slave in Babylon, worker in Brazil). This connection was the explicit justification behind the production of Gershwin's *Porgy and Bess* by the Youth Department at the Hebraica. It is also the theme of a short film released in Brazil in 1999, *Algo em Comum* (Something in common). This film without dialogue was described in promotional literature as "A black child runs desperately through the streets of the metropolis. A chorus of elderly Jews rehearses music from the Holocaust. Barbarity and encounter." The film, by Edú Ramos and Reinaldo Pinheiro, featured the Tradição chorus, a group of elderly Jews who perform songs mostly in Yiddish, who released the first all-Yiddish album in Brazil in 1999. Later in 1999, an innovative Brazilian klezmer group released an album of mostly traditional klezmer music, *Mishmash a Brasileira*, which also included some original compositions that mixed klezmer, a style of music associated with Eastern European Jews, with music styles from the Brazilian Northeast. Although not emphasizing suffering, this music also sought common ground between marginalized peoples.

39. The Casa de Cultura de Israel is located in a new building in the shape of a Torah scroll. Unlike most other Jewish institutions in São Paulo, the building is quite visible from two major roadways, and the front of the building identifies it in both Portuguese and Hebrew as housing the Centro da Cultura Judaica (Jewish Cultural Center). Notably, this center uses the term "Judaica" rather than the more common "Israelita." With education and outreach as its mandate, it would be untenable for this organization to hide behind the unmarked walls or euphemisms common among most Jewish institutions in São Paulo. This does not mean that security is lax; I had to pass through the reinforced, guarded entrance, and then I was stopped by a director when I was taking photographs and had to explain my intentions, exchange business cards, and promise not to photograph the entrance. These issues are discussed further in the following chapter.

40. "*Mangueira*" means "mango tree" and is the name of the hillside *favela* surrounding the Morro da Mangueira, where the association is based and from which the samba school derives its name.

41. *Escolas de samba* are the clublike organizations that plan, prepare, and perform in

the annual *carnaval* parades. In addition to being places of learning, when they perform they are also somewhat like a "school" of fish, with thousands of members in synchronized movement. These schools exist all over Brazil, wherever municipalities sponsor *carnaval* parades. Even though São Paulo's schools have grown and gained notoriety, it is the competition among the fourteen schools in Rio that has national status. For a fuller explanation of the structure and significance of *carnaval* parades, see DaMatta 1991a.

42. The *sambódromo* holds 100,000 spectators.

43. *Jornal O Globo*, October 14, 2002.

44. Gil, a Grammy Award–winning musician, served as minister of culture under the Lula government from 2003 until the end of July 2008.

Chapter 6. Doubly Insecure

1. M. F. Gregori (2000) points out that street children's existence is not exclusively defined by the street, and the term, coined in the 1970s, has misguided scholars and laypeople alike.

2. Not nearly as many take recourse to helicopter commuting as suggested in a sensationalist article that was widely distributed in North American newspapers (Romero 2000).

3. According to the September 5, 1999, *Folha* report on quality of life in São Paulo, 20 percent of families reported that someone in the family had been robbed in the year prior to the research (conducted in 1998), and 6 percent of those interviewed had been robbed in the month of July 1999.

4. The idea of traffic-related violence also encompasses driver aggression and has been identified as a human rights issue and codified into the traffic statutes instituted at the national level under the direction of José Gregori (1998), minister of human rights at the time, before he became minister of justice.

5. In Mexico City rapid abductions are called "*secuestros express*," express kidnappings. This form of kidnapping is becoming more frequent and more brutal elsewhere in Latin America as well, wherever drug gangs have increased their presence, and the targets are increasingly from the middle and lower classes, which do not have access to the elaborate security systems and disguises available to the wealthy (Lacy 2008).

6. The material I cite here from the *Folha* is especially pertinent because it was published during the period of my fieldwork and, as such, reflects the tone of the discourse and concerns of the population that were the context for my research.

7. Nationally, data from the 2000 census reveal that 33 percent of the population lives on less than R$80/month, and there are 22 million (14 percent) indigents, defined as living on less that R$60/month (*Jornal do Brasil*, March 17, 2002).

8. An Instituto Brasileiro de Geografia e Estatística (IBGE) report (*Síntese de indicadores sociais*, Synthesis of social indicators) released in April 2001 concludes that in spite of an improvement in some social indicators, such as infant mortality, Brazil reached the end of the 1990s just as economically unequal as at the beginning. In 1999, the poorest 50 percent of the population held 14 percent of the national income (*renda nacional*), while the richest 1 percent held 13.1 percent, proportions which remained unchanged over the decade.

9. See D. Goldstein 2003 for a discussion of the violence of the everyday for impoverished Brazilians and their response to it.

10. I conducted these interviews in the second half of 1999, before the beginning of the Second Intifada in September 2000. A year and a half later, with a dramatic rise in the numbers of "suicide bombers" in Israel and Israeli military invasions of Palestinian territories, global anti-Semitism had begun to rise. April 2002 brought unprecedented news: anti-Jewish hostility in Rio, with reports of spray painting and rock throwing at Jewish institutions.

11. To make *aliyah* means to step up or return, the same verb used when someone is called to read from the Torah at the *bimah*, the platform or table on which the Torah is placed for reading. Under Israel's "Law of Return," Jews have the right to "return" to Israel and claim citizenship, whether or not they have been there before. This concept of "return" is also employed whenever Jews embrace a deeper observance of Judaism, whether or not they have been observant in the past. Describing the *teshuvah* (religious return) movement in São Paulo, Topel (2008) critiques the use of this concept for what is essentially a conversion process.

12. From 1950 to 1972, 5,619 Brazilians settled in Israel, compared to 22,482 Argentineans, 4,164 Uruguayans, and 1,344 Mexicans in the same period (Avruch 1981:212). For more on Latin American *aliyah*, see Goldberg and Rozen 1988, Herman 1984, and DellaPergola 1987.13. He is also reiterating his middle-class value on consumption, having joined the nearly half million Brazilians who travel annually to Disney World (O'Dougherty 2002:98).

14. As in Portuguese, the "Israelita" in the AMIA's name is another term for "Jewish," not Israeli.

15. The Sephardi community maintains other institutions.

16. At the Hebraica there is a monument memorializing the slain Israeli athletes, one of many commemorative plaques and statues in the club.

17. The September 11 attacks were against both the locus of U.S. power (the Pentagon, with other possible D.C. power centers as intended targets) and the headquarters of global neoliberal economic policy. The targets were not simply symbols of the United States, such as the Statue of Liberty, but locations from which this power was deployed, and hence the act was both symbolic and literal.

18. *Tribuna Judaica* 2, no. 43, 16–30 (October 1999).

19. In the Los Angeles incident, the attacker apparently acted alone but had connections to the Aryan Nation and other white supremacist organizations. When his picture was released, a security guard at the Simon Wiesenthal Center recognized him from a visit to the Museum of Tolerance a few weeks earlier. Apparently, when security was too tight there, and subsequently at the Skirball Cultural Center (which includes a museum of Jewish history and cultures), he was ready to give up when he happened on a little Jewish Community Center just off the freeway in the North Valley where small children were enjoying a summer program. He fired seventy shots and injured five people (four of whom were children), and then killed a Filipino postal worker. This attack was preceded by the other attack in California, the firebombing of a synagogue in Sacramento that caused more than $1 million in damage and was perpetrated by the same brothers responsible for the murder of a gay couple in nearby Happy Valley not long before.

Together with a third white supremacist "killing spree" in the Midwest, these crimes earned those months of 1999 the ignominious label of the "Summer of Hate." Both events occurred while I was conducting fieldwork in São Paulo and reverberated strongly in the Jewish community there. Community leaders considered the security issues, which were also discussed on a Jewish television program and over the Internet; during these discussions, some suggested that the São Paulo community should assist in rebuilding the Sacramento synagogue's lost library, further indication of the strength of these transnational ties.

20. These ties were strengthened with the January 2002 allegation that former Argentinean president Carlos Menem received a $10 million bribe to cover up Iran's role in the 1994 bombing (Sebastian Rotella, *Los Angeles Times*, January 24, 2002).

21. In November 1999, a twenty-six-year-old medical student opened fire with a submachine gun in a darkened movie theater in a shopping center in one of the most upscale regions of São Paulo, the type of crime Brazilians consider typically "American" and a hazard of "First World" living. A young woman interviewed in the *Folha*'s report on the "culture of fear" added in response to this crime: "'I've always said that Brazil is a privileged country because here there are no wars, earthquakes, or psychopathic killers . . . It looks like I'm going to have to take this last one off the list.'"

22. The urgency and anxiety of the event was transmitted in a series of moment-by-moment reports posted to *Folha Online* on October 10, 2000.

23. The April 21, 2002, *Globo* news reported the number as 10,000 *Jews*, equivalent to approximately one-sixth of the community, presuming that all participants were Jewish.

24. The premonitory power of dreams is widely accepted among Jews; see Myerhoff 1978:216–17.

25. The FISESP organized a major antiterrorist protest at the Memorial da América Latina on August 21, 1994, which brought together members of the Jewish community, as well as the mayor, the governor, and the minister of justice (Sundfeld 1996:15).

26. While not one of the explicit commandments, wearing a *kippah* is nevertheless seen as the fulfillment of a *mitzvah* by many Jews.

27. Many synagogues have *kippot* available at the door for those who arrive without one. In Orthodox synagogues, lace kerchiefs may be available for women, though Orthodox married women already have their heads covered with a hat or a wig when out of the house, or in the presence of men other than their husbands. See Dundes 2002 for a discussion of Orthodox women's use of wigs.

28. In addition to religious services and chorus rehearsal, the Hebraica's tiny synagogue, which seated approximately 100, was used for classes and lectures. The synagogue follows a loosely Conservative liturgy and practice, and during services, men and women sit on separate sides of the aisle. However, during choir rehearsal, the altos and basses sit on one side and the sopranos and tenors on the other, mixing up the sexes. Once when I went to hear a lecture in the synagogue, I went to sit on the "wrong" side and was corrected by one of the men and sent over to the women's side in spite of the secular nature of the event. In later conversations about the inconsistencies, several men determined that the chorus was incorrect in allowing men and women to sit together

in the synagogue, but this was not pursued. These inconsistencies are commonplace in a community with highly divergent interpretations of religious practice and meaning.

29. In addition to the liturgical choir, the larger Jerusalém chorus also sang a few liturgical pieces. A couple of the men in the chorus were vigilant about making sure that the other men remembered to put on *kippot* whenever we sang one of them. The discussion about the sacredness of the music continued when we were preparing our program for the performance (*encontro*) with other club choruses at the Sérgio Cardoso Theater in November 1999. The maestro asked whether we thought that the other clubs might be offended if we sang "Adon Olam" (Lord of the World) and "Avinu Malkeinu" (Our Father, Our King), two beautiful pieces of music, the former in eight voices and the latter with a soloist. Our presentation was rounded out with an original piece, "Cantos a la Bella," composed by our maestro, León Halegua, to a poem written by his father, Uruguayan philosopher Isaac Halegua, and three show-stopping pieces from *Porgy and Bess*, including the irreverent "It Ain't Necessarily So." In addition to the many *bossa nova* classics sung by the other choruses, the concert began with the Pinheiros club singing John Lennon's "Imagine" and Bach's "Jesus, Joy of Man," and two gospel tunes. The Paineiras club of Morumbi also performed the gospel song "Happy Day," assuaging any residual doubt that religious music was inappropriate.

30. During one of many commutes home from chorus rehearsal, two women complained that there were no more Jews who were simply Orthodox. "What happened to all the Orthodox Jews?" one asked. "Now they're all ultra-Orthodox." Her comment was both a reference to the fact that when Jews emigrated from Europe, most were "simply" observant Jews, without regard for today's denominations. Not only has Judaism fractured along multiple interpretive lines, but there are movements that encourage increasingly rigorous observance, several of which have gained momentum in Brazil since the early 1990s and are examined in Topel's ethnography of newly Orthodox Jews in São Paulo (2008).

31. I heard about a few incidents of harassment, including from two Orthodox men whose distinctive mode of dress made them highly visible when walking on the Sabbath.

32. See Sedgwick (1990:75–82) and Stratton (2000) for discussions of ethnic, especially Jewish, "passing" and invisibility.

33. In an earlier chapter, I discuss "assimilation" and the way many Jews use the term. Always seen as a "problem," for many people "assimilation" does not carry the full weight of its sociological meaning and is instead reduced to the question of intermarriage. Here I use the term with its more common meaning of cultural and social integration.

34. *Carioca* refers to people from Rio de Janeiro.

35. Though he was a social scientist he was not doing research on the community and was unaware of the full significance of and controversy surrounding the barriers.

Chapter 7. Cosmopolitans at Home

1. Southern (1997) discusses the impressive number of major black performers in the United States who have been part of productions of *Porgy and Bess* and the role that the opera has played as a "milestone" in black music history.

2. In a five-page cover story on the production, "Youth Sings Gershwin," the soloists also discussed the historical importance of Gershwin's opera for black performers and for their individual careers (*Revista "A Hebraica,"* August 1999:17–21). José Gallisa, who played Porgy, had recently returned from studies at the Royal Academy of Music in London, and subsequently rose to prominence in the opera world. The rarity of their opportunities was reiterated by David Marcondes, who played Jake in the production. He was part of the São Paulo Opera Company at the Teatro Municipal and told me once of an incident that occurred outside the opera house when he hailed a taxi after rehearsal one day. The black taxi driver expressed his approval, commenting that he did not often see black people coming out of the opera house. When Marcondes explained that he had not gone to see a production, but that he was in the chorus, the taxi driver was so stunned that he pulled over, stopped the cab, and talked with him for an hour, asking him all about his experience.

3. A *cortiço* is a tenement building, part of the urban landscape, but far less common than the *favelas* where poor Brazilians build their own homes. This translation of the setting into terms familiar to a Brazilian audience is one of the ways that the maestro and theater director bridged the cultural gap.

4. Translation from the script by director Henrique Schafer.

5. See Stack (1996) for a discussion of return migration and the reconstruction of "home" for African Americans within the United States, where these concepts do not depend on crossing national boundaries.

6. Hemsi characterizes this contradiction as being "between the desire for integration in this society and the perception of the differences" (1997:158).

7. Rosaldo extended the concept of cultural citizenship to address the issue of belonging for what he called "hinterland groups" in the Southeast Asian nations of Indonesia, Malaysia, and the Philippines. The peripheries occupied by these ethnic groups pose a slightly different set of questions for political and cultural belonging.

8. There is a deeper European history and multiple iterations of Jews being denied the rights of citizenship that had reverberations in Brazil as well. The Jews forced to convert in the Iberian Peninsula were marked with the identity of New Christians and denied full citizenship (Novinsky 1987:43).

9. It is worth considering the presentation of self of other prominent Brazilian Jews for a moment. Those who have ascended to elected political office have not run as Jewish candidates; this is neither a form of identity politics that has taken hold in Brazil, nor would it be an effective strategy considering the tiny proportion that the Jewish population represents. The best-known Jew in Brazil is Rabbi Henry Sobel, who was head rabbi at the largest synagogue in Latin America, the Congregação Israelita Paulistana, in São Paulo. Until his downfall following a well-publicized scandal in 2008, Rabbi Sobel could be counted on to represent the Brazilian Jewish community at all ecumenical events. He was distinctive because of his bowl haircut and *kippah* perched high on his head, and especially for his accent: after more than four decades in Brazil, and in spite of grammatically perfect speech, Rabbi Sobel still speaks with what is almost a caricature of an American accent—so much so that rumors circulate that he drops the accent in private.

10. In Brazil, *"doutor"* is a title applied to lawyers and professionals, not just medical doctors, but it can be used in many situations that call for respectful address, regardless of the recipient's profession.

11. Tucci Carneiro speculates that because of the presence of censors who kept a close eye on "foreigners," "Jews," and "communists," Malamud was cautious to never criticize the actions of the Brazilian government (1997:20).

12. This contrasted with the experience of Jews in other Latin American nations such as Bolivia, where Jews did not expect to stay (Spitzer 1998), or Mexico, where they kept separate from mainstream society (Roitman 1996).

13. Much later, these articles were translated from Yiddish to Portuguese and published in a collection titled *A Segunda Guerra Mundial na visão de um judeu brasileiro* (The Second World War from the perspective of a Brazilian Jew) (Malamud 1997).

14. Although he complained about short-term memory loss, at ninety-one years old, Doutor Samuel was completely lucid, his memory for the details of deeper history still quite sharp. His memory was probably helped by his having chronicled major events in the history of the Jewish community and his own remarkable life in several publications, including books with such titles as *Documentário* (Documentary, 1992), a collection of his letters and speeches that marked important occasions in the history of the Jewish community in Rio; the autobiographical *Escalas no tempo* (Moments in time, 1986); *Recordando a Praça Onze* (Remembering the Onze Plaza, 1988), a loving, eyewitness "deposition," originally written in Yiddish, on the old immigrant neighborhood that was destroyed in the process of modernizing the city; and *Do arquivo e da memória* (From the Archive and from Memory, 1983), which traces the history of Zionism in general, and in Brazil specifically. In his various capacities as representative and recorder of the community, Malamud documented Jewish life in Rio through the better part of the twentieth century, and these materials have been gathered into a research archive in Rio bearing his name.

15. In 1972, on the 150th anniversary of Brazilian independence, as president of the Jewish Federation of Rio de Janeiro he addressed the State Legislative Assembly of Rio de Janeiro detailing Jewish contributions to the development of Brazil.

16. When one of the international-banking Safra brothers died in Monte Carlo at the end of 1999, a conversation with a taxi driver revealed some confusion about the relationship between Jewishness and national origins. "I thought Safra was Jewish," he said, "but now they're saying he was Lebanese or Syrian or something." He was genuinely amazed when I explained that it was possible to be both.

17. *Borei meorei ha-esh*—he who creates the flaming lights (Frankel and Teutsch 1992:29).

Bibliography

Agosín, Marjorie. 1998. *Always from Somewhere Else: A Memoir of My Chilean Jewish Father*. New York: Feminist Press/CUNY.

Anderson, Benedict. 1991[1983]. *Imagined Communities: Reflections on the Origin and Spread of Nationalism*. London: Verso.

Arendt, Hannah. 1977. *Eichmann in Jerusalem: A Report on the Banality of Evil*. New York: Penguin.

Avigdor, Renée. 2004. "O judaísmo não ortodoxo em São Paulo: Um estudo da Comunidade Shalom." Master's thesis, Universidade de São Paulo.

Avruch, Kevin. 1981. *American Immigrants in Israel: Social Identities and Change*. Chicago: University of Chicago Press.

Bakhtin, Mikhail M. 1968. *Rabelais and His World*. Cambridge, Mass.: MIT Press.

Barbosa, Lívia Neves de H. 1992. *O jeitinho brasileiro, ou a arte de ser mais igual que os outros*. Rio de Janeiro: Editora Campus.

———. 1995. "The Brazilian *Jeitinho*: An Exercise in National Identity." In *The Brazilian Puzzle: Culture on the Borderlands of the Western World*, D. J. Hess and R. A. DaMatta, eds., pp. 35–48. New York: Columbia University Press.

Barth, Fredrik, ed. 1969. *Ethnic Groups and Boundaries: The Social Organization of Culture Difference*. Boston: Little, Brown and Co.

Basch, Linda, Nina Glick Schiller, and Cristina Szanton Blanc, eds. 1994. *Nations Unbound: Transnational Projects, Postcolonial Predicaments, and Deterritorialized Nation-States*. Langhorne, Penn.: Gordon and Breach.

Bastide, Roger. 1978[1960]. *The African Religions of Brazil: Toward a Sociology of the Interpenetration of Civilizations*. Trans. Helen Sebba. Baltimore: Johns Hopkins University Press.

Behar, Ruth. 1985. *The Presence of the Past in a Spanish Village: Santa María del Monte*. Princeton: Princeton University Press.

———. 2007. *An Island Called Home: Returning to Jewish Cuba*. New Brunswick: Rutgers University Press.

Benchimol, Samuel. 1998. *Eretz Amazônia: Os judeus na Amazônia*. Manaus, Amazônia: Valer.

Blay, Eva Alterman. 1997. "Judeus na Amazônia." In *Identidades judaicas no Brasil contemporâneo*, Bila Sorj, ed., pp. 33–66. Rio de Janeiro: Imago.

Boas, Franz. 1912. "Changes in the Bodily Form of Descendants of Immigrants." *American Anthropologist* 14:530–62.

———. 1923. "Are the Jews a Race?" *The World Tomorrow* 6(1):5–6.

———. 1939. "Heredity and Environment." *Jewish Social Studies* 1(1):5–14.

Bourdieu, Pierre. 1977. *Outline of a Theory of Practice*. Cambridge: Cambridge University Press.

———. 1990. *The Logic of Practice*. Stanford: Stanford University Press.

Boyarin, Jonathan. 1996. *Thinking in Jewish*. Chicago: University of Chicago Press.

Brodkin, Karen. 1998. *How Jews Became White Folks and What That Says about Race in America*. New Brunswick: Rutgers University Press.

Brumer, Anita. 1994. *Identidade em mudança: Pesquisa sociológica sobre os judeus do Rio Grande do Sul*. Porto Alegre: Federação Israelita do Rio Grande do Sul.

Buarque de Holanda, Sérgio. 1995. *Raízes do Brasil*. São Paulo: Companhia das Letras.

Bunzl, Matti. 2003. "Travels in Jewish Anthropology." *AJS Perspectives: The Newsletter of the Association for Jewish Studies* (Fall/Winter):14–6.

Burdick, John. 1993. *Looking for God in Brazil: The Progressive Catholic Church in Urban Brazil's Religious Arena*. Berkeley: University of California Press.

———. 1998. *Blessed Anastacia: Women, Race, and Popular Christianity in Brazil*. New York: Routledge.

Caldeira, Teresa P. R. 1999. "Fortified Enclaves: The New Urban Segregation." In *Cities and Citizenship*, James Holston, ed., pp. 114–38. Durham: Duke University Press.

———. 2000. *City of Walls: Crime, Segregation, and Citizenship in São Paulo*. Berkeley: University of California Press.

Caldeira, Teresa P. R., and James Holston. 1999. "Democracy and Violence in Brazil." *Comparative Studies in Society and History* 41(4):691–729.

Câmara Cascudo, Luís da. 1972. *Dicionário do folclore brasileiro*, 3rd edition. Rio de Janeiro: Edições de Ouro.

Canecchio, Otávio. 2003. "Cinqüentão em forma." *Veja São Paulo* (September 24). http://veja.abril.com.br/vejasp/240903/cidade.html.

Cardoso de Oliveira, Roberto. 1976. *Identidade, etnia e estrutura social*. São Paulo: Livraria Pioneira Editora.

Carneiro da Cunha, Manuela. 1986[1979]. "Etnicidade: Da cultura residual mas irredutível." In *Antropologia do Brasil: mito, história, etnicidade*, pp. 97–108. São Paulo: Brasiliense/EDUSP.

Castro Alves, Antônio de. 1971. *Antologia poética*. Rio de Janeiro: Instituto Nacional do Livro.

Chandler, Nahum Dimitri. 2000. "Originary Displacement." *Boundary 2* 27(3):249–86.

Charosh, Paul. 1968. "The Home Song." In *Urbanism in World Perspective: A Reader*, S. F. Fava, ed., pp. 449–56. New York: Thomas Y. Crowell.

Child, Jack. 2005. "The Politics and Semiotics of the Smallest Icons of Popular Culture: Latin American Postage Stamps." *Latin American Research Review* 40(1):108–37.

Clifford, James. 1997. *Routes: Travel and Translation in the Late Twentieth Century*. Cambridge: Harvard University Press.

Cytrynowicz, Roney. 2003. *Associação Brasileira A Hebraica de São Paulo: 50 anos: 1953–2003*. São Paulo: Narrativa Um.

Cytrynowicz, Roney, and Judith Zuquim. 1997. *Renascença 75 anos: 1922–1997*. São Paulo: Sociedade Hebraica Brasileira Renascença.

DaMatta, Roberto. 1987. *A casa e a rua*. Rio de Janeiro: Guanabara.

———. 1991a. *Carnivals, Rogues, and Heroes: An Interpretation of the Brazilian Dilemma*. Notre Dame: University of Notre Dame Press.

———. 1991b. *O que faz o Brasil, Brasil?* 4th edition. Rio de Janeiro: Editora Rocco.

———. 1995. "For an Anthropology of the Brazilian Tradition or 'A Virtude Está no Meio.'" In *The Brazilian Puzzle: Culture on the Borderlands of the Western World*, D. J. Hess and R. DaMatta, eds., pp. 270–91. New York: Columbia University Press.

da Silva, Moreira. "Judia Rara" on *MORENGUEIRA 64*. Odeon: 1964.

Davis, Mike. 1990. *City of Quartz: Excavating the Future in Los Angeles*. London: Verso.

de Andrade, Mário. 2000[1928]. *Macunaíma: O herói sem nenhum caráter*, 31st edition. Rio de Janeiro: Livraria Garnier.

de Andrade, Oswald. 1972. *Obras completas VI: Do pau-brasil à antropofagia e às utopias*. Rio de Janeiro: Civilização Brasileira.

Debert, Guita Grin. 1997. "A invenção da terceira idade e a rearticulação de formas de consumo e demandas políticas." *Revista Brasileira de Ciências Sociais* 12(34):39–56.

Decol, René Daniel. 1999. "Imigrações urbanas para o Brasil: O caso dos judeus." Ph.D. dissertation, Universidade Estadual de Campinas.

———. 2009. "A Demographic Profile of Brazilian Jewry." *Contemporary Jewry* 29:99–113.

DellaPergola, Sergio. 1987. "Demographic Trends of Latin American Jewry." In *The Jewish Presence in Latin America*, Judith Laikin Elkin and Gilbert W. Merkx, eds., pp. 85–133. Boston: Allen & Unwin.

———. 1993. "Modern Jewish Demography." In *The Modern Jewish Experience: A Reader's Guide*, J. Wertheimer, ed., pp. 275–90. New York: New York University Press.

———. 1999. *World Jewry beyond 2000: The Demographic Prospects*. Oxford Centre for Hebrew and Jewish Studies, Occasional Papers. Oxford: Oxford Centre for Hebrew and Jewish Studies.

Demônios da Garoa. "A Promessa de Jacó" on *Trem Das 11*. Lançamento: 2002.

Domínguez, Virginia R. 1993. "Questioning Jews." *American Ethnologist* 20(3):618–24.

Douglas, Mary. 1970. *Natural Symbols: Explorations in Cosmology*. New York: Vintage Books.

Du Bois, W.E.B. 1990[1903]. *The Souls of Black Folk*. New York: Vintage Books.

Dundes, Alan. 1980. "Wet and Dry, the Evil Eye: An Essay in Indo-European and Semitic Worldview." In *Interpreting Folklore*, Alan Dundes, ed., pp. 93–133. Bloomington: Indiana University Press.

———, ed. 1981. *The Evil Eye: A Folklore Casebook*. Vol. 2. Garland Folklore Casebooks. New York: Garland.

———. 2002. *The Shabbat Elevator and Other Sabbath Subterfuges: An Unorthodox Essay on Circumventing Custom and Jewish Character*. Lanham, Md.: Rowman & Littlefield.

Dunn, Christopher. 2001. *Brutality Garden: Tropicália and the Emergence of a Brazilian Counterculture*. Chapel Hill: University of North Carolina Press.

Eakin, Marshall C. 1998. *Brazil: The Once and Future Country*. New York: St. Martin's Griffin.

Egler, Tamara Tania Cohen. 1997. "Trajetórias de vida: Espaços de integração e exclusão." In *Judaísmo: Memória e identidade*. Vol. 1. H. Lewin and D. Kuperman, eds., pp. 111–25. Rio de Janeiro: Universidade do Estado do Rio de Janeiro.

Eisenberg, Joyce, and Ellen Scolnic. 2001. *The JPS Dictionary of Jewish Words*. Philadelphia: The Jewish Publication Society.

Elkin, Judith Laikin. 1998. *The Jews of Latin America*, revised edition. New York: Holmes & Meier.

Faerman, Marcos, and Airton Gontow, eds. 1996. *A Hebraica de São Paulo*. São Paulo: Associação Brasileira "A Hebraica" de São Paulo.

Falbel, Nachman. 1998. "Identidade judaica, memória e a questão dos indesejáveis no Brasil." In *A paixão de ser: Depoimentos e ensaios sobre a identidade judaica*, A. Slavutzky, ed., pp. 215–64. Porto Alegre: Artes e Ofícios.

———. 2008. *Judeus no Brasil: Estudos e notas*. São Paulo: Editora da Universidade de São Paulo.

Fausto, Boris. 1997. *Negócios e ócios: Histórias da imigração*. São Paulo: Companhia das Letras.

———, ed. 1999. *Fazer a América: A imigração em massa para a América Latina*. São Paulo: Editora da Universidade de São Paulo.

Fausto, Boris, Osvaldo M. S. Truzzi, Roberto Grün, and Célia Sakurai. 1995. *Imigração e política em São Paulo*. Série Imigração. São Paulo: Editora Sumaré.

Feldman, Jeffrey D. 2004. "The Jewish Roots and Routes of Anthropology." *Anthropological Quarterly* 77(1):107–25.

Fernandes, Florestan. 1969. *The Negro in Brazilian Society*. New York: Columbia University Press.

Finkielkraut, Alain. 1994. *The Imaginary Jew*. Lincoln: University of Nebraska Press.

Flasher, Lydia V., and Stephen A. Maisto. 1984. "A Review of Theory and Research of Drinking Patterns among Jews." *The Journal of Nervous and Mental Disease* 172(10):596–603.

Foucault, Michel. 1979. *Discipline and Punish*. New York: Vintage.

Frank, Gelya. 1995. "The Ethnographic Films of Barbara G. Myerhoff: Anthropology, Feminism, and the Politics of Jewish Identity." In *Women Writing Culture*, R. Behar and D. A. Gordon, eds., pp. 207–32. Berkeley: University of California Press.

———. 1997. "Jews, Multiculturalism, and Boasian Anthropology." *American Anthropologist* 99(4):731–45.

Frankel, Ellen, and Betsy Platkin Teutsch. 1992. *The Encyclopedia of Jewish Symbols*. Northvale, N.J.: Jason Aronson.

Freyre, Gilberto. 1986a[1933]. *The Masters and the Slaves: A Study in the Development of*

Brazilian Civilization, 2nd English-language, revised edition. Berkeley: University of California Press.

———. 1986b. *Order and Progress: Brazil from Monarch to Republic*. Berkeley: University of California Press.

Fry, Peter. 1982. *Para inglês ver: Identidade e política na cultura brasileira*. Rio de Janeiro: Zahar Editores.

García Canclini, Néstor. 2009. "What Is a City?" In *City/Art: The Urban Scene in Latin America*, Rebecca E. Biron, ed., pp. 37–60. Durham: Duke University Press.

Gilman, Sander. 1991. *The Jew's Body*. New York: Routledge.

Gilroy, Paul. 1993. *The Black Atlantic: Modernity and Double Consciousness*. Cambridge: Harvard University Press.

Glick Schiller, Nina, Linda Basch, and Cristina Blanc-Szanton. 1992a. "Towards a Definition of Transnationalism: Introductory Remarks and Research Questions." In *Towards a Transnational Perspective on Migration: Race, Class, Ethnicity, and Nationalism Reconsidered*, N. Glick Schiller, L. Basch, and C. Blanc-Szanton, eds., pp. ix–xiv. New York: Annals of the New York Academy of Sciences.

———. 1992b. "Transnationalism: A New Analytic Framework for Understanding Migration." In *Towards a Transnational Perspective on Migration: Race, Class, Ethnicity, and Nationalism Reconsidered*, N. Glick Schiller, L. Basch, and C. Blanc-Szanton, eds., pp. 1–24. New York: Annals of the New York Academy of Sciences.

Goldberg, Florinda, and Iosef Rozen, eds. 1988. *Los Latinoamericanos en Israel: Antología de una aliá*. Buenos Aires: Editorial Contexto.

Goldstein, Donna M. 2003. *Laughter Out of Place: Race, Class, Violence, and Sexuality in a Rio Shantytown*. Berkeley: University of California Press.

Goldstein, Eric L. 2006. *The Price of Whiteness: Jews, Race, and American Identity*. Princeton: Princeton University Press.

Gomes, Eugênio, and Hildon Rocha. 1971. "Notas." In *Antologia poética (Castro Alves)*. Rio de Janeiro: Instituto Nacional do Livro.

Gregori, José, ed. 1998. *National Programme on Human Rights*. Brasília: Ministério da Justiça, Presidência da República.

Gregori, Maria Filomena. 2000. *Viração: Experiências de meninos nas ruas*. São Paulo: Companhia das Letras.

Grin, Monica. 1995. "Etnicidade e cultura política no Brasil: O caso dos imigrantes judeus do leste europeu." *Revista Brasileira de Ciências Sociais* 28:139–56.

Grün, Roberto. 1992. *Negócios & famílias: Armênios em São Paulo*. Série Imigração. São Paulo: Sumaré.

———. 1994. "Identidade e representação: Os judeus na esfera política e a imagem na comunidade." *Revista Brasileira de Ciências Sociais* 9:123–48.

———. 1998. "Becoming White: Jews and Armenians in the Brazilian Ethnic Mosaic." *Anthropological Journal on European Cultures* 7(2):107–30.

Guarnizo, Luiz Eduardo. 1997. "The Emergence of a Transnational Social Formation and the Mirage of Return Migration among Dominican Transmigrants." *Identities* 4(2):281–322.

Gupta, Akhil, and James Ferguson. 1997. "Culture, Power, Place: Ethnography at the End of an Era." In *Culture, Power, Place: Explorations in Critical Anthropology*, A. Gupta and J. Ferguson, eds., pp. 1–29. Durham: Duke University Press.

Gurovitz, Hélio, and Ruth de Aquino. 2008. "Samba & holocausto: O desfile da Viradouro levanta uma polêmica: Um genocídio pode ser tema de carro alegórico no carnaval da Sapucaí?" *Revista Época* 507 (posted January 31, 2008, published February 4, 2008). http://revistaepoca.globo.com/Revista/Epoca/0,,EDR81439-6014,00.html.

Harris, Marvin, and Conrad Philip Kottak. 1963. "The Structural Significance of Brazilian Racial Categories." *Sociologia* 25:203–9.

Harvey, David. 2000. "Cosmopolitanism and the Banality of Geographical Evils." *Public Culture* 12(2):529–64.

Heath, Dwight B. 1976. "Anthropological Perspectives on Alcohol: A Historical Review." In *Cross-Cultural Approaches to the Study of Alcohol: An Interdisciplinary Approach*, M. W. Everett, J. O. Waddell, and D. B. Heath, eds. The Hague: Mouton.

Hemsi, Sylvana. 1997. "Identidade judaica: Um modelo paulistano liberal." Master's thesis, Universidade de São Paulo.

Herman, Donald L. 1984. *The Latin American Community of Israel*. New York: Praeger.

Herskovits, Melville J. 1927. "When Is a Jew a Jew?" *The Modern Quarterly* 4(2):109–17.

———. 1960[1949]. "Who Are the Jews?" In *The Jews: Their History, Culture, and Religion*, L. Finkelstein, ed., pp. 1489–1507. New York: Harper & Row.

Herzfeld, Michael. 1997. *Cultural Intimacy: Social Poetics in the Nation-State*. New York: Routledge.

Hess, David J., and Roberto A. DaMatta, eds. 1995. *The Brazilian Puzzle: Culture on the Borderlands of the Western World*. New York: Columbia University Press.

Hinchberger, Bill. 1999. "Christians Believe in Amazon Rabbi." *Jewish Telegraph Agency*. http://www.jta.org/news/article/1999/11/30/14549/Amazonrabbi8217s.

———. 2005. "Brazil's National Dish Goes Kosher." *Jewish Telegraph Agency*. http://jta.org/news/article/2005/08/11/13135/InBrazilcompromis, 8/11/05.

Hintzen, Percy C. 2001. *West Indian in the West: Self-Representations in an Immigrant Community*. New York: New York University Press.

Holston, James. 1989. *The Modernist City: An Anthropological Critique of Brasília*. Chicago: University of Chicago Press.

———. 2008. *Insurgent Citizenship: Disjunctions of Democracy and Modernity in Brazil*. Princeton: Princeton University Press.

Horowitz, Irving Louis. 1974. *Israeli Ecstasies/Jewish Agonies*. New York: Oxford University Press.

Igel, Regina. 1997. *Imigrantes judeus/escritores brasileiros*. São Paulo: Editora Perspectiva.

Jabor, Arnaldo. 1999. "Democracia trouxe revolução da vulgaridade." *Folha de São Paulo*, September 28, p. 8.

Johnson, Paul Christopher. 2002. *Secrets, Gossip, and Gods: The Transformation of Brazilian Candomblé*. Oxford: Oxford University Press.

Kalcik, Susan. 1984. "Ethnic Foodways in America: Symbol and the Performance of Identity." In *Ethnic and Regional Foodways in the United States: The Performance of*

Group Identity, L. K. Brown and K. Mussell, eds., pp. 37–65. Knoxville: University of Tennessee Press.

Karam, John Tofik. 2007. *Another Arabesque: Syrian-Lebanese Ethnicity in Neoliberal Brazil*. Philadelphia: Temple University Press.

Kaufman, David. 1999. *Shul with a Pool: The "Synagogue-Center" in American Jewish History*. Brandeis Series in American Jewish History, Culture, and Life. Hanover, N.H.: Brandeis University Press/University Press of New England.

Kaye/Kantrowitz, Melanie. 2007. *The Colors of Jews: Racial Politics and Radical Diasporism*. Bloomington: Indiana University Press.

Kirshenblatt-Gimblett, Barbara. 1995. "Introduction." In *Life Is with People: The Culture of the Shtetl*, Mark Zborowski and Elizabeth Herzog, eds., pp. ix–xlviii. New York: Schocken.

Klein, Misha. 1999. "Coral litúrgico canta com Moshé Stern." *Revista "A Hebraica"* 40:31–32.

Kleinsinger, Michel. 2000. *Nas asas da esperança*. São Paulo: M. Kleinsinger.

Knupfer, Genevieve, and Robin Room. 1967. "Drinking Patterns and Attitudes of Irish, Jewish and White Protestant American Men." *Quarterly Journal of Studies on Alcohol* 28(4):676–99.

Kroeber, Alfred L. 1917. "Are the Jews a Race?" *The Menorah Journal* 3(5):290–94.

Kushnir, Beatriz. 1999. "São judeus os que aceitam Cristo?" *Boletim da ASA* 10(58):5–7.

Lacy, Marc. 2008. "The Right Thing to Wear at the Wrong End of a Gun." *New York Times*, October 6, p. A12. http://www.nytimes.com/2008/10/06/world/americas/06mexico.html?emc=eta1.

Landes, Ruth. 2006[1947]. *City of Women*, second edition. Albuquerque: University of New Mexico Press.

Lederhendler, Eli. 1999. "New York City, the Jews, and 'The Urban Experience.'" In *People of the City: Jews and the Urban Challenge*, E. Mendelsohn, ed., pp. 49–67. New York: Oxford University Press.

Lesser, Jeffrey. 1991. *Jewish Colonization in Rio Grande do Sul, 1904–1925*. São Paulo: Centro de Estudos de Demografia Histórica da América Latina/Universidade de São Paulo.

———. 1995. *Welcoming the Undesirables: Brazil and the Jewish Question*. Berkeley: University of California Press.

———. 1998. "'Jews Are Turks Who Sell on Credit': Elite Images of Arabs and Jews in Brazil." In *Arab and Jewish Immigrants in Latin America: Images and Realities*, I. Klich and J. Lesser, eds., pp. 38–56. Portland, Ore.: Frank Cass.

———. 1999. *Negotiating National Identity: Immigrants, Minorities, and the Struggle for Ethnicity in Brazil*. Durham: Duke University Press.

———. 2001. "Jewish Brazilians or Brazilian Jews? A Reflection on Brazilian Ethnicity." *Shofar* 19(3):65–73.

———. 2005. "Judeus salvam judeus: Os estereótipos e a questão dos refugiados no Brasil, 1935–1945." In *Os judeus no Brasil: Inquisição, imigração e identidade*, Keila Grinberg, ed., pp. 315–34. Rio de Janeiro: Civilização Brasileira.

———. 2007. *A Discontented Diaspora: Japanese Brazilians and the Meanings of Ethnic Militancy, 1960–1980.* Durham: Duke University Press.

Lesser, Jeffrey, and Raanan Rein. 2008. "New Approaches to Ethnicity and Diaspora in Twentieth-Century Latin America." In *Rethinking Jewish-Latin Americans,* Jeffrey Lesser and Raanan Rein, eds., pp. 23–40. Albuquerque: University of New Mexico Press.

Lévi-Strauss, Claude. 1961. *A World on the Wane.* New York: Criterion Books.

———. 1992. *Tristes tropiques.* New York: Penguin.

Lewis, Herbert. 2001. "The Passion of Franz Boas." *American Anthropologist* 103(2):447–67.

Lima, Paulo, and Bernardete Toneto. 1999. "O Axé de Zumbi." In *The Brazil Reader: History, Culture, Politics,* R. M. Levine and J. J. Crocitti, eds., pp. 487–98. Durham: Duke University Press.

Linger, Daniel Touro. 1992. *Dangerous Encounters: Meanings of Violence in a Brazilian City.* Stanford: Stanford University Press.

———. 2001. *No One Home: Brazilian Selves Remade in Japan.* Stanford: Stanford University Press.

Lispector, Clarice. 1977. *A hora da estrela,* 3rd edition. Rio de Janeiro: José Olympio.

———. 1986. *The Hour of the Star.* New York: New Directions.

Low, Setha. 1997. "Urban Fear: Building the Fortress City." *City & Society:*53–71.

Malamud, Samuel. 1983. *Do arquivo e da memória.* Rio de Janeiro: Bloch.

———. 1986. *Escalas no tempo.* Rio de Janeiro: Record.

———. 1988. *Recordando a Praça Onze.* Rio de Janeiro: Kosmos.

———. 1992. *Documentário.* Rio de Janeiro: Imago.

———. 1997. *A Segunda Guerra Mundial na visão de um judeu brasileiro.* Rio de Janeiro: Aeroplano.

Mandelbaum, David G. 1939. "The Jewish Way of Life in Cochin." *Jewish Social Studies* 1(4):423–60.

———. 1975. "Social Stratification among the Jews of Cochin in India and in Israel." *Jewish Journal of Sociology* 17(2):165–210.

———. 1977. "Caste and Community among the Jews of Cochin in India and Israel." In *Caste among Non-Hindus in India,* H. Singh, ed., pp. 107–40. New Delhi: National Publishing House.

———. 1981. "A Case History of Judaism: The Jews of Cochin in India and in Israel." In *Jewish Tradition in the Diaspora: Studies in Memory of Professor Walter J. Fischel,* M. M. Caspi, ed., pp. 211–30. Berkeley: Judah L. Magnes Museum.

Margolis, Maxine L. 1994. *Little Brazil: An Ethnography of Brazilian Immigrants in New York City.* Princeton: Princeton University Press.

———. 2007. "Becoming *Brazucas*: Brazilian Identity in the United States." In *The Other Latinos: Central and South Americans in the United States,* José Luis Falconi and José Antonio Mazzotti, eds., pp. 213–30. Cambridge: Harvard University Press.

Matsuoka, Hideaki. 2007. *Japanese Prayer below the Equator: How Brazilians Believe in the Church of World Messianity.* Lanham, Md.: Lexington Books.

Milkewitz Trzonowicz, Alberto Samuel. 2006. *Ledor Vador: Construindo identidades judaicas de geração em geração (Estudo exploratório de casos de famílias e escolas judaicas em S. Paulo)*. Master's thesis, Universidade de São Paulo.

Miller, Susan Gilson. 1996. "Kippur on the Amazon: Jewish Emigration from Northern Morocco in the Late Nineteenth Century." In *Sephardi and Middle Eastern Jewries: History and Culture in the Modern Era*, H. E. Goldberg, ed. Bloomington: Indiana University Press.

Mizrahi, Rachel, ed. 1996. *Lembranças . . . Presente do passado: Histórias de vida*. São Paulo: Schmukler.

———. 2003. *Imigrantes judeus do Oriente Médio: São Paulo e Rio de Janeiro*. São Paulo: Ateliê Editorial.

Moraes, Marcus. 2002. "As Awareness of Drug Addiction Grows among Brazil's Jews, So Do Treatments." *Jewish Telegraphic Agency*. http://archive.jta.org/article/2002/05/20/2909639/around-the-jewish-world-as-awareness-of-drug-addiction-grows-among-brazils-jews-so-do-treatments.

Morris, Katherine, ed. 1996. *Odyssey of Exile: Jewish Women Flee the Nazis for Brazil*. Detroit: Wayne State University Press.

Myerhoff, Barbara G. 1978. *Number Our Days*. New York: Simon & Schuster.

Nigri, Shirley. 2001. "Amid the Madness of Carnival Some Yiddishkeit—Just Barely." *Jewish Telegraphic Agency*, March 1. http://archive.jta.org/article/2001/03/01/2902033/amid-the-madness-of-carnival-some-yiddishkeit—just-barely.

Novinsky, Anita. 1987. "Jewish Roots in Brazil." In *The Jewish Presence in Latin America*, J. L. Elkin and G. W. Merkx, eds., pp. 33–44. Boston: Allen and Unwin.

———. 1996. "O racismo e a questão judaica." In *Raça e diversidade*, L. M. Schwarcz and R.d.S. Queiroz, eds., pp. 97–111. São Paulo: Editora da Universidade de São Paulo.

O'Dougherty, Maureen. 2002. *Consumption Intensified: The Politics of Middle-Class Daily Life in Brazil*. Durham: Duke University Press.

Ong, Aihwa. 1996. "Cultural Citizenship as Subject-Making: Immigrants Negotiate Racial and Cultural Boundaries in the United States." *Current Anthropology* 37(5):737–62.

———. 1999. *Flexible Citizenship: The Cultural Logics of Transnationality*. Durham: Duke University Press.

Orsi, Robert A. 2005. *Between Heaven and Earth: The Religious Worlds People Make and the Scholars Who Study Them*. Princeton: Princeton University Press.

Ortiz, Renato. 1985. *Cultura brasileira e identidade nacional*. São Paulo: Brasiliense.

———. 1991[1978]. *A morte branca do feiticeiro negro: Umbanda e sociedade brasileira*. São Paulo: Brasiliense.

Parker, Richard. 1991. *Bodies, Pleasures, and Passions: Sexual Culture in Contemporary Brazil*. Boston: Beacon Press.

Patai, Raphael, and Jennifer Patai. 1989. *The Myth of the Jewish Race*, revised edition. Detroit: Wayne State University.

Pellegrini, Ann. 1997a. "Interarticulations: Gender, Race, and the Jewish Woman Question." In *Judaism since Gender*, M. Peskowitz and L. Levitt, eds., pp. 49–55. New York: Routledge.

———. 1997b. "Whiteface Performances: "Race," Gender, and Jewish Bodies." In *Jews and Other Differences: The New Jewish Cultural Studies*, J. Boyarin and D. Boyarin, eds., pp. 108–49. Minneapolis: University of Minnesota Press.

Perrone, Charles A., and Christopher Dunn. 2001. "'Chiclete com Banana': Internationalization in Brazilian Popular Music." In *Brazilian Popular Music and Globalization*, Charles A. Perrone and Christopher Dunn, eds., pp. 1–38. Gainesville: University Press of Florida.

Pfeffer, Renato Somberg. 1997. "Vidas que sangram história: Do mundo para Belo Horizonte." In *Judaísmo: Memória e identidade*. Vol. 1. H. Lewin and D. Kuperman, eds., pp. 97–109. Rio de Janeiro: Universidade do Estado do Rio de Janeiro.

Pinheiro, Flavio. 2000. "Introdução." In *Próximos 500: As perguntas que o Brasil vai ter que responder*. F. Pinheiro and P. R. Pires, eds., pp. 5–7. Rio de Janeiro: Aeroplano.

Plotnicov, Leonard, and Myrna Silverman. 1978. "Jewish Ethnic Signaling: Social Bonding in Contemporary American Society." *Ethnology* 17(4):407–23.

Pollock, Sheldon, Homi K. Bhabha, Carol A. Breckenridge, and Dipesh Chakrabarty. 2000. "Cosmopolitanisms." *Public Culture* 12(3):577–89.

Prado, Jr., Caio. 1967 [1942]. *The Colonial Background of Modern Brazil*. Berkeley: University of California Press.

Pratt, Mary Louise. 1986. "Fieldwork in Common Places." In *Writing Culture: The Poetics and Politics of Ethnography*, James Clifford and George E. Marcus, eds., pp. 27–50. Berkeley: University of California Press.

Rabinow, Paul. 1996. *Essays on the Anthropology of Reason*. Princeton: Princeton University Press.

Ramagem, Sonia Bloomfield. 1994. *A fênix de Abraão: Um estudo sobre cristãos-novos retornados ao judaísmo de seus ancestrais*. Brasília: Cultura Gráfica e Editora.

Ramos, Alcida Rita. 1998. *Indigenism: Ethnic Politics in Brazil*. Madison: University of Wisconsin Press.

Ramos, Jair de Souza. 1996. "Dos males que vêm com o sangue: As representações raciais e a categoria do imigrante indesejável nas concepções sobre imigração da década de 20." In *Raça, ciência e sociedade*, M. C. Maio and R. V. Santos, eds., pp. 59–82. Rio de Janeiro: Fiocruz.

Rattner, Henrique. 1972a. "Prefácio." In *Nos caminhos da diáspora: Uma introdução ao estudo demográfico dos judeus*, H. Rattner, ed., pp. 7–10. São Paulo: Centro Brasileiro de Estudos Judaicos/FFLCH-USP.

———. 1972b. "Recenseamento e pesquisa sociológica da comunidade judaica em São Paulo—1968: Relatório preliminar." In *Nos caminhos da diáspora: Uma introdução ao estudo demográfico dos judeus*, H. Rattner, ed., pp. 235–56. São Paulo: Centro Brasileiro de Estudos Judaicos/FFLCH-USP.

———. 1977. *Tradição e mudança: A comunidade judaica em São Paulo*. São Paulo: Editora Ática.

———. 1987. "Economic and Social Mobility of Jews in Brazil." In *The Jewish Presence in Latin America*, Judith Laikin Elkin and Gilbert W. Merkx, eds., pp. 187–200. Boston: Allen & Unwin.

Rebhun, L. A. 1995. "Contemporary Evil Eye in Northeast Brazil." In *Folklore Interpreted: Essays in Honor of Alan Dundes*, R. Bendix and R. L. Zumwalt, eds., pp. 213–33. New York: Garland.

———. 1999. *The Heart Is Unknown Country: Love in the Changing Economy of Northeastern Brazil*. Stanford: Stanford University Press.

Reibscheid, Samuel. 1995. *Breve fantasia*. São Paulo: Scritta.

Reis, Paul, ed. 2000. *República das etnias*. Rio de Janeiro: Museu da República/Editora Gryphus.

Roden, Claudia. 1996. *The Book of Jewish Food: An Odyssey from Samarkand to New York*. New York: Knopf.

Roitman, Deborah. 1996. *Jewish Identification among Young Mexican Jews*. Master's thesis, Bar Ilan University.

Romero, Simon. 2000. "Rich Brazilians Rise Above Rush-Hour Jams." *New York Times*, February 15:A:1.

Rosaldo, Renato. 1994a. "Cultural Citizenship and Educational Democracy." *Cultural Anthropology* 9(3):402–11.

———. 1994b. "Cultural Citizenship in San Jose, California." *PoLAR* 17(2):57–63.

Rotella, Sebastian. 2002. "Ex-Argentine Leader Faces Bribery Probe." *Los Angeles Times*, January 24, p. A-1.

Salamon, Hagar. 1999. *The Hyena People: Ethiopian Jews in Christian Ethiopia*. Berkeley: University of California Press.

Schemo, Diana Jean. 1995. "Sao Paulo Journal; The Elevator Doesn't Lie: Intolerance in Brazil." *New York Times*, August 30. *www.nytimes.com/1995/08/30/world/sao-paulo-journal-the-elevator-doesn-t-lie-intolerance-in-brazil.html?scp=1&sq= race+and+soci al+elevator+brazil&st=nyt*.

Scheper-Hughes, Nancy. 1992. *Death without Weeping: The Violence of Everyday Life in Brazil*. Berkeley: University of California Press.

———. 1996. "Small Wars and Invisible Genocides." *Social Science and Medicine* 43(5):889–900.

———. 1997. "Peace-Time Crimes." *Social Identities* 3(3):471–97.

Schwarcz, Lilia Moritz. 1993. *O espectáculo das raças: Cientistas, instituições e questão racial no Brasil, 1870–1930*. São Paulo: Companhia das Letras.

Scliar, Moacyr. 1997. *A majestade do Xingu*. São Paulo: Companhia das Letras.

———. 2000. "Memórias judaicas." In *Entre Moisés e Macunaíma: Os judeus que descobriram o Brasil*. Rio de Janeiro: Garamond.

Scliar, Moacyr, and Márcio Souza. 2000. *Entre Moisés e Macunaíma: Os judeus que descobriram o Brasil*. Rio de Janeiro: Garamond.

Sedgwick, Eve Kosofsky. 1990. *Epistemology of the Closet*. Berkeley: University of California Press.

Seyferth, Giralda. 1996. "Construindo a nação: Hierarquias raciais e o papel do racismo na política de imigração e colonização." In *Raça, ciência e sociedade*, M. C. Maio and R. V. Santos, eds., pp. 41–58. Rio de Janeiro: Fiocruz.

———. 1998. "German Immigration and the Formation of German-Brazilian Ethnicity." *Anthropological Journal on European Cultures* 7(2):131–54.

———. 2000. "As identidades dos imigrantes e o *melting pot* nacional." *Horizontes Antropológicos* 6(14):143–76.

Sheriff, Robin E. 2001. *Dreaming Equality: Color, Race, and Racism in Urban Brazil*. New Brunswick: Rutgers University Press.

Skidmore, Thomas E. 1993. *Black into White: Race and Nationality in Brazilian Thought*. Durham: Duke University Press.

Sorj, Bernardo. 1997. "Sociabilidade brasileira e identidade judaica." In *Identidades judaicas no Brasil contemporâneo*, Bila Sorj, ed., pp. 9–31. Rio de Janeiro: Imago.

Sorj, Bila. 1997. "Conversões e casamentos 'mistos': A produção de 'novos judeus' no Brasil." In *Identidades judaicas no Brasil contemporâneo*, Bila Sorj, ed., pp. 67–86. Rio de Janeiro: Imago.

———. 1998. "Do futuro ao passado: Mudanças nas identidades judaicas contemporâneas." Paper presented at the XXI meetings of the Associação Brasileira de Antropologia, Universidade Federal do Espírito Santo, Vitória.

Southern, Eileen. 1997. *The Music of Black Americans: A History*, 3rd edition. New York: W. W. Norton.

Spitzer, Leo. 1998. *Hotel Bolivia: The Culture of Memory in a Refuge from Nazism*. New York: Hill and Wang.

Stack, Carol B. 1996. *Call to Home: African Americans Reclaim the Rural South*. New York: Basic Books.

Stam, Robert. 1989. *Subversive Pleasures: Bakhtin, Cultural Criticism, and Film*. Baltimore: Johns Hopkins University Press.

———. 1997. *Tropical Multiculturalism: A Comparative History of Race in Brazilian Cinema & Culture. Latin America Otherwise: Languages, Empires, Nations*. Durham: Duke University Press.

Stillman, Norman, personal communication with author, 2011.

Stratton, Jon. 1997. "(Dis) placing the Jews: Historicizing the Idea of Diaspora." *Diaspora* 6(3):301–29.

———. 2000. *Coming Out Jewish: Constructing Ambivalent Identities*. London: Routledge.

Sundfeld, Roberta Alexandr, and Marly Rodrigues, eds. 1996. *FISESP 50 Anos: Uma trajetória coletiva*. São Paulo: R. A. Sundfeld.

Tavares de Sá, Hernane. 1947. *The Brazilians: People of Tomorrow*. New York: John Day.

Titãs. "Homem Primata" on *Cabeça Dinossauro*. WEA: 1986.

Toneto, Bernardete. 1999. "The Church Tries to Combat Prejudice." In *The Brazil Reader: History, Culture, Politics*, R. M. Levine and J. J. Crocitti, eds., pp. 384–85. Durham: Duke University Press.

Topel, Marta. 2008. *Jerusalem & São Paulo: The New Jewish Orthodoxy in Focus*. Lanham, Md.: University Press of America.

Truzzi, Osvaldo M. S. 1992. *De mascates a doutores*. Série Imigração. São Paulo: Editora Sumaré.

———. 1997. *Patrícios: Sírios e libaneses em São Paulo*. Estudos Brasileiros, Vol. 31. São Paulo: Editora Hucitec.

Tucci Carneiro, Maria Luiza. 1988. *O anti-semitismo na era Vargas: Fantasmas de uma geração (1930–1945)*. São Paulo: Editora Brasiliense.

———. 1997. "Introdução." In *A Segunda Guerra Mundial na visão de um judeu brasileiro*, by Samuel Malamud, pp. 17–27. Rio de Janeiro: Aeroplano.

Unterman, Alan. 1991. *Dictionary of Jewish Lore and Legend*. London: Thames and Hudson.

Veloso, Caetano. "Sampa" on *Muito (Dentro Da Estrela Azulada)*. Philips: 1978.

Veloso, Mariza, and Angélica Madeira. 1999. *Leituras brasileiras: Itinerários no pensamento social e na literatura*. Rio de Janeiro: Editora Paz e Terra.

Veltman, Henrique. 1996. *A história dos judeus em São Paulo*. Rio de Janeiro: Editora Expressão e Cultura.

Vex, Susan Lind, and Sheila B. Blume. 2001. "The JACS Study I: Characteristics of a Population of Chemically Dependent Jewish Men and Women." *Journal of Addictive Diseases* 20(4):71–89.

Vieira, Nelson H. 1995. *Jewish Voices in Brazilian Literature: A Prophetic Discourse of Alterity*. Gainesville: University Press of Florida.

Warren, Jonathan W. 2001. *Racial Revolutions: Antiracism and Indian Resurgence in Brazil*. Durham: Duke University Press.

Wilk, Richard R. 1999. "'Real Belizean Food': Building Local Identity in the Transnational Caribbean." *American Anthropologist* 101(2):244–55.

Wolff, Egon, and Frieda Wolff. 1988. *Guia histórico da comunidade judaica de São Paulo*. São Paulo: Editora B'nei B'rith.

Worcman, Susane, ed. 1991. *Heranças e lembranças: Imigrantes judeus no Rio de Janeiro*. Rio de Janeiro: Associação Religiosa Israelita do Rio de Janeiro/Centro Interdisciplinar de Estudos Contemporâneos/Museu da Imagem e Som.

World ORT. 2008. "Brazil Honours Samuel Malamud z"l." http://www.ort.org/asp/article.asp?id=702, posted 8/15/2008, downloaded 11/1/2008.

Yelvington, Kevin A. 2000. "Herskovits' Jewishness." *History of Anthropology Newsletter* 27(2):3–9.

Zborowski, Mark, and Elizabeth Herzog. 1995[1952]. *Life Is with People: The Culture of the Shtetl*. New York: Schocken Books.

Zenner, Walter P. 1991. *Minorities in the Middle: A Cross-Cultural Analysis*. SUNY Series in Ethnicity and Race in American Life. Albany: State University of New York Press.

Zweig, Stefan. 1942. *Brazil: Land of the Future*. A. St. James, trans. London: Cassell.

Index

African Americans, 18, 20–21, 125, 193–94, 229n1, 230n5. *See also Porgy and Bess* (Gershwin)

African Diaspora, 13

Afro-Brazilians, 1, 18, 21, 37, 80, 84, 88, 97, 107, 141, 155–56, 192–94, 217n26, 221n9, 225n38, 230n2

Albert Einstein Hospital, 127, 212n28

Alcohol, 123, 149–50, 223nn30–33

Aleichem, Sholem, 57

Aliyah (step up; return), 227n11; Jewish Brazilians and, 173, 197, 227n12

AMIA. *See* Asociación Mutual Israelita Argentina

Anderson, Benedict, 13, 195–96

Andrade, Mário de, 220n3

Andrade, Oswald de, 18–19

Anthropophagy (*antropofagia*), 18–19, 198

Anti-Semitism: anthropology against, 210n8; in Argentina, 176–79, 228n20; in Brazil, 46, 94–95, 163, 170–72, 176, 183, 196, 204, 213n12, 227n10; Brazilian law against, 172; Iran and, 179, 228n20; and Israel, 176–79, 227n16; Jewish identity and, 98, 182, 184; march against, 181–82, 228n23; Second Intifada and, 181, 227n10; Security and, 175–76, 180–81, 184–90, 228n22; transnationalism and, 172, 176–81, 185, 189–90; in U.S., 179, 227n19

Architecture: of Hebraica Club, 32, 151, 211n28; of maid's quarters, 106; modernist, 157, 182, 210n17, 211n28; racism and, 107–8; social class and, 106–7

Arendt, Hannah, 166

Argentina, 47, 176–79, 227n15, 228n20

Argentinean Jews in Brazil, 48, 113, 197

ARI. *See* Associação Religiosa Israelita

Armenians, 45, 97, 213n8, 222n13

Ashkenazi Jews, 6, 53–54, 56, 58, 95, 135, 203; braiding, meaning of, 12–13; definition of, 73, 209n4; food, 12, 38, 85, 118; immigrants, 26, 79; racialization of, 73–75, 80, 96–97; religious practice of, 77–78; Sephardi Jews, relations with, 38, 54, 73–75, 78–81, 215n4; *shtetl*, meaning of, 57–58. *See also* Intermarriage; Yiddish

Asociación Mutual Israelita Argentina (AMIA), 176–79, 227nn14–15, 228n20; Brazilian Jewish response to bombing of, 185, 224n35; protest against bombing of, 25, 182, 228

Assimilation, 46, 73, 81, 172, 185, 196, 200, 208, 229n33. *See also* Intermarriage

Associação Brasileira "A Hebraica" de São Paulo. *See* Hebraica Club

Associação Religiosa Israelita (ARI, Rio de Janeiro), 215n6

Avenida Paulista, 41, 54–55, 65, 182

Baal korei (master of the reading), 148, 223n28

Bakhtin, Mikhail, 224n34, 224n37

Bar Mitzvah, 116, 147, 219n17, 223n28

Basch, Linda, 14

Bat Mitzvah, 219n17

Behar, Ruth, 36

Belonging, 12, 13, 16–17, 21, 130, 196, 199–201, 210n14, 230n7; Jews in Brazil, 2, 26, 69, 74, 88, 93, 95, 130–31, 143, 163–64, 173, 184, 189, 192, 198, 206

Ben-Gurion, David, 138, 140, 205, 221n8

Binyan Olam, 216n20

Blanc-Szanton, Cristina, 14

Bloch, Adolfo, 33

B'nai B'rith, 6, 209n3

Boas, Franz, 9–10, 19, 210n8

Bom Retiro (neighborhood), 50, 53–54, 56, 58, 62–63, 76, 86, 100–101, 213n17, 227

Bonder, Rabbi Nilton, 215n6

Boyarin, Daniel, 92, 217n35

Boyarin, Jonathan, 217n35

Branqueamento (*embranquecimento*) (whitening), 46, 97

Brazil: anniversary of European arrival, 21, 50, 133–34, 220n1; Catholicism in, 1, 5, 7–8, 25, 132–33, 151–52, 171, 209n5; Chinese Brazilians in, 44, 85, 211n19; class stratification in, 20–21, 56, 99, 101, 106–12, 123–26, 130, 152, 164, 168–70, 175, 226nn7–8; clubs in, 31–32, 61, 63, 99–102, 138, 149, 152, 154, 214n22–23, 229n29; contradictions in, 18, 24, 41, 93–94, 110–11, 166, 172, 175, 189, 191–92, 198–99, 200, 217n26, 230n6; currency in, 49, 113, 116, 214n29, 218n3; educational system in, 112–13; ethnicity in, 4–5, 17, 24, 31, 61, 72, 83, 85, 87–88, 91, 97, 159, 172, 175, 183–84, 186–87, 195–96, 211n18, 211n26, 218n6; flag of, 210n17; food in, 3–4, 83–90, 119, 164, 216n18; German Brazilians in, 63; historical revision of, 50, 133–35; holidays, 3–5; immigration and, 4, 7, 21, 25–26, 44, 46–47, 50, 52, 97, 134, 204, 211n18, 212n3, 213n10, 217n35; Italian Brazilians in, 3–4, 7, 44, 55, 63, 83, 85, 212n3; Japanese Brazilians in, 4, 21, 41, 63, 80, 83, 85, 97, 209n5, 211n19, 215n3;

Korean Brazilians in, 58; Middle Eastern Brazilians in, 4, 21, 32, 41, 45, 85, 97, 136–37, 179, 209n6, 211n19, 213nn9–10, 216n18, 221n6, 222n13; modernism in, 18–19, 198, 220n3; "myth of three races," 19, 21, 50, 97, 133–34; national identity, 8, 17–24, 50, 83–84, 87–88, 91, 155, 172, 184, 195–96; race, cultural construction of, 17–21, 97, 171, 201–2; regional discrimination in, 94, 217n26; religions in, 7, 25, 47–48, 78, 136, 159, 209n5, 218n6; street, meaning of, 152, 164, 182. *See also* Racial democracy; São Paulo

Brazil effect, 79–82

Brazilian Jews. *See* Jewish Brazilians

Buarque de Holanda, Sergio, 210n17

Cabral, Pedro Álvarez, 217n24

Caldeira, Teresa P. R., 165–66, 169–70, 180, 185, 199

Câmara Cascudo, Luís da, 87, 217n27

Cardoso, Fernando Henrique (president), 55, 140, 142, 214n29, 221nn9–10

Cardoso de Oliveira, Roberto, 214n20

Carioca (from Rio de Janeiro), 203, 215n6, 229n34

Carnaval, 2, 5, 151–52, 155–61, 209n1, 225n41; charity and, 158–59; at Hebraica Club, 152–54, 224n35; Jewish themes in Rio parades, 154–61, 224n37; Jews' celebration of, 101, 152–54; and national identity, 154–55

Carneiro da Cunha, Manuela, 182, 214n20

Casa de Cultura de Israel, 156, 159, 225n39

Castro Alves, Antônio Frederico de, 43

Cavaquinho (ukulele-like instrument), 42, 212n1

Centro da Cultura Judaica (Jewish Cultural Center), 225n39

Cesta basica (basic basket), 3

Cestas de natal (Christmas baskets), 3–5

Chabad, 78, 91–92, 95–96, 139, 150, 216n20

Chai (living), 82–83, 147, 223n24

Chain migration, 44–45, 212n5

Charitable organizations, 116–17, 126–27, 131; Albert Einstein Hospital, 127, 212n28; OAT, 127; ORT, 207–8; Ten Yad, 127–28, 159; UNIBES, 121–23, 125, 127–29, 159

Charosh, Paul, 41

Chaverim (friends), 32, 127

Chazzan (cantor), 49, 77, 141, 145–46, 148, 221n12, 223n26

Chevra kadisha (funeral society), 120–22, 220n25

Children, 108, 110, 128, 145, 168, 219n11; services for, 145, 148, 223n20; street, 165, 226n1. *See also* Education; Youths

Christianity, 3–5, 69, 158–59, 171, 209n5, 211n23; Messianic Christian churches, 82–83, 216n14; rabbi saint for, 132–33; symbols of, 136–37, 220nn4–5, 224n37

Churrasco (Brazilian barbeque), 100, 119, 120, 149

Chutzpah (brazenness), 218n2

Cidadania (citizenship), *tzedakah* and, 129–31, 198

CIP. *See* Congregação Israelita Paulistana

Círculo Israelita de São Paulo (Jewish Circle of São Paulo), 62–64, 66

Círculo-Macabi Club, 66–67, 153, 214n23

Citizenship, 191, 203–6; *aliyah* and Israeli, 197, 227n11; and belonging, 93, 130, 200; charity related to, 129–30; *cidadania*, 129–31, 198; cultural, 17, 130, 200–203, 206, 208, 230nn7–8; flexible, 15, 201; formal compared to substantive, 108; military service and, 204

CJB. *See* Congregação Judaica do Brasil

Clifford, James, 13, 15

Close, Roberta, 93–94, 216n23

Cochin, India, 10, 97–98, 210n9; Indira Gandhi and, 142–43, 222n16

Colégio Renascença, 49–50, 56

Comunidade Shalom, 76, 127, 145, 215n6

Confederação Israelita Brasileira (CONIB), 27, 181, 207, 228n23

Congregação Israelita Paulistana (CIP), 56, 78, 215n5, 216n9, 230n9

Congregação Judaica do Brasil (CJB, Rio de Janeiro), 215n6

CONIB. *See* Confederação Israelita Brasileira

Conservative Judaism, 56, 76, 215n5, 228n28

Convivência (conviviality), 79–80, 82, 94

Cosmopolitanism, 17–19, 198–99

Costs: of Hebraica Club membership, 102, 218n3; of High Holy Day seats, 219n18; of Jewish burial, 120–22; of Jewish education, 113–14, 219nn13–14; of keeping kosher, 115–22; of *mezuzah* parchment, 115–16, 219n16

Covas, Mário, 140–41, 221n11

Crypto-Jews, 82, 210n10, 221n9

Cultural citizenship, 17, 130, 200–203, 206, 208, 230nn7–8

Culture, 97–98, 156, 225n38, 225n39; cannibalism of, 18–19; diversity of, 6; idealizations within, 57–58; Judaism as, 9–10, 210nn8–9; poetry, 43; public art, 139; race with, 9–10, 22; self-definition within, 11–12; Tropicália for, 41. *See also* Music

Cursinhos (private post-secondary schools), 112–13

DAIA. *See* Delegación de Asociaciones Israelitas Argentinas

DaMatta, Roberto, 88, 184, 224n37

Davis, Mike, 165–66

Death. *See* Jewish burial

Decol, René Daniel, 33, 47, 197

Delegación de Asociaciones Israelitas Argentinas (DAIA), 176

DellaPergola, Sergio, 31, 72–73, 173, 211n22

Democratization, 167, 198–99

Demônios da Garoa, 43–44, 212nn3–4

Diaspora, 2, 13–17, 195–96, 199–200, 210n12, 216n7; identity and, 13–14, 16–17, 24–25, 33–34, 196; Israel related to, 14, 173, 176, 197; Jewishness and, 16–17, 79; transnationalism compared with, 13–17, 197, 206

Discrimination: and antidiscrimination ideology, 20, 94–98; laws against, 107, 135, 172, 178, 211n26, 218n6; prejudice as, 95–96, 98, 171–72, 217n27, 218n6; regional, 94, 217n26; social class and, 107–8, 218n6

Disney World, 101, 174, 218n1, 227n13

Domestic employees (*empregada doméstica*). *See* Maids

Domínguez, Virginia, 8

Dona (title), 213n14

Douglas, Mary, 88

Doutor (title), 231n10

Dundes, Alan, 216n13, 222n17, 228n27

Eakin, Marshall, 210n17
Economic status, 2, 111, 131; elitism and, 63, 65, 99–100, 105; impoverishment, 122, 126–27, 129; inequality, 20–21; Jewish burial and, 121–22; materialism and, 105–6, 124–25, 129; neighborhood and, 104–5
Education: in Brazil, 112–13. See also Jewish education
Elkin, Judith, 61, 215n4
Endogamy. See Intermarriage
Escolas de samba (samba schools), 152, 155–57, 225n41
Ethnicity, 11–12, 23, 38, 61–62, 70, 182, 199, 214n20; and economic status, 131; and national identity, 17, 22–25, 91, 97, 172, 195–96, 210; symbolism, 82–83, 88, 95, 182–84
Evil Eye, 216n13, 222n17, 223n24

Falbel, Nachman, 171, 214n23
Fausto, Boris, 46, 51, 61
Favelas (shantytowns), 126–27, 230n3
Federacão Israelita do Estado de São Paulo (FISESP), 153, 180–81, 185, 187, 228n25
Feffer, Leon, 65, 214n24
Feijoada (national dish), 87–88, 90; adaptations of, 90–92; Jews and, 88–90; kosher version of, 91–92
Ferguson, James, 23
Fernandes, Florestan, 20
FISESP. See Federacão Israelita do Estado de São Paulo
Folha de São Paulo, 168, 181, 226n3, 226n6
Foods: Arab, 85, 216n18; bagels, 86; Brazilian, 84, 86–90; cesta basica, 3; cesta de natal, 3–4; cholent, 91; feijoada, 87–92; gefilte fish, 36–39; at Hebraica Club, 85, 87, 119–20, 220nn23–24; immigrant influence, 85–86; language and, 84, 124; music and, 84; race and, 84; restaurants, 86–87, 119; sushi, 85, 120, 220n23; symbolism of, 12, 83–84; vegetarianism, 119, 220n22. See also Kosher (kashrut)
Fortuna, 32, 212n29
Frank, Gelya, 210n9
Freidlin, Jairo, 213n19

Freyre, Gilberto, 19, 106, 210n17
Fry, Peter, 88, 220n4

Galut (exile), 16, 210n12
Gandhi, Indira, 142–43, 222n16
Gefilte fish, 36–39
Geiger, Paulo, 208
Gematria, 146–47
Gender: ethnicity and, 217n35; language and, 212n32; religious practice and, 77, 182–83, 215n6, 228nn27–28
Gershwin, George, 193–94, 223n21, 230n2. See also Porgy and Bess (Gershwin)
Gil, Gilberto, 160, 225n38, 226n44
Gilman, Sander, 217n35
Glick Schiller, Nina, 14
Goldfarb, José Luiz, 102, 145–46, 148, 151, 158–59, 218n4
Goldman, Claudio, 145, 221n12, 223n21
Goldstein, Donna, 219n8, 227n9
Gregori, José, 226n4
Gregori, Maria Filomena, 226n1
Gruman, Sara, 216n14
Grün, Roberto, 222n13
Guarnizo, Luiz Eduardo, 15, 197
Gupta, Akhil, 23

Halegua, León (maestro), 27, 70, 147, 192–93, 223n26, 229n29, 230n3
Harvey, David, 198
Hassidic Judaism, 216n20
Havdalah, 12–13, 208, 231n17
Hebraica Club, 30–34, 54, 66–68, 70–72, 79, 211n26; architecture of, 32, 151, 211n28, 222n19; Carmel Festival at, 71–72, 221n8; carnaval at, 151–54, 159, 224n35; charity at, 67, 102–3, 127, 130–31, 159; Christmas baskets at, 3–5; Círculo-Macabi Club compared to, 67; as community center, 27, 32, 66–67, 71, 151, 211n24, 227n16; and continuity, 31, 65, 67, 70–72, 102–3; cost of, 102; elderly at, 32, 67, 71, 81, 103, 212n30; food at, 32, 85, 87, 119–20, 220nn23–24; history of, 62–63, 65–66, 214n24, 214n29; Jewish education at, 32, 71, 219n12; nannies at, 110, 219n9; non-Jewish members, 72, 211n26; non-Jewish

staff at, 3, 5, 72, 103; politicians at, 32, 67, 140–43, 145, 154, 188, 221nn8–14; security at, 67, 165, 170, 180–81, 188; social class and, 66, 67, 101–4, 111; synagogue in, 32, 127, 145–46, 182, 218n4, 223n22, 223n28, 228n28; youth and, 32, 49, 65–67, 71–72, 96, 102–3, 145, 147–51, 180, 192, 215n3, 218n4, 223n29, 225n38

Hebraica Club's High Holy Days, 33, 49, 140, 144–46, 222nn18–19, 223n20, 223n22, 223nn26–28; choir for, 27, 49, 147–48, 180, 223n26; party after, 149–51, 223n29; politicians at, 140–42, 221nn10–13. *See also* Rosh Hashanah; Yom Kippur

Hebraica-Rebouças train station, 137–38

Hebrew (language), 53, 77, 83, 113, 115, 135, 146–47, 148, 212n32, 215n6, 223n26

Hemsi, Sylvana, 211n24, 219n11, 230n6

Herskovits, Melville, 9, 11, 210n9

Herszkowitz, Gerson, 145

Herzfeld, Michael, 22

Herzl, Theodore, 138

Herzog, Elizabeth, 57

High Holy Days, 129, 143, 145–46, 151, 178, 181, 219n18, 222n17. *See also* Hebraica Club's High Holy Days; Rosh Hashanah; Yom Kippur

Higienópolis neighborhood, 27–28, 50, 54–59, 66, 77, 83, 86, 101, 104–5, 139, 213n19

Hinchberger, Bill, 91

Holidays. *See specific holidays*

Holston, James, 69, 108, 130, 198–99

Horowitz, Irving Louis, 111

Humor, 4–5, 36–38; as critique, 93–94, 100, 124–25, 174; about Jewishness, 60, 73–74, 80–81, 89, 96; in music, 42–44; as survival strategy, 165–67, 191, 218n2

Hybridity, 18–19. *See also Mestiçagem*

IBGE. *See* Instituto Brasileiro de Geografia e Estatística

Identity, 69–70; Brazilian, 19–22, 24, 198; cosmopolitan, 198–99; diaspora, 13–14, 16–17, 195–96; ethnicity and, 199; Hebraica Club as expression of, 30–31, 34, 96; Jewish Brazilian, 8, 69–70, 78, 93, 134–35,

140, 142, 163, 172, 184, 203–4, 207–8; multiple, 17, 199; of researchers, 9, 29; and social class, 105, 121–25; symbolizing, 82–84, 88–89, 115, 139, 154–56, 160, 182, 184; transnational, 15–16, 23, 91, 163, 190, 195–96, 210; urban, 59, 61–62, 164, 184, 186. *See also* Jewish identity; National identity

Igel, Regina, 217n32, 219n7

Immigrants, 10, 21; aid organizations for, 44, 46, 59, 126; Brazilians abroad, 91, 213n15, 218n1; Brazil's quincentenary and, 50–52, 134–36; of color, 201, 207; culinary influences of, 4, 84–86; economic niches of, 44–45, 58, 213n6; Egyptian, 64–65; German, 63; Jewish, 25–26, 42–44, 46–47, 79, 203, 205, 210n16; Korean, 58; Latin American, 48, 210n16; neighborhoods, 50, 53–54, 56, 58–59, 85, 203, 212n3, 218n5, 231n14; nostalgia of, 38, 56–57, 59–60; population of, 46–47; representations of, 43–44, 47, 50–54, 134, 213n6; rural settlement of, 46, 213n11. *See also specific immigrants*

Immigration: to Brazil, 7, 21, 25–26, 41, 47, 134, 204–5, 211n19; chain migration, 44, 212n5; contrasted with diaspora, 13–14, 196; experience, 15, 50–52, 231nn11–12; generation of, 48; quotas on, 46–47; as rite of passage, 51; to U.S., 47, 52, 213n15; whitening related to policy, 46, 97

India: Brazil compared with, 142, 222n15; Jews of, 10, 97–98, 142–43, 210n9, 222n16

Indigenous peoples in Brazil, 1, 13, 21, 134, 167, 209n6

Instituto Brasileiro de Geografia e Estatística (IBGE), 226n8

Intermarriage, 21, 72–75; with non-Jews (exogamy), 72–73, 215n4, 219n10, 229n33; between Sephardim and Ashkenazim, 73–75, 79–81, 215n4

Iran, 179, 228n20

Islam, 136–37, 209n6

Israel, 132, 139, 173–74, 192, 205, 220n2, 221n8; *aliyah* to, 173, 197, 227nn11–12;

Israel—*continued*
consul in Brazil, 65, 205; diaspora related to, 14, 17, 173–74, 176–78, 181, 197–98, 210n13; emigration from, 48, 113; and Jewish identity, 6, 11, 73, 153, 172–73, 178, 197–98, 205–6; violence related to, 173, 175–79, 181, 185, 224n35, 227n10, 227n16. *See also specific organizations*
Israelita vs. *israelense*, 95, 227n14

Jabor, Arnaldo, 20
JACS. *See* Jewish Alcoholics, Chemically Dependent Persons and Significant Others
Jardins neighborhood, 54, 74, 86, 167
Jewish Alcoholics, Chemically Dependent Persons and Significant Others (JACS), 150, 224n32. *See also* Alcohol
Jewish Brazilians: and *aliyah*, 173, 197, 227n12; and Brazilian food, 86–90; Brazilianness of, 23–24, 70, 90, 93, 124–25, 131, 134–35, 154–61, 163, 172, 185, 196, 199, 208; contradictions for, 5, 24, 30, 69, 71, 80, 88–91, 93, 105–6, 110–11, 139, 146, 151, 154, 172, 175, 187, 189–92, 198–99, 222n13, 230n6; *convivência* among, 79, 82, 94; from Egypt, 64–65; identities of, 8, 69–70, 78, 93, 134–35, 140, 142, 163, 172, 184, 203–4, 207–8; immigration of, 25–26, 42–44, 46–47, 79, 203, 205, 210n16; from Morocco, 25–26, 132, 220n3; national identity of, 70, 89–94, 134–35, 142, 184, 189, 205–8; as *paulistanos*, 48–49, 54, 73, 100–101, 164–65, 174, 183, 187, 222n13; in politics, 222n13, 230n9; population of, 26–27, 47–48, 211n22; religious denominations among, 23, 76, 183, 229n30. *See also* Malamud, Samuel; *specific religious denominations*
Jewish burial, 115, 120–22, 132, 220n25
Jewish clubs, 61. *See also specific clubs*
Jewish education, 111–15, 219nn11–14
Jewish identity, 11, 29, 61–62, 89–90, 92, 95–96, 98, 196; alcohol and, 150, 224n31; anti-Semitism and, 98, 172, 182, 184, 228n24; *carnaval* and, 153–54; exclusivity of, 206, 231n16; and food, 88–92, 117–18;

Jewish law on, 211n25; multiple origins of, 73, 87; national identity and, 100, 172, 182–84, 189, 196, 207, 217n32; poverty and, 122–25; and race, 10, 98, 196; secular, 61, 90–91, 104, 196; social class and, 105, 119, 121–25, 131; and youths, 71–72, 95–96, 217n31. *See also* Diaspora; Identity; Transnationalism
Jewish National Fund (JNF), 220n2
Jewishness, 1, 60–61, 71, 88, 193–94, 206; Brazilianness and, 5, 21–25, 61, 79, 89–91, 131, 163, 199; diaspora and, 16–17. *See also* Jewish identity
Jewish New Year. *See* High Holy Days; Rosh Hashanah; Yom Kippur
Jewish symbols, 12, 38, 82–83, 88–89, 115, 135–36, 139, 144, 146–47, 154–56, 160, 182, 184, 222n17, 223n27
Jews, 209n9; anthropology and, 8–13; continuity of, 31, 65, 67, 70–73, 81, 102, 199, 214n26; cosmopolitanism of, 17, 198; definition of, 11; elderly, 9, 32, 36–38, 67, 71, 81, 103, 209n7, 212n30; imaginary, 171–74; of India, 10, 97–98, 142–43, 210n9, 222n16; racialization of, 73–75, 80, 96–97, 217n35; solidarity of, 61, 92, 105, 153, 224n31; terms for, 95–96, 104, 171, 217nn27–30, 217n32, 225n39, n227n14. *See also specific countries; specific subethnicities*
JNF. *See* Jewish National Fund
Jokes. *See* Humor

Kabala, 146–47, 178
Kaddish (mourners' prayer), 202
Karam, John Tofik, 216n18
Keren Kayemet LeIsrael (KKL), 135, 220n2
Kidnapping, 167, 226n5
Kippah (*kippot* pl.) (skullcap), 215n6, 228nn26–28, 229n29; symbolism of, 160, 182–84
Kirshenblatt-Gimblett, Barbara, 58, 210n8
KKL. *See* Keren Kayemet LeIsrael
Korean Brazilians, 58
Kosher (*kashrut*) (fit, proper), 220n19; costs of keeping, 115–22; explanation of, 117, 220n20, 220n22; *feijoada* version, 91–92;

food at Hebraica Club, 32, 120, 220n23; keeping, 119–20, 220n22; restaurants, 32, 87, 91–92, 119–20

Kroeber, Alfred L., 9–10

Kushnir, Beatriz, 214n14

Ladino (Judeo-Spanish), 33–34, 54, 73–74, 212n32

Language: multilingualism, 53, 203. *See also* Hebrew (language); Ladino (Judeo-Spanish); Yiddish

Lar Golda Meir (Golda Meir Home for the Elderly), 36–38

Latin American Jewish studies, 22–24

Lederhendler, Eli, 58, 59

Lesser, Jeffrey, 22, 23, 47, 171, 183, 211n19, 216n9, 218n5, 221n9

Lévi-Strauss, Claude, 11, 40

Lispector, Clarice, 109, 219n7

Livraria Sêfer (Jewish bookstore and press), 28, 116, 197, 213n19

Low, Setha, 166, 170

"Lula" da Silva, Luiz Inácio (president), 141, 161, 168, 221n10

Macabi club. *See* Círculo-Macabi Club

Maestro. *See* Halegua, León (maestro)

Maids, 106–10, 219n8; as "*shikses*," 110–11, 118. *See also* Nannies

Malajovich, Hugo, 207–8

Malamud, Samuel, 202–8, 231n11, 231nn13–15

Mandelbaum, David, 10, 97–98, 142–43, 210n9

Mangueira (samba school), 156–61, 225n40

Margolis, Maxine L., 213n15

Marranos. See Crypto-Jews

Marriage, 62, 72–75, 101, 104, 185, 222n17; dowries for, 74, 215n5. *See also* Intermarriage

Mascates (traveling salesmen), 43, 45, 201–2, 213n6

Materialism, 105–6, 124–25, 129, 131

McDonald's, 120, 220n24

Meir, Golda, 138

Menem, Carlos, 228n20

Messianic Christian churches, 82–83, 216n14

Mestiçagem (racial mixing), ideology of, 19–21, 74, 80, 82

Mexico, 216n10, 226n5, 231n12

Mezuzah (*mezuzot* pl.), 77, 115–16, 184, 219n16

Mikvah (ritual bath), 215n6, 222n17

Minimum wage (monthly) (*salário mínimo*), 3, 37, 218n3, 219n13; prices compared with, 102, 114, 116, 218n3

Mitzvah (*mitzvot*, pl.) (commandment), 115–16, 127, 130, 228n26; Bar Mitzvah as, 116, 219n17; Jewish burial as, 120–22; *mezuzah* as, 115–16, 184. *See also Kosher* (*kashrut*); *Tzedakah*

Mizrahi Jews (Middle Eastern Jews), 54, 58, 73, 78, 79, 212n3

Moreira da Silva, Antônio (Morengueira), 42–43, 212n2

Moroccans, 25–26, 132, 220n3

Mosaico (TV show), 27

Music, 135; benefit concerts, 32, 128; chorus ("Jerusalém"), 27, 165, 182–83, 192, 229n29; Demônios da Garoa, 43–44, 212nn3–4; food and, 84; Fortuna, 32, 212n29; Gil, Gilberto, 225n38, 226n24; at Hebraica Club, 32, 149; klezmer, 225n38; liturgical, 49, 145, 147–48, 182–83, 194, 223n26, 229n29; opera, 229n1, 230n2; popular, 2, 39, 42–43, 84, 128, 152, 224n36, 225n38; *samba de breque*, 42–43, 212nn1–2; Titãs, 40–41, 84; Tradição chorus, 225n38; Tropicália, 41; Veloso, Caetano, 40–41; Yiddish, 37, 192, 225n38. *See also* Halegua, León (maestro); *Porgy and Bess* (Gershwin); Samba

Muyal, Rabbi Shalom Emanuel, 132–33

Myerhoff, Barbara, 9, 29, 36, 39, 60, 209n7

Nannies, 74; at Hebraica Club, 110, 219n9

National identity, 13, 93, 100, 195, 216n21; of Brazilians, 17, 50, 91, 131, 134–35, 163; *carnaval* and, 154–55; ethnic identity related to, 17, 22–25, 70, 87, 91, 195, 199; and food, 83, 87–88, 90–91; of Jewish Brazilians, 70, 89–92, 100, 134–35, 142, 163, 182–84, 189, 205–8; Jews and,

National identity—*continued*
98, 133, 135, 143, 182–84, 216n21; in Latin
American Jewish studies, 22–23; racial
mixture and, 19–22, 198; transnationalism
and, 23–24, 163, 172, 190, 196, 207; unity
for, 195–96
Nationalism: anti-Semitism related to,
17–19, 176, 205; cosmopolitanism
and, 17–19, 198; secular, 143. *See also*
Transnationalism
Native Americans, 13, 19. *See also* Indigenous peoples in Brazil
Neighborhoods, 55, 59, 61–62; Bom Retiro,
50, 53–54, 56–58, 62–63, 76, 86, 100–101,
213n17, 227; economic status and, 104–5,
218n5; Higienópolis, 27–28, 50, 54–59,
66, 77, 83, 86, 101, 104–5, 139, 213n19;
immigrant, 50, 53–54, 56, 58–59, 85, 203,
212n3, 218n5, 231n14; Jardins, 54, 74, 86,
167; Morumbi, 54, 229n29; Pinheiros, 54,
67, 181; security in, 168
New Christians (*cristãos novos*), 25, 93,
210n10, 211n21, 217n24, 230n8
Nicknames, 44, 76, 86–87, 96, 104–5,
217n33, 218n5
Nigri, Shirley, 155
Nobre (noble), 54, 125, 220n26
Nossa Senhora Aparecida (Our Lady of the
Apparition), 55

OAT. *See* Oficina Abrigada de Trabalho
O'Dougherty, Maureen, 124, 218n1
Oficina Abrigada de Trabalho (OAT), 127
Ong, Aihwa, 14–15, 201
Organização, Reconstrução e Trabalho (Or-
ganization, Reconstruction, and Work)
(ORT), 207–8
Orsi, Robert, 12
ORT. *See* Organização, Reconstrução e
Trabalho
Orthodox Jews, 72, 76, 91, 202, 229nn30–31;
Binyan Olam, 216n20; flexibility among,
76–78; Jewish education for, 113; practices
of, 23, 76–78, 92, 144, 183, 202, 219n17,
222n17, 228n27; relations with non-
Orthodox Jews, 70, 79, 92, 150. *See also*
Chabad; Hassidic Judaism

Ortiz, Renato, 19–20, 88, 161
O Shil, 91, 216n19

Passover, 5, 85
Patrícios (fellow countrymen), 45, 212n5
Paulista (from the state of São Paulo), 31,
211n27, 217n26
Paulistano(s) (from the city of São Paulo),
34, 46, 142, 168, 181, 186, 211n27; Jewish
Brazilians as, 48–49, 54, 66, 78–79, 95,
100–101, 105–6, 110–11, 124–25, 163–65,
174, 183, 187
Pellegrini, Ann, 217n35
Peres, Shimon, 141, 221n8
Peyot (sidelocks), 202
Pinheiro, Flavio, 134
Pinheiros, Esporte Clube, 32, 63, 138, 154,
214n22, 229n29
Pitta, Celso, 141, 221n10
Political Economy, 14–15
Politics: at Hebraica Club, 140–43,
221nn8–14; Jewish Brazilians in, 99,
139, 222n13, 230n9
Pollock, Sheldon, 198, 199
Porgy and Bess (Gershwin), 192–95,
223n21; chorus participation in, 27,
147, 192–95, 229n29, 230nn2–3; race in,
192–93, 225n38, 229n1, 230n2
Porto Alegre, 26, 213n11
Poverty, 123–24, 217n26, 226nn7–8;
Brazil and, 1, 20–21, 35, 56, 99, 103, 109,
168–69, 198, 218n3, 226nn7–8; crime
related to, 169; economic instability
for, 126–28; *favelas*, 126–27, 230n3;
immigrant, 46, 58–60; Jewish identity
and, 119, 122–26, 199; pride related to,
128–29. *See also* Charitable organizations; *Tzedakah*
Prado Júnior, Caio, 210n17
Prejudice, 217n26, 218n6; abstract, 171–72;
Brazil as country without, 20, 95, 98,
110. *See also* Anti-Semitism
Prestações (purchasing in parceled payments), 45, 213n7

Rabin, Yitzhak, 140, 221n8, 224n35
Rabinow, Paul, 198

Race, 201, 217n35; anthropology and, 9–11, 210n8; in Brazil, 17–21, 46, 80, 84, 97, 107–8, 133–34, 171, 191, 196–97, 201–2, 218n6; hypodescent, 17–18; Jews as a, 9–11, 24, 98, 155–56, 210n8, 217n35, 225n38; whitening and, 46, 97. *See also* Brazil: ethnicity in

Racial democracy, 20, 73, 80, 94–95, 160–61, 191, 217n26

Racialization: of Jews by non-Jews, 96–97; of Jews by other Jews, 73–75, 80, 96–97, 217n35

Racism, scientific, 217n35

Radio stations, 109, 166

Rattner, Henrique, 48–49, 105, 214n26

Reform Judaism, 76, 127, 215n6

Reibscheid, Samuel, 54, 213n17

Rein, Raanan, 22, 23

Rio de Janeiro (city), 26, 40, 41, 229n34, 231n15; anti-Semitism in, 227n10; *carnaval* in, 154–55, 224n27; Jewish institutions in, 186, 215n6, 224n27, 231n15; security in, 186–87. *See also Carioca*; Malamud, Samuel

Roden, Claudia, 87

Roma (gypsies), 13–14

Rosaldo, Renato, 130, 200–201, 210n14, 230n7

Rosh Hashanah, 5, 33, 49, 116, 129, 141–44, 219n18, 221nn10–12, 222n18, 223n27

Salário mínimo. See Minimum wage (monthly)

Samba de breque (music style), 42–43, 212nn1–2

Samba schools, 155, 224n37, 225n41, 226n42; Mangueira, 156–60, 225n40. *See also Escolas de samba*

Sambódromo (samba stadium), 157, 226n42

Santos, Silvio, 155

São Paulo (city), 26–27, 36–42, 46, 55, 211n27, 212n3, 226n2; history of, 39–42, 62–63; Jewish population in, 14, 26–27, 46–48; Rio de Janeiro compared to, 40, 186–87; security issues in, 54, 164–70, 185, 226n3. *See also* Neighborhoods

Sapir, Edward, 9

Scheper-Hughes, Nancy, 166

Scliar, Moacyr, 51–52, 135, 213n6

Second Temple, 216n7

Security, 2; of Jewish institutions, 50, 56, 67, 77, 139, 170, 175–81, 184–90, 225n39; privatization of, 167–68; in Rio de Janeiro, 186–87; in São Paulo, 54, 164–70, 185, 226n3. *See also* Violence

Sephardi Jews, 25–26, 54, 58, 73–74, 85, 91, 95, 96, 135, 211n20, 212n29, 212n32, 227n15; Ashkenazim and, 38, 54, 73–75, 78–81, 215n4. *See also* Intermarriage; Racialization

Sequestros relâmpagos (lightning kidnappings), 167

Serra, José (minister), 141, 142, 221nn10–11

Servants. *See* Maids

Shabbat (Sabbath), 6, 12–13, 38, 49–50, 75–76, 78, 89, 91–92, 122, 148, 208, 222n17, 229n31; Havdalah, 12–13, 208, 231n17

Shalom Brasil (television program), 126–27, 211n23

Sheriff, Robin, 160–61

Shikse (non-Jewish woman), 110–11, 118, 219n10

Ship brothers (*irmãos de navio*), 51–52

Shofar (ram's horn), 148, 223n27

Shtetl, 57–59, 60, 61

Simchat Torah, 149–50

Sobel, Henry, 230n9

Social class: architecture and, 106–7; Brazil and, 20–21, 56, 99, 101, 106–12, 123–26, 130, 152, 164, 168–70, 175, 226nn7–8; crime related to, 169; discrimination and, 107–8, 218n6; Hebraica Club and, 66, 67, 100–104, 111

Sorj, Bernardo, 20, 210nn16–17

Sorj, Bila, 60, 105, 215n4

Southern, Eileen, 229n1

Souza, Márcio, 135, 220n3

Stack, Carol, 230n5

Stam, Robert, 18

Stamps, commemorative, 136–39, 142, 220n5

Star of David, 82–83, 121, 139, 155, 214n23

Stern, Moshe (*chazzan*), 49, 141, 145, 147–48, 223n26

Stillman, Norman, 38
Stratton, Jon, 14, 229n32
Street sellers, 213n6
Sukkot (Festival of the Tabernacles), 220n23
Symbolism, 83, 136, 143, 160, 184, 189, 195, 200; of violence, 177–78, 227n17. *See also* Foods; Jewish symbols
Synagogues, 3, 32, 50, 56, 60, 75–77, 81, 135, 211n24, 215n6, 219n18, 228n27; Hebraica Club's synagogue, 32, 127, 145–46, 182, 218n4, 223n22, 223n28, 228n28; Knesset Israel, 56, 60–61; Syrian, 77–78, 216n8. *See also specific synagogues*

Tallit (prayer shawl), 155–56, 215n6
Tashlikh (ceremony), 144, 222n17. *See also* High Holy Days
Tefillin (phylacteries), 70–71, 127, 155–56, 215n2
Ten Yad, 127–28, 159
Terms of address, 214n1
Teshuvah (religious return), 227n11
Topel, Marta, 76, 78, 92, 217n31, 227n11, 229n30
Transnationalism, 2, 6, 163–64, 197, 218n1; anti-Semitism and, 172, 176–81, 185, 189–90; citizenship of, 130, 201–2; definitions of, 14–15; diaspora compared with, 13–17, 197, 206; identity, 15–16, 23, 91, 163, 190, 195–96, 201, 207–8; and multilingualism, 53, 203; and national identity, 23–24, 163, 172, 190, 196, 207; violence and, 175–85, 187, 196
Tucci Carneiro, Maria Luisa, 205, 231n11
Tzedakah (righteousness, charity), 120, 130, 159; *cidadania* and, 129–31, 198

União Brasileiro-Israelita do Bem-Estar Social (UNIBES) (Jewish-Brazilian Social Welfare Association), 121–23, 125, 127–29, 159
United States (U.S.), 21–22, 200–201, 221n7, 230n5; anti-Semitism in, 179, 227n19; Brazil's racial and ethnic relations compared to, 17–18, 96, 125; immigration policies of, 47, 97; immigration to, 47, 52, 197, 213n15; Jewish community centers in, 32; Jewish foods in, 85–86; violence against, 177, 179, 227n17, 227n19; wages in, 218n3

Vargas, Getúlio (regime), 46, 64, 205
Veloso, Caetano, 40–41
Violence, 2, 99, 127, 160, 166–67, 169, 228n21; normalization of, 165–66, 180–81, 191; by police, 167, 169; in Rio de Janeiro, 186–87; symbolism of, 177–78, 227n17; traffic-related, 226n4; transnational, 175–85; against U.S., 177, 179, 227n17, 227n19. *See also* Anti-Semitism
Voloch, Adão, 217n32

Warchavchik, Gregory, 211n28
Whitening. *See Branqueamento*
Wilheim, Jorge, 211n28
Wolff, Egon and Frieda, 138, 221n7

Yarmulke (skullcap). *See Kippah* (*kippot* pl.)
Yiddish, 32, 33–34, 37, 53–54, 58, 73, 74, 95, 148, 192, 205, 231nn13–14; mixed with Portuguese, 43, 110–11, 124, 131, 216n19, 217n29; polyglots and, 33, 203; as synonym for Jewish, 95, 104, 217nn29–30; Tradição chorus, 225n38
Yizkor (mourners' prayer), 202
Yom Kippur, 143–45, 223n27; party after, 149–51, 223n29. *See also* High Holy Days; Rosh Hashanah; Hebraica Club's High Holy Days
Youths: Hebraica Club for, 32, 49, 65–67, 71–72, 96, 102–3, 145, 147–51, 180, 192, 215n3, 218n4, 223n29, 225n38; movements, 57, 174; Orthodox outreach to, 95–96, 119–20, 216n20, 217n31

Zborowski, Mark, 57
Zionism, 173, 197–98, 205, 208, 210n13, 220n2, 231n14. *See also* Israel; *Aliyah* (step up; return)
Zumbi, 155, 224n36
Zweig, Stefan, 20, 39–40, 138, 207, 210n17

Misha Klein is associate professor of anthropology at the University of Oklahoma.

The University Press of Florida is the scholarly publishing agency for the State University System of Florida, comprising Florida A&M University, Florida Atlantic University, Florida Gulf Coast University, Florida International University, Florida State University, New College of Florida, University of Central Florida, University of Florida, University of North Florida, University of South Florida, and University of West Florida.

More Than Black: Afro-Cubans in Tampa, by Susan D. Greenbaum (2002)

Carnival and the Formation of a Caribbean Transnation, by Philip W. Scher (2003)

Dominican Migration: Transnational Perspectives, edited by Ernesto Sagás and Sintia E. Molina (2004)

Salvadoran Migration to Southern California: Redefining El Hermano Lejano, by Beth Baker-Cristales (2004)

The Chrysanthemum and the Song: Music, Memory, and Identity in the South American Japanese Diaspora, by Dale A. Olsen (2004)

Andean Diaspora: The Tiwanaku Colonies and the Origins of South American Empire, by Paul S. Goldstein (2005)

Migration and Vodou, by Karen E. Richman (2005)

True-Born Maroons, by Kenneth M. Bilby (2005)

The Tears of Hispaniola: Haitian and Dominican Diaspora Memory, by Lucía M. Suárez (2006)

Dominican-Americans and the Politics of Empowerment, by Ana Aparicio (2006)

Nuer-American Passages: Globalizing Sudanese Migration, by Dianna J. Shandy (2006)

Religion and the Politics of Ethnic Identity in Bahia, Brazil, by Stephen Selka (2007)

Reconstructing Racial Identity and the African Past in the Dominican Republic, by Kimberly Eison Simmons (2009)

Haiti and the Haitian Diaspora in the Wider Caribbean, edited by Philippe Zacaïr (2010)

From Douglass to Duvalier: U.S. African Americans, Haiti, and Pan Americanism, 1870–1964, by Millery Polyné (2010)

New Immigrants, New Land: A Study of Brazilians in Massachusetts, by Ana Cristina Braga Martes (2010)

Yo Soy Negro: Blackness in Peru, by Tanya Maria Golash-Boza (2011; first paperback edition, 2012)

Trance and Modernity in the Southern Caribbean: African and Hindu Popular Religions in Trinidad and Tobago, by Keith E. McNeal (2011; first paperback edition, 2015)

Kosher Feijoada and Other Paradoxes of Jewish Life in São Paulo, by Misha Klein (2012; first paperback edition, 2016)

African-Brazilian Culture and Regional Identity in Bahia, Brazil, by Scott Ickes (2013; first paperback edition, 2015)

Islam and the Americas, edited by Aisha Khan (2015)

Building a Nation: Caribbean Federation in the Black Diaspora, by Eric D. Duke (2015)

www.ingramcontent.com/pod-product-compliance
Lightning Source LLC
Chambersburg PA
CBHW031437280326
41927CB00038B/490